Marv Christensen
NCREL

D0090553

REAL
CHANGE
LEADERS

REAL

HOW YOU CAN CREATE

CHANGE

GROWTH AND HIGH

LEADERS

PERFORMANCE AT YOUR COMPANY

JON R. KATZENBACH AND THE RCL TEAM

FREDERICK BECKETT, STEVEN DICHTER, MARC FEIGEN, CHRISTOPHER GAGNON, QUENTIN HOPE, AND TIMOTHY LING

TIMES BUSINESS

RANDOM HOUSE

Copyright © 1995 by McKinsey & Company, Inc., United States

All rights reserved under International and Pan-American Copyright Conventions.
Published in the United States by Times Books, a division of Random House, Inc., New
York, and simultaneously in Canada by Random House of Canada Limited, Toronto.

Library of Congress Cataloging-in-Publication Data

Katzenbach, Jon R.,
    Real change leaders : how you can create growth and high
performance at your company / Jon R. Katzenbach and the RCL Team,
Frederick Beckett . . . [et al.]. — 1st ed.
      p. cm.
    Includes bibliographical references and index.
    ISBN 0-8129-2626-9 (hard cover)
    l. Executive ability.   2. Leadership.   3. Middle managers.
4. Management.   I. Title.
HD38.2.K39   1996
658.4'092—dc20   95-34405

Manufactured in the United States of America
Design by Leon Bolognese

98765432

First Edition

To the dozens of change leaders
who made this possible

P R E F A C E

SUCCESSFUL ORGANIZATIONAL CHANGE IS BECOMING EVERYONE'S PROBLEM. CEOs are held accountable for it. Customers require it. Shareholder performance demands it. Continued growth depends on it. Literally thousands of jobs from the front line to the executive suite ride on the outcome. Increasingly, middle manager jobs are the most at risk.

For many, this is a battle for survival that rages on two fronts: workers and middle managers are fighting for their jobs, while their leaders struggle to change their organization to improve performance. Both sides appear to be losing their respective battles for closely related reasons. Top leaders are in a bind because they cannot attain required productivity and growth objectives by simply eliminating jobs. Workers and middle managers are unable to adapt their skills and approaches to fill the kinds of roles that create continuing growth, productivity, and employment. Both are frustrated, if not discouraged.

In the midst of this struggle, a new breed of manager is emerging. The new managers are change leaders who are making a difference because they have learned new skills and approaches for changing the behaviors of people that generate better and better results for customers faster than the competition. This book describes how these mid-level leaders have adapted to the need for change and what they do that works. They are the first wave of what successful managers and leaders will be like in the future. We call them RCLs—real change leaders.

C O N T E N T S

REAL
CHANGE
LEADERS

INTRODUCTION

WHEN YOU MEET A REAL CHANGE LEADER LIKE GEORGE DEVLIN YOU UNDERSTAND why some companies are winning the battle for survival.

George was born in 1953 in Ayr, Scotland—home of Scotland's famous poet Robert Burns, who wrote what is now everybody's favorite New Year's Eve ballad, "Auld Lang Syne." George is quick to point out, of course, that Burns was also a prominent psychologist and sociologist of his day. When you deal with people the way that George does, these disciplines become more than academic curiosities.

George was the very first employee in Compaq's manufacturing operation in Erskine, Scotland, hired in January 1987 when the current plant was "nothing more than a field." From that pristine beginning, George advanced to lead a manufacturing effort that, from 1992 to the present, brought the price of a "box" (his term for Compaq's personal computer) from 100 to 33 on an index basis—in an environment in which volumes rose more than 60 percent, product life cycles shortened from years to months, and new-product introductions tripled. It was a huge change both for the Erskine operation and the company. To achieve these gains, George had to change everything about the way Compaq in Scotland thought about and went about making the boxes. Moreover, it was not until October 1991 that anybody at Compaq even suspected the need for a miracle.

George doesn't look the part of miracle worker, however. Nor does he fit the traditional mold of "good general manager." He is bold, direct,

3

and plain in appearance. He speaks in rapid-fire Scottish brogue so heavy that no McKinsey secretary in North America could transcribe tapes of his interviews. He charges around his domain (the plant) with unrestrained enthusiasm, showing off his prized cell-manufacturing layout to visitors with obvious pride. One minute he is explaining the process, the next he dashes off to check out the circuit board line. Back again in the blink of an eye, he picks up the tour. And all the while, he is talking with everyone on the floor as though they were members of his immediate family. He is a real change leader.

Officially speaking, Devlin is the managing director and vice president for all of Compaq's Scottish operations (around 80 percent of the company's European products are made in Erskine). This is obviously a job for a strong general manager, right? George, however, is not your traditional manager. He has no MBA, no operational expertise of note—he is not even a legitimate engineer! The best he can claim is a one-year advanced course in personnel management at the Glasgow College of Technology. His first management job was as a line supervisor in a dyeing and finishing plant in Manchester, England, which he describes as "pure Dickensian—a dark union mill." From there he went to the Digital Equipment Company, where he picked up some high tech and general manager skills. Unfortunately, they were not enough for what he would soon face— and what taught him the management lesson of his life—when he had to close the plant.

> Once you've closed a plant and seen the hurt and pain you cause so many hardworking people, you question everything you know about management. You never want that to happen again.

While closing a plant is not necessarily the way to acquire change leader capabilities, at least it makes one determined to find a better way. Finding the better way is exactly what the entire Compaq organization had to do in 1991. The company had been the darling of Wall Street in the 1980s, as the "David that slayed the IBM Goliath." Unfortunately, as George points out, the company became so absorbed in its success that it did not recognize the threat of others coming up from behind—"to do unto us as we had done unto IBM."

> Customers loved our product, our reliability, and our service. But they were not prepared to pay 40 percent more for it. We had giz-

mos and quality and reliability—but people were not prepared to pay for it.

The main source of denial at Compaq's manufacturing operations turned out to be their key measure—cost per unit—because it continued to look good as long as the volume growth was masking the cost growth. Few wanted to hear about this, however, and George struggled to get the message understood. Even when he was able to get compelling numbers to prove his point, it still was not easily received. As a result:

> The next level required a revolution. We had to get more out of our people. So we introduced "cell manufacturing." We ripped out the main conveyor and replaced it with cells [teams] of workers.

This approach not only worked, it has set a model throughout Compaq—once George could convince headquarters in Houston. In fact, he couldn't really convince headquarters at first, so he just went ahead and took the risk. Luckily, cells turned out to be incredibly powerful in increasing productivity and performance. Compaq operations have reduced costs from 100 to 33 on an indexed scale; Devlin expects to get to 25 and then keep on going. George sums it up as follows:

> It was bloody and painful and it still is. . . . There is the current state and there is the future state. Between them is the *delta state,* according to the textbook. The delta state is blood, sweat, and tears. You can't prepare for the sort of pain that comes from changing people's roles and changing the physical structure—all while trying to get the existing people to step outside their daily jobs and look at the new processes and systems for a new world as well as achieve record growth.

Simply put, real change leaders learn how to survive and win in the delta state, while traditional managers can only survive in the current state or the future state. Compaq is perhaps an extreme example of the intensity of the delta state, but only in the sense that the change cycle is so rapid in the computer industry. Companies in every industry will face the same challenges as Compaq, but most won't have enough George Devlins.

Why is it that so few managers have learned how to bring about change in the behavior and skills of people as well as overall performance, when that is exactly what leaders at the top are so desperately seeking? The consequences of this failure are clear: thousands of middle managers lose their jobs every month, and top management continues to lose its battle for major change.

Most top executives are in a real bind. There is no more pressing problem than changing the responsiveness of their organizations—and they don't have enough real change leaders in the middle to make it happen. The change being demanded by most of their constituents—and increasingly required in their marketplaces—is beyond top management's capacity to accomplish. Still, their constituents as well as their boards hold them responsible.

The solution to this bind appears to be simple, yet is ultimately profound: It is not the heroic CEO, but a new breed of manager that is already emerging to fill the need. These new managers are the Real Change Leaders (RCLs) about whom this book is written. RCLs are very different from traditional middle managers, even the good ones. Their recent appearance reflects the fact that the need for change has never been greater—and is increasing rapidly.

WHAT IS MEANT BY MAJOR CHANGE

Simply stated, we define *major change* as those situations in which corporate performance requires most people throughout the organization to learn new behaviors and skills. These new skills must add up to a competitive advantage for the enterprise, allowing it to produce better and better performance in shorter and shorter time frames.

Change, of course, can refer to the efforts of large and small organizations to do a wide variety of different things, not all of which are heavily dependent on people. Major change can encompass an entire workforce or simply most of the people in a particular function or a single line of business. It can also refer to dramatic shifts in asset configurations or market concentrations that are *not* particularly people intensive. Finally, it can be focused on downsizing, layoffs, and replacement of people—or on growth, innovation, and skill development of people. And it can be a combination of some or all of the above.

Real change leaders do not care if the change effort is fast or slow, empowered or controlled, one-time or recurring, cultural or engineered—or all of the above. *They only care that it is people intensive, and performance oriented.* Today's business environment is forcing company after company to focus on these kinds of change efforts. For example:

■ Forest products giants like Weyerhaeuser and Georgia Pacific, whose tree resources used to carry the day, now pursue self-directed work teams to sustain their competitive advantage.

■ Technology brain trusts like Kodak and Merck must rely less on patent protection and more on the speed of their product development and the effectiveness of their distribution.

■ Marketing giants like Sears and IBM now find themselves outpositioned by marketers like Home Depot and Compaq that are razor-sharp market segmenters and service providers.

"Reinvent government," says Vice President Al Gore; "reengineer the corporation," says Michael Hammer; and "rediscover leadership," says Peter Drucker. Fully two thirds of the Fortune 100—and probably an equally significant proportion of small and mid-size companies as well—claim to be in the midst of some kind of revamping or major change that is aimed at the behaviors and skills of hundreds to thousands of people at all levels. The same can be said for institutions in the public and nonprofit sectors of the economy. And all are struggling with the challenge of recurring major, if not *continuous*, change. Even those who are winning among large corporations—General Electric, Motorola, Procter & Gamble, British Airways, Asea Brown Boveri—all say they have more change ahead of them than behind them. Few top leaders are claiming victory yet.

Even more troubling, however, the results that most are claiming have the potential to slowly and systematically undercut their enterprises' future ability to adapt, in two very important ways:

■ First, top managers are laying off thousands of workers, at least some of whom have the skills and potential to be superior workers—in a competitive environment in which superior skill is the name of the game.

■ Second, the past decade has seen a remarkable thinning of the middle ranks of managers and business professionals, many of whom have the leadership potential and capacity that will be invaluable in generating change and future growth.

As a result, the ranks of the unemployed are growing, and the sources of temporary, or rental, skills are virtually exploding. In short, top management risks losing its ability to sustain a competitive advantage based on a superior workforce, because it is inadvertently weeding out both the better workers and the mid-level leadership capacity necessary to build superior competitive capabilities.

A NEW BREED EMERGING

The business press fuels the flames of corporate layoffs and firings, as top management appears determined to destroy the middle bureaucracy. And why not? Everybody knows that is where the waste, duplication, layering, overhead costs, and hidden resistance to change are embedded. Too many middle managers have become information transmitters, compilers, syndicators, and administrators; they do little real work that translates into value for the customer, the shareholder, or the employee. Yet our recent work and research clearly indicates that the key to changing performance capability in dozens of dynamic companies is a new breed of manager and professional in the middle: the *real change leader*.

These mid-level change leaders are every bit as essential to creating high-performing organizations as are the more visible and dynamic leaders at the top. In industries as varied as banking, telecommunications, oil exploration and production, personal computers, public transportation, hospitals, and many others, RCLs are breaking the mold and establishing new patterns of what is considered good management practice. Their distinctive combination of tough, balanced performance standards and a fresh sense of how to motivate and mobilize the better workers makes them uniquely in tune with today's changing business culture and marketplace forces.

Real change leaders are the linchpins connecting three critical forces for organizational change and performance: top leadership aspirations (what are we trying to become?); workforce energy and productivity (how will we climb the mountain?); and the marketplace reality (what do our target customers truly seek, and what can and will our potential competitors really do?). Simple as it may sound, making this linkage work is what separates the high-performing companies from the also-rans in industry after industry.

WHAT ARE REAL CHANGE LEADERS LIKE?

The best way to appreciate who change leaders are is to get to know a few—in addition to George Devlin. We have been fortunate to meet and learn from dozens of change leaders in scores of different change situations in all kinds of different industries. These leaders do not fit into a neat set of job categories or organization levels—some are line managers, some are staff department heads, some are special-assignment team leaders, and some are mavericks and champions. They come in an endless variety of shapes and sizes, but their most common attribute is that they know how to achieve high standards of performance by changing the behaviors and skills of lots of people.

While in very short supply in most large organizations, they are surprisingly easy to identify. You simply ask executives for the names of people with a reputation for improving performance through people—and for exceeding expectations along the way. They are the ones who always get the tough jobs done quickly and well. Everybody knows who they are. Somewhat surprisingly, however, theirs are not always the names you get if you ask which people have the highest potential for promotion. First, top management still makes advancement decisions and judges leadership potential against traditional general management criteria, which too often do not include change leader capability or aptitude. Second, a number of RCLs do not fit the acceptable advancement patterns in many organizations because they are outspoken nonconformists and do not always play by the rules for getting ahead. When you meet them, you will see what we mean.

Mom's Best Communicator

Tom Timmins of Mobil Oil is no longer on Mobil's short list of high-potential future leaders (simply because he is nearing the end of his career); he is, however, at the top of their short list of real change leaders. He was recently asked to take on the difficult task of spearheading the

corporate-wide implementation of a set of reengineering recommendations, the first part of which was to downsize the corporate staff. This effort
is part of the new CEO's (Lou Noto) well-publicized efforts to reshape the
management approach for the organization, and change both profitability
and people productivity all across the company. The part that Timmins is
leading is aimed at revitalizing and energizing thousands of Mobil's people
around the world.

Since he was a small boy, the toughest tasks have attracted Timmins
like a bee to honey. Much of his love for tackling the impossible comes
from his ninety-year-old mother, Lucille, who still manages to reinforce
Tom's determination to do what is right and to do it the right way. Mom is
also largely responsible for his reputation as one of the "best formal and
informal communicators" in the company because she urged him into
speech training when that was the last thing he wanted to do. Even though
his natural interests were sports and science, "she figured I'd better learn
how to communicate, so I did."

He joined Mobil after graduating from MIT with a degree in nuclear
engineering, even though he never intended to practice as such. When he
joined Mobil, he went into the technical side of exploration and production, but his questioning mind and bias for action quickly led people to
seek him out for difficult management problems. Charlie Spruell, who also
played a critical change leader role in the turnaround in Mobil's exploration and production operations, describes Timmins as

> . . . objective, open and honest. He can take criticism a lot better
> than most because he looks at the facts like a scientist. Yet he is a
> real people person, and probably the best communicator I have
> ever known—both informally and with large groups. He always
> makes the messages clear to people in terms and ways they can
> understand and relate to—no matter what their level or back-
> ground.

In 1989, when the executive leaders of Mobil's worldwide exploration and production activity needed someone to lead the demanding
change in the exploration and production organization approach in the
United States, they turned to Timmins. Walt Piontek, the head of North
American E&P who picked Tom for the job, loves to talk about his "maverick" change leaders. His eyes light up and his voice takes on a combination of enthusiasm, pride, and mild surprise in retrospect:

Now you take Tom Timmins, for example. Here's a guy who never expected to be a manager of operations, much less some kind of change leader. We plucked him out of Dallas research, where he was well along in a technical career path. He has really grown in the last few years—almost to the point where I don't think he even recognizes himself anymore.

Timmins would agree. The effort changed the leadership approach of several people before it was over, and it resulted in a lot more than just downsizing. It moved Mobil's E&P from near the bottom to the top among its major and large independent competitors, maximized cash flows without reducing the ultimate value of the business—and reestablished the pride and enthusiasm in the workforce. Tom credits the leaders above him for their vision, support, and guidance, the leaders below him for their initiative, courage, and risk-taking, and those who followed him to inspire ongoing conviction and energy from the workforce. Without him, however, the critical connections among his change teams would not have occurred.

When the Canadian E&P effort seemed like a similar change challenge, it was Timmins again. In both cases, the performance results were worth millions of dollars to Mobil. Now, just when most people in Tom's career situation would be shifting toward a retirement glide path, Timmins is taking on the corporate reorganization implementation—one of the toughest change tasks Mobil has ever faced. He is leading a corporate-wide change effort that purports to shape a new performance culture across one of the world's largest corporations. He certainly cannot claim success yet, but we would not bet against him because he knows how to motivate and mobilize people for high performance. "Unless you can communicate with all of your people about the urgency of the task, as well as the value to them as individuals, you cannot get these kinds of things done. And that is a day-in, day-out effort that never ends."

THE UNEXPECTED RISK TAKER

"So I have decided to move to a team-based approach in leading my department," concluded Sally Beck of Enron. She is a soft-spoken department manager who looks more like a thoughtful corporate planner than an aggressive change leader. Sally had just finished presenting her new plan for converting the leadership of her forty-person department to a handful of real teams. She was met with complete silence from the other supervisors and superiors in the room. While Sally was not surprised, she had hoped for more. She realized, however, that what she was suggesting sounded very risky in an environment that was completely driven by the numbers and individual accountability.

For more than five years now, Enron has been "knocking the cover off of the ball" with its Capital and Trade Resources group. The company's innovative financing and energy-service efforts have left competitors eating its dust. But it is running in a fast race where catch-up by the enemy is always a threat—and its top leaders are committed to a set of financial numbers that put virtually everybody in the company under stringent time constraints and financial-performance pressures. Enron's leaders do not mind the idea of teams, and, in fact, have a lot of them running about doing good things in their pipeline operations, power plants, and development groups. But for the most part, these are teams with a single leader who is clearly accountable for the numbers. Few are real teams.

Sally was talking about real teams, in which leadership and accountability are shared, performance potential is materially higher than in single-leader working groups, and performance results always include more than just financial numbers. This notion was scary to others in the room, particularly her supervisors, who could envision being hung from the Enron yardarm should Sally's team experiment cause them to miss their numbers. The meeting ended on an awkward note.

But Sally firmly believes that the only way she can expect to keep her department climbing higher and higher in the results column is to open up leadership capacity without adding people. She also believes that the most practical way to do so is to take the time and the personal risk to reshape her leadership approach around a few real teams. She is well aware of both the difficulty and the chance she is taking. But those factors are secondary to her determination to get the full performance potential out of all of her people, and thereby keep delivering higher results.

COMMON CHARACTERISTICS

So what are RCLs like? They are all different—except in their determination and ability to achieve better performance results through people.

They share a set of common characteristics that helps explain how they accomplish these results.

1. Commitment to a better way.   They share a seemingly inexhaustible and visible commitment to a better way, and believe deeply that the company's future is dependent upon the change—particularly their part of it—being successfully executed. They see the change target as exciting, worthwhile, and essential to the future success of the institution, as well as to their own personal satisfaction.

2. Courage to challenge existing power bases and norms. They develop the personal courage needed to sustain their commitment in the face of opposition, failure, uncertainty, and personal risk. While they do not welcome failure, they do not fear it. Above all, they demonstrate the ability to rise again, and thereby build courage in those around them.

3. Personal initiative to go beyond defined boundaries.   They consistently take the initiative to work with others to solve unexpected problems, break bottlenecks, challenge the status quo, and think outside the box. Setbacks do not discourage them from trying again—and again. Certainly, they are responsive to top leadership's inspiration, but they do not wait around for it to move them to action.

4. Motivation of themselves and others.   Not only are they highly motivated themselves, but they have the ability to motivate, if not inspire, others around them. They create excitement and momentum in others and provide opportunities for people around them to follow their example and take personal responsibility for changing.

5. Caring about how people are treated and enabled to perform. They really care about other people, but not to the extent of blind self-sacrifice. While certainly not the corporate equivalent of Mother Teresa, they are fair-minded and sensitive to helping other people succeed. They are also intent on enabling the performance of others as well as their own. They do not knowingly manipulate or take advantage of others.

6. Staying undercover.   They attribute part of their effectiveness to keeping a low profile; grandstanding, strident crusading, and self-promotion are viewed as sure ways to undermine their credibility and acceptance as change leaders. In fact, many RCLs expressed concern about not "blowing their cover" by being interviewed for this book.

7. A sense of humor about themselves and their situations. This is not a trivial trait. A sense of humor is often what gets them through when those around them start losing heart. It is also what enables RCLs to help others stay the course in the face of confusion, discouragement, and the inevitable failures that change produces.

A critical mass of such leaders seems to be essential in every institution striving for major change. The chart below summarizes briefly where you find them, and what they do.

REAL CHANGE LEADERS (RCLs)

Where you find them	What they are doing
Business-unit leadership teams	Designing/spearheading change initiatives
Manufacturing operations	Leading a plant or a production line
Product design groups	Managing new-product design teams
Strategic planning groups	Benchmarking competitors
Quality improvement programs	Facilitating front-line teams
Corporate headquarters	Developing strategic plans
Field offices	Managing field salespeople
Marketing departments	Running customer-service task forces
Finance departments	Reshaping performance targets

WHAT WE DID

Until recently, we really did not understand the unique characteristics of these emerging change leaders. Moreover, as we probed our experience in working on change from the top, we could not fully explain why the bulk of the change efforts in large organizations became stalled somewhere down the line. Nor could we explain fully why so many good managers were frustrated, if not defeated, by today's change situations. So we put together our own team of change leaders to find a better explanation. The team set out to find out why so many efforts were floundering and few were succeeding.

We began by reviewing our combined experiences with large-scale, people-intensive change situations. Some of the change efforts seemed to be making excellent progress, although no leaders would claim to have completed their change efforts yet. A few had already thrown in the towel or simply declared victory early. Most, however, were still struggling— with the final outcome unpredictable. We found it difficult to explain why seemingly well-crafted change efforts became mired down in the middle. The answer was not found at the top.

So we began talking in-depth with dozens of down-the-line leaders in all kinds of change situations. We wanted to understand how they see major change and to learn what they are doing that works, as well as what they try that does not work. This task would have been more difficult five years ago, simply because there were not nearly as many major change experiences to explore. After all, it is only within the last few years that large institutions have been seriously trying to improve enterprise performance by systematically changing the capabilities of their people. Previously, top management focused more on allocating resources and making strategic decisions than on changing the behaviors and skills of hundreds of people. The emphasis was on smart decisions at the top, not on broad-based people initiatives at the bottom. Most leaders paid lip service to culture change, but they devoted minimal resources to it. In total, we have researched and probed into the specific experiences of close to 150 down-the-line change leaders across nearly thirty challenging situations over the last three years, many of which did not involve our clients. A summary of the specific database used is shown in the Appendix.

WHAT WE FOUND

A *new breed* of leaders is emerging to fill the need in the middle of major change situations. These leaders think and act differently from traditional middle managers, even the good ones. As a result, they have a unique capability to help create better-performing organizations by changing the skills and behaviors of lots of people! Hence, building a critical mass of RCLs is increasingly the challenge for creating the high-performance organization.

The basic top management principles for achieving broad-based change are mostly valid, but they are applied in significantly different ways down the line. What works for RCLs is not the same as what works at the top, although the contributions of both dimensions are critical in making a permanent change in any organization's performance capability.

We also found that RCLs tend to be fundamentalists in disguise—albeit a thin disguise. By fundamentalists, we mean that they instinctively believe and practice what early management thinkers discovered many years ago—that a successful business is both a social and an economic institution and must be led as such. More specifically, they believe in the following:

1. Tough standards of performance, but not just financial performance; customer value and workforce rewards are important as well.

2. A set of democratic principles that tap the creative power inherent in every person; but they also enforce consequence management, believing they can truly empower people only by requiring results in return.

3. The essence of self-governance is joint accountability (among leaders and constituents alike) for creating new opportunity; the basic approach is open dialogue and interaction to resolve conflicts by working to obtain the best contributions from multiple points of view.

These ideas originated with people like Peter Drucker, Edwards Deming, and Mary Parker Follett many decades ago.* Today's change leaders are rediscovering these principles and applying them in new and aggressive ways to today's challenges—because they carry the practical burden for changing people's behaviors across the broad base of any large organization. This leads to our definition of RCLs as:

Individuals who lead initiatives that influence dozens to hundreds of others to perform differently—and better—by applying multiple leadership and change approaches.

---

* Peter F. Drucker, *The Best of Peter Drucker on Management* (New York: HarperCollege, 1977) and *The Age of Discontinuity: Guidelines to Our Changing Society* (Transaction Publications, 1992); W. Edwards Deming, *Out of the Crisis* (Cambridge: Massachusetts Institute of Technology, 1986); E. M. Fox and L. F. Urwick, eds., *Dynamic Administration: The Collected Papers of Mary Parker Follett* (New York: Pitman, 1973).

RCLs Differ From Traditional Managers

Real change leaders are clearly different. They do not look, sound, or act like the mid-level managers of the past. They are younger, more diverse in gender and race, and more casually dressed. They are more likely to have nonbusiness backgrounds, and they talk without buzzwords. In addition, they delegate less, do more real work, and get their hands much dirtier than those of their predecessor professional managers.

They go for the facts, but they do not do a lot of unnecessary analyses. They track and measure their performance against more than financial numbers. They are unafraid to make decisions and judgment calls that go beyond their comfort zones and that place them and their careers at risk. They work with, through, and around the hierarchy. They anticipate that their careers will take them through several different enterprises—and this does not concern them. They believe they have the skill sets to survive beyond their current employers.

Many RCLs today do not have an MBA and may not even have strong functional experience of any kind. Most of them have been working in multidisciplinary teams and working groups; their roles have varied greatly depending on the situation at hand. As one developing change leader with a computer technical background told us, referring to his first leadership assignment over sixty personal-computer technologists, "I have never done anything like this before." And not too surprisingly, he approaches the role a bit differently than your standard-model MBA. Anita Ward, an RCL of Texas Commerce Bank (TCB) in Houston, Texas, proudly counts her roots in anthropology as more useful than her MBA.

Many top executives do not yet fully understand these emerging change leaders. This is not all that surprising since the two groups often come from different backgrounds and experience bases. The typical top executive today graduated from college with a degree in business administration, engineering, marketing, or finance. The most successful are typically "left-brain"-focused (i.e., logical, analytic, and quantitative); many have MBAs and have reached their positions by serving in apprenticeship management roles, then managing larger and larger groups of people, products, markets, and assets. They have advanced on the corporate ladder by delivering cost, revenue, and earnings results, and by making smart decisions in a variety of general management positions. They are elitists by nature, believing in the age-old maxim of "a few good men." The majority have spent their professional careers in two or three companies at most.

They are impressive, organized, and tough decision makers. A few mavericks and scientists like George Fisher* make the CEO roster, but most have been professional managers throughout their careers. This is not bad, it is just different from RCLs, who come from a different experience base, speak a different language, and share a different mind-set. RCLs are populists by nature, believing in the gospel of getting the most out of everyone. With RCLs, their right brain is continually working with their left brain, as they try to focus on emotions and feelings as well as facts and analysis. In light of these differences, it is no wonder that these two essential forces of change—top-management change leaders and RCLs—sometimes pass each other by like ships in the night. This often results in top management imploring prospective mid-level change leaders to do things they do not know how to do.

A HANDBOOK FOR RCLs

A separate "Real Change Leader's Handbook for Action" containing a compendium of frameworks, approaches, and diagnostic tools for prospective change leaders is available. Page 346 describes how it can be obtained free of charge.

---

* Formerly CEO of Motorola, currently CEO of Eastman Kodak.

THIS BOOK IS ABOUT REAL CHANGE LEADERS BELOW THE TOP LEVEL. WE LEARNED, however, that such leaders have much to say of value to top management struggling with major organizational change. For that reason, we urge you to continue reading beyond this introductory summary and explore what the RCLs themselves have to say about change and performance. We learned a lot from them. We are sure that potential RCLs will also learn a lot, and we are convinced that top management can obtain valuable insights about how to develop their own cadre of RCLs, as well as how their individual leadership approaches can be modified to take advantage of the RCL potential.

We believe this book is worth your time for three reasons:

1. It shows how a new breed of down-the-line leaders of change are getting the job done:

   - It reflects the process of change through their eyes and in their words.

   - It describes what they do that works, and what they try that does not work, in leading change efforts of many different kinds.

   - It explores how and why their views and behaviors differ from the current general prescriptions for how top management can bring about major change.

   - It explains how their skills and leadership approach also differ from those of most good general managers, past and present.

2. It demonstrates why RCLs are an important source of new leadership capacity for change and performance, since they are:

   - Already as important to major change as top management.

   - Fast becoming the best top management prospects in an increasing number of high-performance organizations.

■   Already having a profound influence on how top management shapes its own role in leading change.

3. It indicates what your organization can do to develop a cadre of such leaders, because they:

■   Differ markedly from mid-level managers in most corporations, and therefore require a different kind of nourishment.

■   Bring a different set of skills and experience to the table, even though some of them are simply battlefield converts who were good managers before coming under fire in one or more people-intensive change situations.

■   Are in short supply and high demand by a growing number of performance-driven organizations facing different kinds of change.

If your change effort is going well, this book may be unnecessary for you or your people. You probably already have a critical mass of such leaders functioning effectively. On the other hand, if yours is like most large corporate change efforts today, this view-from-the-coal-face may be worth reading. Since we are more experienced with the top management point of view, we found that there is nothing like hearing it straight from the RCLs themselves. This book will also help you understand better why the skills and mind-sets of traditional managers are no longer adequate for the challenges of major change.

(The table opposite contrasts the skills and attributes of traditional mid-level managers with those of RCLs. It is followed on p. 22 by a one-page quiz to assess whether you are an RCL or potential RCL.)

DIFFERENCES BETWEEN "GOOD MANAGERS" AND RCLs

Key issues	Traditional GM view	Emerging RCL view
Basic mind-set	*Analyze, leverage, optimize, delegate, organize, and control it— I know best.*	*Do it, fix it, try it, change it—and do it all over again; no one person knows best.*
"End-game" assumptions	1. Earnings per share 2. Market share 3. Resource advantage 4. Personal promotions **Always make the numbers**	1. Value to customers, employees, and owners 2. Customer loyalty 3. Core skill advantage 4. Personal growth **Satisfy customers and workers**
Leadership philosophy	1. Strategy driven 2. Decide, delegate, monitor, and review 3. Spend time on important matters 4. Leverages his/her time **A few good men will get it done for me**	1. Aspiration driven 2. Do real work 3. Spend time on what matters to people 4. Expand leadership capacity **I must get the best out of all my people**
Sources of productivity and innovation	1. Investment turnover 2. Superior technology 3. Process control 4. Leverage the people **People = exploitable resource**	1. Productivity 2. People superiority 3. Process innovation 4. Develop the people **People = critical resource**
Accountability measures	1. Comprehensive measures across all areas 2. Clear individual accountability **I hold you accountable**	1. A few key measures in the most critical areas 2. Individual and mutual accountability **We hold ourselves accountable**
Risk/reward trade-offs	1. Avoid failure and mistake at all cost 2. Rely on proven approaches 3. Limit career risks 4. Analyze until sure **I cannot afford to fail – or to leave**	1. Expect, learn from, and build on "failures" 2. Try whatever appears promising 3. Take career risks 4. If in doubt, try and see **I can work here – or elsewhere**

ARE YOU A REAL CHANGE LEADER (RCL)?

1. **Does your institution face major change?**

   A. Is your organization, or your part of the organization, underperforming relative to its competitors or its aspirations—from a financial, customer, or employee viewpoint?

   B. Does closing the performance gap require major changes to the skills, behaviors, or attitudes of a large portion of the people throughout the organization?

   C. Does upper management seem more interested in eliminating jobs than in motivating growth and new ideas and initiatives from middle management?

2. **Are you an RCL or potential RCL?**

   A. Has top management asked you to lead or participate in any initiative designed to improve the individual and collective performance capabilities of many other people?

   B. Do you have the ability to influence—directly or indirectly—how others perform their work?

   C. Do you believe that changing the people/performance capabilities of your organization is central to future success?

   D. Are you willing to take some personal risks to increase the change capacity of your organization?

3. **Should I read this (yet another!) book on change?**

   A. Are you dissatisfied with your organization's pace in improving people performance?

   B. Do you see lots of talk and activity about change, but no results?

   C. Do you worry that top management's change vision and initiatives are not reaching the front line?

   D. Are lack of middle management change skills a major bottleneck?

   E. Do you understand the difference between managing your people and enabling them to change?

   F. Do you know the skills and approaches that are most likely to bring about change in the people you work with?

PART I

PEOPLE-
INTENSIVE
CHANGE

PERFORMANCE

DELIVERING RESULTS

BEYOND THE BOTTOM LINE

CHANGE LEADER DILEMMAS*

What is "performance" supposed to mean around here anyway?

- *I guess it is earnings per share, but all we ever work on are costs. Can head-count reduction drive major change?*

- *Customers complain and competitors eat our lunch; still, we seem to make money. How long can it last?*

How do I make the corporate goals motivate my front-line people?

- *Our stated goals are cash flow, market share, and people productivity; do most people really see any personal benefit in achieving these goals?*

How can I tell which of these change "activities" will hit the bottom line?

- *With dozens of activities to choose from, which ones really count? How do I measure their real impact?*

How do I keep people fired up for more than a few months?

- *Our goals are tough, and once we achieve them, they will just be raised again. . . . Is there any light at the end of this tunnel?*

Why do we need all this culture change if our financial returns are okay?

---

*Each chapter begins with a box that cites the dilemmas that trouble most prospective change leaders facing the subject covered in the chapter; subsequent chapter boxes are not labeled.

"PERFORMANCE" IS A WORD THAT VIRTUALLY EVERY BUSINESS, SPORTS, AND GOVernment leader advocates these days. If you are not performing, your life must be a hollow shell. To Jack Nicklaus, performance means shooting under par at Augusta; to Tom Hanks, it is winning the Academy Award; and to Donald Trump, it is resurrecting the Central Park ice skating rink. Performance is some clear indication of a superior achievement that makes you stand out above the crowd. Naturally, performance must be the objective function of major change—when you can figure out what that means. To the real change leader, performance is simply *delivering results (value), that matter to shareholders, customers, and employees.*

Performance is a question of balance. Recently, the front page of *The New York Times* called attention to Japan's growing concern about an educational system supposedly second to none in performance; that is, if performance means accelerating the number of smart young people who get the highest grades on college entrance exams—and excel at the best schools in the world.* How can that be bad? Because it is out of balance. Japanese young people spend so much time hunched over desks that they "resemble the stereotype of the computer nerd: brilliant, driven, but utterly lost when in human company." The article goes on to point out that, while the students were absorbing ever greater amounts of information, they never really "learned what human beings are or developed into mature personalities." They memorize masterfully, but think narrowly.

Obviously, there is more than one kind of smarts required for the balanced human being. You cannot simply rely on test scores to determine the success of an educational system; the human-value and societal-contribution scores count as well. Nor can you rely solely on financial scores to determine the success of a business; the customer and workforce scores are equally important, even though you cannot measure them as precisely. Performance is clearly a question of balance over time.

Real change leaders (RCLs) are the scarce resources in large organizations attempting major change, largely because they are the best positioned to score for all three of the institutions' constituencies: shareholders, customers, and employees. RCLs are the formal and informal leaders below top management levels who always seem to find ways to get the difficult jobs done. And they do it by energizing and focusing people down the line

---

* Sheryl WuDunn, "Japanese Critics Say Schools Pushed Best and Brightest Into Sect's Arms," *The New York Times,* 22 May 1995, sec. A, page 6.

on collective actions that yield higher performance results in all three areas. We think of RCLs as unique *linchpins* who connect:

1. Marketplace realities (i.e., customer and competitor behaviors);

2. Top management aspirations; and

3. Workforce energy and initiative.

When the connection succeeds, it produces an unbreakable chain of events that leads to faster and better performance results. To make the connection work, RCLs ensure that primary attention is given to those few things that will have the greatest direct impact on performance results in each of the three areas—over both the short term and the long term. This is not as simple as it sounds, because finding and focusing on the few right things is difficult.

Ironically, much of the problem stems from the traditional, tough general manager attitude: What's the bottom line here? How many times have you heard that? Invariably, it means, how much money will this effort make or lose this year? Hard-nosed businesspeople are always focused on this year's bottom line. However, unless their view of the bottom line delivers customer results, and workforce job and skill enhancement as well as financial results, it eventually falls short in today's intensely competitive markets. Understanding this is the crux of a short-term versus a long-term management view. Financial results will certainly make the shareholders happy, but they seldom motivate either customers or employees. Consequently, if you only measure against the financial dimension, people invariably neglect the other two dimensions, and, over the long run, all three decline.

For example, competitors take market share when management becomes overly absorbed in short-term cost concerns; sound strategic direction goes unheeded when it seems abstract and meaningless to the front line; and the workforce feels little urgency to change when it has incomplete knowledge of marketplace changes. As a linchpin, the RCL can make sure that connections among the marketplace, top management, and the workplace remain solid.

Real change leaders open people's eyes to marketplace realities and convert higher-level objectives into actionable priorities for everyone in the organization. Obviously, RCLs in the middle need top management help. Change leaders may be able to recognize what is going on in the marketplace on their own, but they probably cannot establish and meet higher corporate performance standards by themselves, nor can they determine the right balance for overall enterprise performance. Fortunately, more and more top leaders recognize that bottom-line annual profit is no longer a sufficient target. Change leaders in the middle help people in their organizations pay attention to customers, competitors, and employees. To accomplish that, they:

1. **Learn what matters in the marketplace**—and clarify why.

2. **Measure the change effort by its performance results**—and ensure that activities alone do not become a surrogate for results.

3. **Strive for better and better results**—over time and against multiple standards.

1. LEARN WHAT MATTERS—AND CLARIFY WHY

Real change leaders go into their marketplaces first to assess their performance situations in light of firsthand customer and competitor reactions. They seek answers to four simple, critical questions:

- How do our products/services stack up against customer needs and competitor offerings?

- What does the marketplace require for us to earn higher performance results?

- What marketplace rationales can support strategic priorities and convince our people?

- What specific individual and collective results and measures must we pursue?

This sounds simple enough, but addressing and answering the implications of these questions require honesty, determination, initiative, and hard work. Most people can live with unpleasant truths about customers and competitors, and some thrive on them—provided they understand how these truths affect enterprise performance and why that matters to them. Not every change situation is fortunate enough to have an exciting upside; in fact, in many mature businesses, RCLs have to find ways to motivate themselves and others without any positive long-term opportunities to draw on. Real change leaders find, however, that even in such situations, it is possible for people to work together and take pride in their accomplishments. Consider the case of Mobil's Exploration and Production Division in the United States (MEPUS). Major oil companies are not particularly renowned for their ability to bring about major changes in workforce behaviors and performance. MEPUS is clearly an exception worthy of note, largely because of the unique role played by its change leaders.

COMPETITIVE REALITIES AT MOBIL

In 1990, a major reality at MEPUS was downsizing—and had been for years. The company was not unique in this regard. Since before 1980, downsizing had been the performance imperative for the exploration and production operations of virtually every major oil company in North America. Running out of domestic reserves, the industry was in decline. It was not so easy to cast change in a positive light for people who knew that job opportunity was shrinking at both company and industry levels. MEPUS's position among its industry peers was even bleaker. Despite three downsizings since 1985, MEPUS in 1990 was still at a 20 to 30 percent cost disadvantage versus its best competitors, and its cash generation was well below the norm. Return on assets was 4 percent versus a 12 percent target. To those who find financial percentages tedious, this means that MEPUS earned less on investors' money than it would have earned at the local bank. If you were supervising workers on the oil rigs in East Texas, the signs of shrinking business and job opportunities were all too clear. The picture was not a pleasant one.

RECOGNIZING THE NEED FOR CHANGE

Despite this bleak outlook, however, opinions varied within MEPUS on the need for major change. Companies like Mobil, whose names are household words, do not like to believe that the approach that made them successful originally no longer works. Thus, some contended the problem was simply another round of abnormally low crude oil prices, which were bound to rise again and bring back strong returns. Others argued that the problem was simply not quite enough good managers to manage in the tight market conditions. Still others feared doing anything too drastic, lest it cripple a proud, capable organization that had taken decades to build.

A few within top management, however, were convinced that a fundamentally different, higher-performing organization would be needed to survive: price increases were not going to save the day and past practices were no longer viable. The highly functional organization with its strong hierarchical culture was simply too unwieldy and expensive. The old command-and-control philosophy must give way to a new engaged-and-empowered paradigm. Forward thinkers at the top had not only read about new-paradigm organization approaches, they had already used many of the new tenets successfully. As a result, some in top management focused high-priority attention on developing into a high-performing organization.

Unfortunately, these early efforts suffered from a lack of clear performance emphasis and balance. While directionally correct, people lacked fundamental industry insights about the differences between core and noncore assets, as well as clear performance objectives. As a result, it would have been surprising to discover very many RCLs at work. A number of managers, however, were asked to work with outside process consultants to redesign twenty or more business processes. The resulting structure was flatter and organized around asset teams that managed geographic groupings of oil and gas fields. Again, however, these were top-down-driven and staff-designed programs and changes; few change leaders were involved, and fewer still were committed.

Consequently, despite what surely appeared to be extensive changes, chronic performance problems persisted. The company's cost structure remained out of line even after the downsizing and reorganizing. Return on assets continued below any reasonable set of expectations. Words and reporting structures changed, but old attitudes and behaviors changed only modestly, and morale remained low. Expected increases in productivity in the field did not materialize, and while some progress was made through process changes, the initiatives were unintegrated and left MEPUS largely uncompetitive with what others seemed to be able to achieve. In short, well-intentioned major change efforts from the top were not producing results, nor were they energizing very many people. Top management was not sure what to try next, so they decided to step back and take another look at the market.

A Hard Look at the Market

This time, however, top management decided to ask twenty of its best middle managers to take a fresh look at the business in an effort called the North American Asset Review (NAAR). Most of this group turned into change leaders, since they were picked on the basis of knowing how to get tough jobs done and had an acknowledged dissatisfaction with the status quo. Ken Miller, a soft-spoken Scotsman, is a good example of how attitude and values separate potential RCLs from ordinary managers.

Ken began his career with Mobil in various engineering assignments in the North Seas of Britain. Working the North Sea platforms in those days was anything but easy. From that challenging work he moved through assignments in Mobil's worldwide technical trouble-shooting center based in Dallas and then in planning at their Fairfax, Virginia, headquarters. The planning assignments focused on worldwide acquisitions, giving Ken his first opportunity to look objectively at companies as a whole, including some that were being broken up for sale. It was a new, broader perspective that would serve him well in his later change work. From there he became one of the new asset team leaders in the MEPUS reorganization. When it came to NAAR, Ken was an obvious choice because he thrived on tough assignments. As one of the new asset team leaders, he saw merit in the new organization approach, but he understood senior management's dilemma about continued poor performance. Ken reasoned that:

> They picked us to have somebody different take a look at the whole system, all of our oil and gas fields, and show that this [problem] is more than an organizational issue. We had done all this downsizing stuff, and we still were not getting satisfactory performance.

The NAAR team first looked at the basic unit of Mobil's business—the individual oil and gas fields the company owned and operated. In particular, it probed the value-adding attributes of each group of assets, asking:

> Which fields do we really want? Which ones fit our skills so that we add value to them? Which ones look like cash cows to us but would actually be more valuable to someone who could operate them at lower cost? Should we just cash them out in the market? If so, when and how? Could/should we just sell everything?

The team began looking at industry-cost benchmarks to determine cost rankings. Most MEPUS managers had seen such data before, but they had simply explained away their poor rankings by claiming that inaccuracies in the data and recent reorganizations made the information irrelevant. This time, however, the review team allowed no such excuses:

> The new 1991 data still said that we were one of the highest-cost operations. It slowly started to sink in, so this time we said, "Look, there has got to be something in these numbers."

When it became clear that on a value-added basis Mobil could just sell off as many as two thirds of its fields, "the idea didn't sit well up the line," Ken recalls. "But, we had the analysis behind us and could say, 'Look, we either have got to manage these fields completely differently—or sell them!' " This was a hard pill for top managers, but they swallowed it.

Obviously, the special-review team of change leaders had surfaced a fundamental insight about the business: MEPUS's costs were out of line largely because the company was treating all fields the same when it came to allocating both human and capital resources. This was understandable, if not laudable. Mobil's decades of pride in its sophisticated engineering and technical experience in developing fields virtually guaranteed a mind-set of investing its very best in every situation. If a field was new or still being developed, Mobil's sophisticated skills, highly experienced resources and capital dollars added great value. Yet, nearly two thirds of the fields simply needed to be efficiently depleted. The need was for low-cost operations, not sophisticated technical skills and incremental investment. This was a very hard reality for proud engineers to face.

In pressing to sell off the mature fields, the NAAR team got right to the heart of the competitive dynamic in its industry. In Mobil's marketplace (the maturing oil and gas fields in the U.S.), the winner would be whoever could extract the most, at the lowest unit cost, over the entire life cycle of any given field. Moreover, there were lots of players, from big multinationals to small independent operators, who could operate mature fields more cheaply than MEPUS could. Unless the company could find a way to beat its competitors, it might as well cash out now.

Amazingly, it was this gloomy insight that actually began to energize the potential RCLs and those around them. Proud people who wanted the source of their pride back, they began to view—and manage—core, versus noncore, assets differently. (Core fields were those with development potential, in which MEPUS skills and experience were of high value; non-core fields were those being depleted, in which low-cost operation and minimal investment were everything.) People realized they would have to learn to manage both types of fields differently, and that became a new, dynamic challenge: to be the best by retaining existing skills in developing fields, and by building new skills to operate mature fields at the lowest cost.

The effort of the initial review team led to a second team, named SONAAR,* that would classify each field as core or noncore. To expedite the task, the team broke into subteams. One subteam pushed the NAAR team's initial look at benchmarks down to excruciating detail to see just how far Mobil would need to cut costs to be the low-cost operator of the noncore fields. Another subteam looked into selling the fields. In the end,

---

* SONAAR was officially an acronym for Selecting Options for North American Asset Restructuring; unofficially it was known as Son of NAAR, the original initiative team.

Mobil found legitimate ways to keep most of the fields, largely by committing itself and its people to doing whatever was necessary to operate each field competitively. The company reorganized its asset teams around either core or noncore fields (the 1990 reorganization had grouped both types together). Those chosen to lead the new noncore teams had a clear charter: get to the low-cost benchmark. The core teams were also challenged. While they added value through their technical skills, costs were still a factor and they had benchmarks to hit as well. After all, the challenge was to extract the most, at the lowest cost, for all types of fields.

The result was an entirely different mind-set from the one in which quality engineering and superior technical know-how had set the standard. Now, it was cash flow, workforce productivity, and return on the asset base that set a new standard. It was all driven by a growing competitive spirit and relentless determination to be the best.

DEFINING PERFORMANCE PRIORITIES

The potential change leaders in these two special-review-team efforts succeeded because:

- They clarified the true competitive picture, weeding out corrosive denial among their people—no more explaining away unfavorable analysis.

- They surfaced the real organizational issue, which was not empowerment, but rather the imperative of managing different types of fields differently—no longer would a single management approach work!

- They got the newly reorganized asset teams strongly committed to specific cash flow and cost-improvement targets.

Instead of targeting some elusive culture change, the potential change leaders went after specific performance improvements based on building new skills and attitudes, managing with more than one approach, and getting commitment from all hands.

Obviously, the various RCL teams addressed immediate performance issues. But they also went well beyond the near term by clearly articulating what Mobil would need to do to survive over time. This took the form of three long-term themes:

1. *Become the lowest-cost producer.* In a maturing commodity business, this is the only way to survive. And Mobil had to develop new capability to win in that game over time.

2. *Tailor the approach to fit each asset base.* Core and noncore called for very different skills, staffing, investment, and performance requirements. Each had to be managed differently to add value.

3. *Develop superior flexibility and agility.* As fields mature and prices change, the asset teams must be able to quickly restructure their operations and portfolios, and change their skills and leadership approach to stay ahead of the competition.

Each theme had a compelling marketplace rationale that gave it widespread credibility as one of MEPUS's key long-term performance priorities. In fact, the buzzword management often uses for such themes is *key drivers,* meaning those actions, interactions, or decisions that have the most influence on performance results. Sometimes the key drivers in a major change situation are well known; sometimes they must be identified through creative analyses; and sometimes they require collective judgments. Almost always they require a constructive reexamination of old, established assumptions. Whatever it takes, however, RCLs must consciously identify their situation's equivalent of the key drivers and focus the change efforts directly and relentlessly on them.

Facing the stark reality of what needed to be done is what eventually led to a new pride and competitive spirit throughout the organization. People now realized that MEPUS would have to become a far more capable organization in order to have the agility and flexibility needed to extract the most value from its fields. More important, they became convinced that they could help do it! But they also realized that a rigid command-and-control, cost-cutting exercise would not produce this result. This gave RCLs the rationale they needed to convince people to change Mobil into an innovative organization with performance teams in key places that could continuously reduce costs through bottom-up initiative. Now there was a clear rationale for developing the high-performance organization to which their leaders had originally aspired.

Moreover, their pride was increasingly on the line. Seeing their poor cost position relative to the competition constantly reminded people of their challenge and of Mobil's opportunity to be an industry leader again.

This renewed competitive spirit was reflected in the overall vision the RCLs eventually developed in several areas for MEPUS, to be "the one others copy." (More on this in chapter 2.)

THE FINAL CONNECTION

By this time, Ken Miller and the growing cadre of change leaders were making the critical linchpin connections, that is, accepting top management's downsizing and economic imperatives and linking them to the unvarnished realities of the marketplace to define the critical performance priorities. The final connection was to translate the broad business priorities into something meaningful to, and actionable for, people at all levels—all the way out to the rigs.

Greg Cox, another asset team leader, was one of many RCLs who started to make the key workforce connection required for better results. Greg's role was leading the implementation program designed to capture $300 million in cost reductions—the three-year target set by top management based on the benchmark data. He had twenty years of engineering and operations experience in the construction and petroleum industries and was used to working in a world of linear thinking and logical relationships. But despite his background of engineering precision and logic, he was a remarkably sensitive people leader—who believed that, without the initiative of people across the front line, this game could not be won. To Greg, the job was always more than managing a project to a schedule, although he was plenty good at that. Greg had to convey the new MEPUS performance challenge to others in both rational and personal terms—terms that would produce commitment as well as initiative. Yet why should the rig operators and roustabouts care about more downsizing and job elimination?

Greg spent a tremendous amount of time with asset team members—both one-on-one and in small groups—going through the earlier team analysis findings and explaining why he believed they could, and must, cut costs by $300 million. He faced a tough audience in a tough set of circumstances, with not much to build on. In fact, the very first step toward the goal was yet another downsizing that would deliver but a small fraction of the target. Much more had to come from the unproven efforts of front-line, problem-solving teams, which were expected to generate and implement hundreds of improvement ideas to bring down costs. (Energizing large numbers of people through such structured performance improvement processes is the subject of chapter 4.)

The essence of Greg's message is painfully familiar to many change leaders today: "Because there will now be fewer of us, we will have to perform far better: work harder and smarter—with no promises of greater rewards!" But he kept working the message, building the trust and confidence of the potential change leaders within the asset teams, and developing many of them into RCLs who could take the message further into the organization. It was fundamentally a simple message of pride in doing the toughest of jobs well. This time it worked.

It worked not only because Cox was sensitive and convincing, but because he found people like Charles Bennett. Bennett had just become a production foreman at Mobil's High Island plant off the Gulf Coast. He was a hardworking, respected production technician who had worked his way up from a start with Mobil in 1981 fresh out of Louisiana Tech with a degree in petroleum engineering technology. Charles was a no-nonsense person who believed he had to put all the cards on the table for his new production crew. In his view, you do not get much out of a bunch of production hands by peddling some top management boilerplate about cost efficiency, empowerment, and shareholder wealth. So Charles began by simply talking to his people directly about the layoffs and the hard work ahead.

> Okay, guys, we just went through a layoff here and saw our friends go down the road. Do you understand why that happened and what caused it? We were uncompetitive; our production costs were out of line; so this came down. Our stake in this is a three-year deal: three years to get to deliver on our share of the $300 million target. The ball is in our court. Now, we can do something about it. We can't make any guarantees that it will save our jobs, but we can sure go down swinging.

Right on the heels of this sobering message, Charles also shared the details of MEPUS's actual cost position and how management looked at the business. He felt it was critical that his crew clearly understand the kind of business they were in, difficulties and all. It was a very unpleasant message, but it had to be delivered.

> I said, "Look, guys, I don't want to make accountants out of you, but you've got to understand the business, and how what you do every day affects these indicators. We had lifting costs in '91 at High Island of $1.52 BOE [barrels of oil equivalent]. Guys, we

have to do better than that." I was consciously talking business in front of them. What does lifting costs mean? What does cash flow mean? They had never seen any of these kinds of numbers before or how they affected them.

Most important, however, by comparing MEPUS's cost position with those of specific competitors, Charles showed his people what could be in it for them. He helped them to believe that they could be the cheapest operator in the Gulf of Mexico, and thereby expect to actually take over operations for other companies, which would mean jobs for more people:

> We can beat these guys! And every time we do, it means more jobs, so let's do it! We can get better here at High Island, we can be the very best in our area. Now, if we do that, guys, that equals jobs.

This was not a one-time talk plus a follow-up memo by Charles. It was talking to a lot of people, over and over again. "They don't get it in one presentation; they get it sitting on the handrail of the drilling platform with you out there drinking coffee with them, and you ask them, 'What do you think about this? Does it make sense?' You've got to live it with them everyday. It takes a lot of intense focus to influence people."

Charles Bennett demonstrates one of the unique attributes of the better change leaders: they find a way to turn brutally unpleasant facts into team performance! Only such RCLs are in a position to convince the front line to abandon comfortable behaviors in favor of developing a more stringent and demanding set of performance standards. Only they can help their people adjust to, and live with, difficult competitive and business situations. Ordinary managers may be able to do benchmarking analysis and financial projections, or disseminate results of customer-satisfaction surveys. But it is only the RCL who can sense the true feelings in the minds and hearts of his or her people, find the simple words that calm anxieties and instill courage, and maintain the trust that brings about lasting change. They take the time, again and again, to shape messages that convert skeptics up and down the line. Without this RCL connection, performance results under difficult circumstances simply do not hold. Fortunately, people like Charles were there to make it hold at MEPUS.

REMARKABLE RESULTS

In just over two years, a critical mass of change leaders at MEPUS had not only emerged to do battle on its own terms, but it had also enabled management to completely reverse previous performance trends. By the end of 1993, MEPUS had reduced annual expenses by more than $250 million while increasing production volumes. Industry benchmarking figures showed MEPUS moving from close to a bottom-quartile position in unit operating costs to that of the lowest-cost producer among the majors and large independents. Few people, in or outside of Mobil, had really believed it could be done. This is not the kind of change that the shrinking business segments of large behemoths are noted for. No wonder MEPUS alumni remain proud of their achievements to this day.

In retrospect, there was a simple snowball phenomenon at work. Top management asked a small team of potential change leaders to take a fresh, hard look at the marketplace reality. That fresh look started the snowball of energy that turned into a critical mass of RCLs who, with the unwavering support of top leaders, simply rolled on to confront their competitive shortfalls in cost and productivity—and get management and the entire workforce to face them as well. From there the effort snowballed into a deep-seated recognition of the need to establish new and clear performance priorities, both at the top and down the line. The link between RCLs and top management was critical in forging a clear, long-term view of the business. Likewise, the link between the RCLs and the front-line organization was critical in energizing hundreds of people to reach out and strive to regain a leadership position in the industry. For MEPUS to survive, top managers had to stick to their original operating-cost course (including further downsizing), and with the help of RCLs like Ken, Greg, and Charles, they were able to add the positive objectives of achieving industry leadership and pursuing a truly high-performing organization. Most important, of course, a growing critical mass of RCLs kept believing they could do it, and they did.

2. MEASURE CHANGE BY PERFORMANCE RESULTS

Sometimes an unfiltered awareness of what is really going on in the marketplace is enough. If the facts are compelling and straightforward, most people will respond—unless of course, they are otherwise constrained or diverted. Because the marketplace is both dynamic and complex, however, RCLs are seldom content to let the facts speak for themselves. Instead, they want to be sure that all individuals in the organization clearly understand what the marketplace reality means for them and their work. Accordingly, RCLs distill what the marketplace wants into a few performance priorities that are actionable, as well as motivating. To that end, RCLs strive for tight linkages between results tracked against performance priorities and the day-to-day change activities of people throughout the organization. These linkages take the form of simple measures and goals, and clear accountabilities for performance results, at both individual and team levels. Unfortunately, it is not always possible to measure important results with simple numbers—but RCLs still find "measures." For example, sales account teams sometimes assess customer-service reactions by multiple interview comparisons, which, while not exactly quantifiable, constitute valid measures. Whether or not results are quantifiable, RCLs measure them in ways that their people can understand, and will align their actions to achieve.

Two very different change situations are used to illustrate this process. The first involves Sealed Air Corporation, best known for the plastic bubble wrap used in the protection of breakable shipments. Sealed Air's performance in the specialty and protective packaging industry—more than twenty-five years of remarkable growth and high shareholder returns, plus the unique CEO leadership of T.J. Dermot Dunphy—is well known to most business analysts. The second situation involves the world's largest telecommunications enterprise, AT&T (specifically, the sales force change effort of its multibillion dollar Business Communications Services organization). These situations are as different as night and day when it comes to company size, business characteristics, and competitive situations; yet each illustrates how and why RCLs establish individual- and team-accountability measures by doing two simple things:

1. Establishing measures, assessments, and goals that put real meat behind the change effort, and link it to performance priorities that people can understand.

2. Avoiding "the activity trap," in which lots of measured actions are viewed as surrogates for results.

Accountability measurement is not nuclear physics, but it does require tough and unrelenting discipline. The wrong measures will not work, too many measures will impede progress, and conflicting measures can be worse than none at all. At the same time, important changes must often be rigorously assessed, if not measured, in other than financial numbers. The best RCLs are very sensitive to, if not wary of, past measures with which people appear overly comfortable; such measures often miss or distort what is important. RCLs find ways to measure what standard reports do not.

MEASURES PEOPLE CAN UNDERSTAND

Since 1960, Sealed Air has consistently outperformed its competitors and generated attractive returns for its shareholders. The impetus for launching its recent performance-improvement efforts, therefore, was somewhat "self-induced." In 1989, Sealed Air's dynamic CEO, T.J. Dermot Dunphy, was concerned that the company's success was lulling people into complacency at a time of pending change. Complacency was not an acceptable notion to Dunphy. Too many factors cried out for proactive rather than reactive change: key patents were running out, the acquisitions that had fueled earlier growth were much harder to find, and competitors were catching up. As a result, he created an environment uniquely friendly to the emergence and exploitation of RCLs. While this book is for, about, and by RCLs, it would be incomplete without recognizing the crucial partnership between RCLs and top management—and what top management does that energizes RCLs. Sealed Air clearly illustrates that kind of partnership.

THE WAKE-UP CALL

In the Dermot Dunphy school of management, a threat of complacency means it's time for a serious wake-up call. Intent on destroying internal complacency and heightening the urgency for change, Dermot took all of the company's cash, borrowed much more, and then declared an extraordinary dividend of $40 per share in 1988. This recapitalization was roughly analogous to launching a major reengineering effort, and then writing checks to the shareholders up front for the full value of the expected improvement.

Left with heavy debt and negative shareholder equity, down-the-line management had no choice but to find ways of greatly increasing cash flow and boosting earnings to avoid bankruptcy. This was challenging enough, it would seem, but, in addition, big new-volume opportunities were limited and margins were being squeezed by increased competition. The only remaining avenue of sustainable competitive advantage open to the company was increased manufacturing productivity, a broad direction that Dermot titled World Class Manufacturing (WCM), borrowing from the book of the same name by Richard Schonberger.*

ADAPTING WCM TO FIT SEALED AIR

The general concept of World Class Manufacturing was clear enough, but how to measure and hold people accountable for achieving it turned out to be another matter. Fred Smagorinsky is Sealed Air's director of performance improvement (his background and story are described in chapter 4). As he looks back admiringly at the early work done on WCM before he signed on, he sees it as an unusual adaptation of Schonberger's concept, because:

> You won't find a chart in Schonberger's book where he says, here are the disciplines and here's how you measure each one. . . . He doesn't talk about how you measure them and why it's important to measure them.

Don Tate, who was directly involved in the launch of WCM as a regional manufacturing manager, points out how important it was to adapt (or "Sealed Airize" as they called it) Schonberger's original disciplines. First, he and a group of Sealed Air's line managers added a disci-

---

* Richard J. Schonberger, *World Class Manufacturing: The Lessons of Simplicity Applied* (New York: Free Press, 1986).

pline of their own: safety, because safety had always been important for Sealed Air employees and they feared its getting lost in all the new thinking. The resulting six disciplines became Sealed Air's way of taking a broad management mandate (manufacturing productivity) and breaking it down into actionable performance priorities. The second step Don recalls in making WCM their own was setting very specific measures and goals.

> We got together and said, "What are our goals for next year for each one of these disciplines? Let's make them tangible and meaningful . . . let's pick things that really matter . . . just three [per discipline] so we don't get lost. And let's keep it simple . . . easy to measure, easy to chart, not a lot of work, not hard to understand."

The Sealed Air table on the next page highlights both the measures and their ties to WCM priorities. The RCLs have kept them pretty much this way for over five years now—you see them in any Sealed Air plant and find the plant summaries in the corporate conference room (their "war room"). (More of the story of how Don Tate "just got started" with WCM at Sealed Air is told in chapter 7.)

Note the clarity, simplicity, and tight linkages running across the disciplines, objectives, and measures in the table. Even more important, however, were the annual goals set within each plant with respect to these measures. This table and its attendant goals were largely developed by Sealed Air's RCLs rather than top management—which helps explain the chart's long-term usefulness, the RCLs' commitment, and the fact that almost every member of the workforce has internalized this picture of success. You will see the same pattern in the General Electric Motors case at the end of this chapter.

Change leaders "paper the walls" in their people's minds with such specifics because they have learned the hard way that nothing much really happens until top priorities and mysterious acronyms—like TBQ (Time-Based Qualitivity at General Electric), TQM (Total Quality Management at dozens of companies), CLQ (Customer-Led Quality at Browning-Ferris Industries), Six Sigma (Motorola's famous quality motto), as well as WCM—are translated into specific actions and measures at every level and unit. Change may well be a game of feelings and emotions, but you still need a way to keep score! Without a scorecard, World Class Manufac-

World Class Manufacturing—Sealed Air Version

Discipline	Objective	Targets (Measures)
Employee involvement	To push information, decisions, and accountability down as far as possible in the organization (empowerment)	■ Suggestions ■ Customer and vendor visits ■ Absences
Total quality control	To manufacture products that meet and exceed customer expectations and requirements at a competitive cost	■ Conformance to specifications ■ Customer credits
Just-in-time	To eliminate all delays in the chain of supply between our vendors and end users	■ Lead times ■ Inventory turns ■ On-time and complete
Total preventive maintenance	To maximize the time each machine is available to run production	■ Machine uptime ■ PM "batting average" ■ Operator training
Total materials usage	To minimize the generation and disposal of waste products	■ Machine yields ■ Dumpster hauls ■ Usage of scrap
Safety	To eliminate the conditions and practices that lead to accidents and lost time	■ Total accidents ■ Lost-time accidents ■ Safety program compliance

turing is nothing more than a brilliant concept. *Translating concepts into scorecards is a key task of the RCL.* As Fred says,

> If you just introduce the principles in the abstract, it does not work. We want to have faster machine changeovers—who cares? But if people believe and understand why you need cash, and realize that the cash is in your inventories, then many abstractions take on tangible meaning.

TYING BACK TO BUSINESS PRIORITIES

The chart above illustrates how RCLs translated the WCM concepts at Sealed Air into tangible scorecards that were clear to everyone down the line. It is also a good example of keeping a plant-level program closely tied to top management priorities. The WCM disciplines, objectives, and measures were tightly linked to the recapitalization imperative to increase earnings and cash flow. While many of the measures are clearly focused on cost reduction (machine yields), others protect the revenue side by assuring customer satisfaction (on-time and complete), and still others are mindful of the employees from whom productivity gains come (suggestions, safety compliance, and operator training).

It has always been important at Sealed Air for people to clearly understand why and how the WCM disciplines generate results that make good business sense. In the early days of the program, Don Tate and other change leaders from the middle of the organization, including Ted Bell, a vice president of engineering, and Randy Gouveia, head of operations, were especially clear about how WCM would improve cash flow. For example, they focused people's attention directly on the best places for getting cash out of operations, including something that was visible to everyone: "a very, very, fat inventory," according to Tate. Reducing inventory led directly to the principle of *just-in-time*. By focusing here first, a back pressure was created which brought the other principles into play. Lower inventories meant shorter production runs, requiring quicker machine setups and higher machine availability. This meant that *preventive maintenance* now had relevance (before, it was a low priority). Quick changeovers also required trained and *involved employees*. Meeting tighter delivery schedules meant there was no time to waste producing and then reworking defective products. Accordingly, *total quality control* now had clear relevance.

The payoff from this early focus on business priorities was important. For example, between 1988 and 1993 inventory turns increased 42 percent and earnings before operating profit rose 98 percent! What was truly significant about this achievement, however, was that it was the result of change leaders' determination to address an immediate financial challenge in a way that would also build long-term capabilities for the company. It is one thing to squeeze out short-term financial results by working people harder and shouting louder. It is another to get short-term and long-term benefits by tying overall business priorities to a set of measures that work for both the front-line worker and senior management, and, therefore, sustain better performance results over time. That is what RCLs do.

In summary, three very simple things made this Sealed Air story an RCL-driven effort:

1. It was the change leaders themselves who decided they needed the measures in the first place (which built a sense of urgency).

2. It was the change leaders who determined what the measures should be (which is why they were simple, clear, and few).

3. It was the change leaders who kept each other accountable (which is what produced both individual and mutual commitment). Top management's role was secondary, which is not normally the case in traditional manager situations.

AVOIDING THE ACTIVITY TRAP

In major change situations, it is all too easy to become overwhelmed by what many change veterans refer to as "the *activity trap*," in which people pursue dozens of activities that don't produce results. Worse yet, there is no time to discover why there are no results, so the activities proliferate. The change game is often characterized by top management's setting some high-level aspiration that triggers an explosion of activities. While these activities sound good because lots of people are involved, they are seldom focused on the key drivers of performance, and this snares the organization into an activity trap.

As a result, the change effort is at risk of being defeated by some combination of system overload, misplaced emphasis, and diversionary confusion. Most RCLs have had to take top management's high-level direction a step closer to firing-line realities by breaking their piece of the problem into more manageable (and understandable) chunks. Take the case of Michael Keith, a change leader within AT&T's Business Communications Services (BCS).

Meaningful Chunks at AT&T

As the newly designated head of nationwide sales of network services (long-distance, 800 number service, and data lines) to medium-size businesses, Michael's direction from top management was clear—to raise share—but not all that helpful. Everybody already knew that AT&T could do better in this middle-market segment, so Michael figured that just yelling "sell more" wouldn't help much. It would just throw people into panic and confusion. He also knew that the sales organization had a history of spawning one special initiative after another with no thought about their eventual impact. (A recently completed inventory of such initiatives filled a three-inch binder.) Determined to avoid activity without results, he broke the problem into more manageable and meaningful chunks, focusing on those few that would really impact results:

1. **Simply knowing who the potential customers were—and how to reach them.**

   Somewhat surprisingly, there were a lot of companies out there we did not yet even know about! And if we didn't know 'em, we sure couldn't sell to 'em. They were hiding from us like Waldo in the well-known *Where's Waldo?* children's books.

2. **Calling on customers—more regularly and more frequently.**

   We needed both to make more regular calls and to have more salespeople if we were going to cover the market. I knew that if we could just find the customers, we could justify adding more salespeople.

3. **Selling effectively—by emphasizing specific values that mattered to each customer.**

   Once you're with the customer, you have to understand their needs and show them real value. There was important work to do here, but I felt it was appropriate to handle it through normal management channels.

Not surprisingly, this simple breakdown kept the sales force effort coordinated and focused on performance in two ways. First, it was painfully clear and compelling. Everyone knew that doing these three things well would lead to more sales, so emphasizing them prevented people from going off on tangents (e.g., new sales techniques or call-management software). Second, it helped to sort out which units or parts of the organization would take care of what. The first two pieces were national concerns and lent themselves to common processes and top-down special initiatives. The third, involving very individual skills, fell logically to regular management processes of the local sales branches.

Simple and compelling as it was, however, this breakdown alone was not enough to locate the lost Waldos. It also took a change leader's relentless dedication to measure both progress and results.

FINDING WALDO

Ray Butkus reported to Mike Keith and led BCS's middle-markets Eastern Region. He volunteered to lead the effort to "Find Waldo," which by now had become the energizing slogan for the group charged with finding all potential customers. "I just felt it was a critical task, clear enough to get our teeth into," he said. Like many potential RCLs, Ray was initially distracted by the seemingly endless list of activities and ideas being suggested to surface Waldos. Brainstorming sessions were held, hundreds of ideas spewed forth, surveys were designed, forms filled out, databases created—even Bell Labs' awesome analytic and number-crunching powers were brought to bear on the problem. Everybody was working hard and doing many things, all of which made sense, but somehow Waldos remained in hiding. People spent more energy discussing how to find Waldos than they did working to flush them out.

Ray, however, was not the type to be distracted for long. He had been a lieutenant in the army during the Vietnam War, so he already believed that individual and joint accountability tied to a few measurable tasks invariably got things moving. As Ray says, "I decided that we could be doing all the right things, but if we didn't have the branch managers feeling accountable for finding Waldos, we'd never get there." A little staff work led to a rough estimate of the number of Waldos that each branch manager should have in his or her area. Armed with these estimates, Ray called the branch managers together and dispatched them to "find and verify their target number of Waldos within a month."

Ray was not really sure the estimates were all that accurate, but he was sure that they were close enough to get something started. He was also not sure that all the targets were fairly assigned across branch managers. But again, they were close enough, simply because Ray saw finding Waldo as a collective responsibility, as well as a clear set of individual assignments.

> We emphasized that we were placing a big bet. We were out building new branches, hiring branch managers for six figures

per year, adding sales managers and account executives—all based upon the proposition that those accounts were there. So we had to say, "Your slice of that bet is 1,200 accounts and $50 million of opportunity."

Ray did not entertain individual arguments about whether one branch should have a hundred more or fewer Waldos as its target. In his view, "we are all in this together." In pulling "Find Waldo" out of the activity trap, Ray drew directly from his army experience.

> This stuff is like "fields of fire" in war. Let me explain. When you are setting a defensive position in, you must teach your soldiers to "lay in fields of fire," that is, you stake out positions for each foxhole, and you define the areas they are to watch and fire into. If you don't do this, you or your buddies get killed. In fact, you can endanger the whole perimeter. However, it requires more than logic to get people to do it. The commander's responsibility is not just to present the logic, but it is to go around and specifically make sure that everyone does it and to keep communicating why.

But understanding what and why is not always enough. People had failed in this attempt before; clearly, Ray would need to try something different. He knew he needed a better way to screen local business lists and to identify high-likelihood Waldos. His salespeople would also need a new set of sales tools to reach and convince the customers. Without such tools, change leaders cannot expect to achieve performance goals that others have found to be out of reach before.

With clear direction, individual and joint accountability, and new tools and approaches for branch managers—lo and behold, Waldos began appearing. Ray built further momentum by regularly tracking and reporting progress across branches: people wanted to keep up with their peers. Within the allotted time, 24 percent more Waldos than expected were found. Both Mike and Ray succeeded where other change efforts had failed, largely because they were careful to "lay in their fields of fire"—specific areas of individual and joint accountability. Thus, they translated top management goals into clear priorities and measurable targets for people at all levels, and they provided timely feedback. This is obvious, perhaps, but it works.

In some ways, Mike and Ray sound like standard-model good managers just doing their jobs. However, three things set them apart as change leaders:

1. Relentless determination to measure the results that matter, rather than simply keeping track of multiple activities that diffuse and confuse;

2. Willingness to take a risk and go with "close enough" fields of fire; and

3. Insistence on joint, as well as individual, accountability.

As a result, they cut through the ivy-like bureaucratic behavior patterns that choke most organizations, and accelerated the pace of change to ensure timely performance gains. Most important, however, they kept working with, and through, their people until they created new levels of commitment, understanding, and individual initiative—and until they were working with *all* of the sales force, not just a few obvious winners. Good managers and change leaders may look alike until you get beneath the surface and compare the focus, speed, initiative, momentum, and enthusiasm that you find among their people—and their collective performance results (more, better, and faster).

3. BETTER AND BETTER OVER TIME

"Ay, there's the rub . . . ," to quote a little Shakespeare. It is one thing to focus people on achieving higher results for a few months. It is quite another to continue building on initial accomplishments and keep people energized and aligned over time. Continuous performance improvement is a lot tougher than it sounds. Those who seem to be doing it literally lock in to customer and competitor behavior patterns and set out clear performance priorities and measures that reflect how they intend to change those patterns. More important, perhaps, they consistently find ways to energize and reenergize the workforce to take on stretch targets with a sense of collective responsibility.

Of the many change situations explored for this book, there are few that better exemplify the kind of market-driven performance ethic that ongoing change requires than that of the Motors and Industrial Systems business of General Electric (GE Motors), headquartered in Fort Wayne, Indiana. It is a difficult, commodity-based business (low-tech electrical motors), with very tough competition and modest growth prospects at best, and it is a far cry from the high-growth, glamour units that most good managers seek out. GE Motors also offers an excellent example of the partnership between RCLs and top management that is characteristic of the most successful change efforts.

ZERO TO 20+ PERCENT IN THREE YEARS!

GE Motors makes a wide range of electrical motors and related control systems for a variety of customer groups, whose current product offerings range from household appliances to golf carts to steel mills. When Jim Rogers took over as CEO at GE Motors, he found an organization floundering somewhere in between discouragement and denial. Its financial performance and market position were well below acceptable levels to GE. In Rogers's words, "my job was easy; if you are at *zero* percent return on total capital, everybody knows your house is burning and there is no place to go but up." Well, at GE there is one other place—out! It is common knowledge that GE does not play for fun, and businesses that are not delivering competitive returns are addressed—one way or another.

So here was an industrial tortoise creeping along with its commodity line of plain old electric motors. How long could it last in GE's tough performance culture? Furthermore, as Rogers points out, "an electric motor is not much more than copper wire, steel, and sweat," so virtually any boy scout knows how to make one. As if that weren't enough, GE Motors competes with the likes of Toshiba and Emerson Electric, who would be among the tougher competitors in anybody's book. Obviously, this constitutes a set of marketplace realities that nobody enjoys facing. But you will find little or no denial anywhere within GE Motors.

MOTIVATED BY MARKETPLACE REALITY

Virtually everything people do at GE Motors is rooted in this tough marketplace reality; for its RCLs, there is no other way. They immerse themselves in the marketplace situation daily through a rigorous combination of facts, informal reports, and direct observation. What their customers and competitors think and do is the common focal point: it is where everything about performance begins and ends for them. They seek every opportunity to utilize the marketplace to engage the workforce, find new performance imperatives, maintain a sense of urgency, and regain their bearings when efforts fail.

Bob Turko is a typical GE Motors version of the RCL. An extremely energetic leader, he is a member of the leadership team of the heating, ventilating, and air-conditioning (HVAC) business unit. When Turko discusses his business, team, and job, his enthusiasm fills the room. Since 1992, his HVAC fan team has increased its market share by 15 points, with a combination of everything from new-product introductions to increasing inventory and receivable turnover. Bob says, "We are winning in a marketplace where there are only two or three horses; unfortunately, you cannot afford to rest much in this kind of horse race!" But Bob thrives on competition, loves to tackle the impossible, and takes great pride in his team getting things done faster and better than ever before. Just listening to him describe the race is enough to tire you out.

Exposure to the marketplace is the primary way in which RCLs engage the workforce in performance improvement. Bob (and the rest of the leadership team for HVAC) sees marketplace exposure as the key to expanding employees' frames of reference and skills. "We have to make them into different people, and we cannot do that if we keep them behind terminals and efficient workstations." So he and his team get their people, engineers, and hourly workers out with customers. Their contacts are not mere tours or courtesy calls. They go out to solve real problems and to advise customers on how they can better use HVAC products. They leave behind their business cards and their credibility—and they expect to be called again.

Bob's team has recently borrowed a Wal-Mart idea as another means of keeping the marketplace foremost in everyone's mind. Every Monday morning they hook up the HVAC team leaders, all the salespeople (about a dozen), three plant managers, the customer service reps, and representatives of the hourly workers—about thirty people in all—on a conference call for what they call a "quick market intelligence" session. The call lasts about fifty minutes; it is tightly structured and action oriented, as everyone shares whatever competitor or customer intelligence they have obtained over the preceding week. In Bob's mind:

> It gives everyone a chance to know what's going on. You can feel the rhythm; you know when the market is going up and when it is going down, when we're winning and when we're losing, and I think the people love that. Now, we can take all those little bits of competitive information and put it all together to paint a coherent picture.

That coherent picture is the key benefit of the call. The discussions yield a tremendous amount of information that can be acted upon both to preempt weekly competitive moves and to deliver unexpected on-line value to customers. Bob believes that much of the unit's success depends on their ability to know information a day or two ahead of the competition or customers. For example, since they serve a broad market, they often know better than some of their customers when the housing market is soft in one part of the country.

> This, from a competitive standpoint, is absolutely terrific. There are some great stories to tell. . . . We found out about a competitor's die-casting problem. We were able to act on this information before our competitor reached their customers. We jump in that void and are ready to serve quickly. We get two gold stars for being the guy on the spot.

This constant market focus often has the effect of pushing GE Motors to achieve unimagined performance objectives. At the same time that it doubled net income, it also achieved enviable increases in receivables and inventory turnover. Increasing inventory turns, however, was not part of its original objective. GE Motors improved turns because that was the only way it could meet the unprecedented demand created by its new product offerings—and the company was not about to disappoint customers or lose out to competitors because of inventory constraints. As Bob says, "sometimes you need something to blast you out of your mind-set" before you realize what you can accomplish.

Bob and the other RCLs at GE Motors have found their answer to the question of how to maintain a sense of urgency. They just keep looking outward to the market. Jim Rogers contends that they can create a continual sense of urgency by appealing to competitive instincts (there is always a new threat on the horizon) and always examining themselves from the customer's perspective (they can count on frequent blasts of reality to reset internal assumptions).

The real test of market focus comes when a high-profile initiative falls short. It is easy at that point to either look internally for scapegoats or externally for excuses. Rick Tatman, HVAC's manager of ECM programs,* did neither. Two years ago, the leadership team of this business staked out a virtually impossible aspiration: to become a $100-million business by 1995. By late 1994, it was clear that ECM would miss the target by a wide margin. This was a very serious situation for Rick and his team, but rather than explain away the shortfall, they looked back into the marketplace to find their mistakes.

> We should have taken a few more months to study the market. We assumed that the initial enthusiasm we were hearing from our customers meant that once we had the right product, nothing could stop us. We should have gone to our customers' customers. We got the products all right, but we overlooked the time it would take for our customers to change their basic platforms to be able to maximize the value from our products. We simply outran our customers.

Rick and his teammates are now reformulating their strategy with a new level of market understanding in mind. Just as the marketplace is the

---

* Electric Commutator Motors found in major appliances and heating and air-conditioning (HVAC) products.

first place that RCLs at GE Motors go for a performance focus, it is likewise their point of return when they stumble. And they determine their success and progress by a set of measures that link tightly to the marketplace requirements.

Clearly Connected Measures

The focal point of GE Motors' dramatic turnaround and continued performance improvement is a clear set of performance priorities that include more than financial bottom-line results. These performance priorities are GE Motors' continuing themes of change. They go under the GE banner of time-based qualitivity (TBQ), which Jim Rogers relentlessly reinforces.* The entire GE Motors effort—teams, nonteams, business units, champions, technical support groups, and staff specialists—must perform against the key externally focused TBQ measures. Not only does everybody understand this, but they also know the specific implications of these themes relative to behaviors at individual, team, and business-unit levels.

The TBQ elements at GE Motors may initially seem rather commonplace, but as they are specifically translated to different areas and levels of the business, they become very uncommonplace.

These are priorities "that all teams, all managers, and all plants will monitor," says Jim. Everybody from Jim down believes that the lefthand column describes the few things that matter for performance in their business. As one change leader told us, "you cannot succeed by doing wrong on these things, and if you do these things right, you will succeed." Moreover, a person can count on these being the priorities month after month, year after year.

As the next table clearly indicates, the performance priorities at GE Motors go well beyond the higher-level, hard-to-argue-with elements. Each change leader in every unit and segment of GE Motors has taken these elements, determined the specific implications for his or her part of the institution, and translated them into something people care about. The rock-solid link between Rogers's performance priorities and the production plant and marketing teams' priorities is what ensures alignment in the actions and activities of the entire workforce. There is really nothing new

---

* TBQ is a company-wide focus on speed, quality and cost relative to the rising expectations of customers and the changing benchmarked performance of competitors.

about the idea of a few closely watched numbers. What is special at GE Motors is the work of the RCLs in translating the TBQs into something tangible and meaningful for every person in every situation.

General Electric Motors

TBQ elements	Market-based team measures	Production plant team measures
Customer service	■ Customer satisfaction surveys ■ Customer requests met ■ Promises kept	■ Promises kept
Speed	■ Order to delivery cycles ■ Inventory turnover	■ Manufacturing cycle time ■ Inventory turnover
Quality	■ Customer-driven measurements ■ Total cost of quality (i.e., parts per million)	■ Plant cost of quality ■ Simulated customer acceptance test

Productivity	■ Total cost of productivity
	  –Variable
	  –Base
		■ Total cost of productivity (plant)

Employee involvement	■ Survey results ■ Quality training	■ Survey results ■ Environmental, health, and safety measures

The other striking aspect of GE Motors is the discipline with which nearly everyone really lives the numbers. TBQ at GE Motors is never out of view or out of mind. It is physically present on four-by-six-foot boards, where results for particular work areas are tracked over time. It is talked about repeatedly in weekly meetings in which managers and workers discuss firsthand how they are doing and what more needs to be done. Customers hear about it too. TBQ provides the common language across all functions and units for discussing what is happening with customers and competitors anywhere in the business.

RCLs, through clear performance measures like GE Motors' TBQ, or Sealed Air's WCM principles, make performance a precision drill that everyone knows by heart. The power of this repeated drill is in the extraordinary degree of focus and alignment achieved across the organization. Very little energy is lost by people wondering what is important, what they should do, or how well they are doing. Somewhat surprisingly, however, the measures measure more than financial results.

BEYOND THE FINANCIALS

The most intriguing element of TBQ is employee involvement, which demands that the work environment be viewed positively by the workforce. Most financial performance turnarounds do not take time to worry about team or worker feelings, much less find a way to track and measure them. In marked contrast, Jim Rogers says his RCLs and teams are what make the difference in both speed and performance. The people component of performance results is critical here. In fact, Jim claims to measure the performance of his managers against a set of numbers that includes how their people feel about working there:

> We try to keep it simple. We survey everybody who works here once a quarter and rank them in one of three categories:
>
> 1. *The sun is shining:* My job is great; I really like working here.
>
> 2. *It's a bit cloudy and overcast:* My job is OK, the pay and benefits are good—guess I'll stay.
>
> 3. *It's raining, the sun never shines:* My job stinks, and I hate the place.

Any part of the business that is trending down on this set of people measures cannot be considered a good performer no matter what the financial numbers say. Moreover, Jim claims there is substantial evidence all around General Electric of good financial performers being replaced because they do not get their financial results "the right way."

There is little question that the performance aspirations (short term and long term) of companies like GE Motors have become multidimensional. The three dimensions (shareholders, customers, and employees) form a "closed loop," i.e., shareholders gain wealth *only* when customers perceive and reward a better product or service package, which can happen *only* if a company gets better work out of its people. Managers today widely recognize the importance of this three-way interplay, but most often it is the people dimension that gets only cursory attention. Measures in this dimension typically consist of an annual employee attitude survey whose tabulation becomes a one-time agenda item for discussion and some remedial action. Attention then shifts back to short-term-cost and headcount reductions.

RCLs, however, are in the performance game for the long run, and they know it requires motivating people as well as delivering quarterly earnings. For them performance is a matter of both how much and how it is achieved. RCLs realize their real source of productivity improvement is in the motivation and initiative of their people. They are, therefore, demanding of themselves and others in setting performance measures and objectives for developing and creating job opportunity for their people. For most companies, this is an area where much work remains undone. GE Motors' "weather report" is among the truest efforts to give the same attention and consequences to people measures as to hard numbers, yet even this company would admit it hasn't yet achieved the full focus and rigor required. Nonetheless, GE Motors' effort is all a part of continually stretching the limits of the company's capability—and always pushing to advance that capability. The habit of stretch is deeply ingrained.

THE HABIT OF STRETCH

The change leaders at GE Motors constantly practice the habit of reaching for stretch targets. In Jim Rogers' words, "I prefer that we miss high-stretch goals now and then rather than discourage the stretch by punishing all shortfalls. We try to celebrate the hell out of achievement and progress here, even when some of it falls short of what the team goals may have been to begin with." This was certainly the spirit of Rick Tatman's ECM team cited earlier, when it set its initial objective. "The only pressure we felt was the pressure we put on ourselves. We wanted to get to $100 million as fast as possible because we felt that anything less than that size is not really a viable business at GE."

Beyond propelling the sort of business breakthroughs the ECM team was seeking, stretch targets also break the day-to-day logjams that occur when people are simply reluctant to think differently or to try new approaches. This has been the experience of Mike Pulick, manager of capital equipment sourcing, who came to GE Motors "because it was a business in trouble, and I knew there would be plenty of change and opportunity." When he recently led a major improvement project on capital equipment acquisition, his team encountered lots of resistance to changing established procurement practices. Objections to the team's redesign proposals came to a head over a new capital proposal to add capacity to the HVAC production line. At first people were against even the idea of getting competitive quotes on the business, but the TBQ targets for the business made it clear that a vast improvement in performance was needed—far more than existing practices could deliver. As Mike says, "That's the whole idea of stretch. It gets people to try things that they would not have tried otherwise." As it turned out, the company ended up buying all its new capacity from world-class vendors it had never used before, successfully adding the line capacity in half the usual time and at far lower cost.

The stretch mind-set also means that accountability works off a broader base that not only includes multiple goals, but demands a mutual as well as an individual accounting.

BROADENING THE BASE OF ACCOUNTABILITY

The ultimate state in accountability is when people begin to say "we hold ourselves accountable" rather than "our leader holds us accountable." That, of course, is how real teams do it all the time—but the same phenomenon is appearing in larger groupings at companies like GE Motors, Sealed Air, and Mobil. The best RCLs are able to obtain true mutual accountability across some surprisingly large groups—and it makes a big difference in performance.

*The Wisdom of Teams** cites several necessary conditions for developing mutual accountability within a team: hearing and expressing views openly and constructively, having a common purpose and approach, earning trust from others, and taking the risks associated with trusting others. These are the same conditions that RCLs work to develop across their entire organizations. Jim Rogers actually believes that entire manufacturing and marketing operations—even entire business units—can perform as a unified team through a commitment to a common, stretch set of performance goals, and by focusing on a common enemy. While this environment might be better described as a team-like state, there is no quarrel

---

* Jon R. Katzenbach and Douglas K. Smith, *The Wisdom of Teams: Creating the High Performance Organization* (Boston: Harvard Business School Press, 1993).

with Jim's basic point: people will perform beyond expectations when they truly believe in what they are doing—and when they recognize their interdependency in that endeavor.

There is clear evidence at GE Motors that this, in fact, is the atmosphere Jim and his RCLs are creating across the organization. It begins with the open environment, in which information of all types, from company financials to competitor tactics, is widely shared and actively discussed. Dick Krause exemplifies this openness in his All Hands meeting, in which he brings together all 900 of the employees of the Fort Wayne manufacturing operations in a local gymnasium every three months. He openly talks about where the business stands and invites questions and discussion in a true town meeting atmosphere.

The ubiquity of TBQ provides the common purpose and approach that can be seen across the organization. Shahbaz Malik, a young engineer, experienced this unifying effect in his first assignment at GE Motors, serving on an account team that included people from sales, marketing, applications development, and manufacturing. "Every team at GE Motors has a cost, quality, and speed target. That is what allows you to work with a spirit of mutual accountability. You know you have a well-defined objective with positive accountability, and it is easier to get people to do real work." TBQ not only helps mutual accountability within a team, but across teams. Everyone knows that they have their TBQ targets to meet. *They are all in the same boat, so they row together.*

Risk taking works at GE Motors because failure is tolerated, for the right reasons. Rick Tatman knows this from his experience with the ECM business. Certainly, he recognized the severity of missing the $100 million target, and the difficulty of the changes his team would need to make to recover; however, there was no fear, intimidation, or concern about retribution. To Rick, "it was simply a matter of getting on with the job. We are all in this together, and we have to hold up our end of the effort. You just have to admit mistakes, face reality, and figure out what you are going to do about it." At GE Motors, people do not expect failure, but they accept it along the way. They do not, however, accept it with respect to their overall aspirations.

While widespread mutual accountability is the general state sought by RCLs, they do not overlook individual accountability. Performance is recognized and rewarded in multiple ways. Likewise, nonperformance is penalized, but not disproportionately to the offense. GE Motors creates significant personal and professional growth opportunities for its people—

giving them a chance to fail and to learn, but not suffering laggards gladly. The company steps up to tough people-decisions sooner rather than later, but tries to do it in a way that is in the best interests of both the organization and the person whenever possible. High-performing companies with strong performance ethics are both challenging and personally rewarding, though not necessarily comfortable, places to work. These are the actions commonly associated with *consequence management,* as practiced by the very best managers. RCLs go further, however, by using a broader definition of accountability (both individual and mutual), one which is reflected in GE Motors' use of the weather-report survey in evaluating overall performance. Simply making the financial and market numbers is not sufficient; how the numbers are made counts too.

PERFORMANCE WRAP-UP

It is probably premature to fully describe what works for continuous improvement, since there are few efforts of adequate duration to warrant the label. Nonetheless, to the extent that the experience of front-runners such as GE Motors proves valid, several things are working for RCLs who are continuing their climb to higher results:

1. Keeping the marketplace foremost in mind and always in current focus.

2. Developing a clear set of performance priorities, translating them into meaningful measures, and really living by those numbers.

3. Ensuring that all change efforts are clearly focused on performance priorities—not on activities.

4. Redefining the meaning of the bottom line by giving the same rigorous attention to involving and developing people as good managers have traditionally given to meeting financial numbers.

5. Developing the habit of setting stretch performance targets, meeting them most of the time, and learning from occasional failures.

6. Broadening collective accountability within the organization by building an atmosphere of openness, common purpose, and trust.

The atmosphere of performance created by change leaders that encompasses these attitudes and actions can best be described as a performance ethic that permeates the organization in a very tangible way. To be sure, such an ethic requires a top management team that walks the talk, but it is even more important to have RCLs who can foster it within the organization.

CHAPTER 2

WORKING
VISION

Do we have a "change vision" or not? Our latest version is so lofty that I have no idea what is supposed to change at my level.

■ *Should I use it, ignore it, or fix it?*

How can I energize people about something that means nothing to them?

■ *Lucite-encased copies of our vision sit proudly on executives' desks. They are as inspiring as a row of tombstones. In fact, nobody even looks at them anymore.*

What are the words and reasons that will motivate our people to change?

■ *Should I use fear? Competitive spirit? Dare to be great? Hope? Survival? What will work best? How can I help people develop a personal reason to change?*

Is there some simple, proven process for developing a vision that works?

■ *Sitting around all day in another "group visioning" session cannot be the answer. People feel it's a phony exercise; they have better things to do with their time.*

Won't a few simple reminders work better than some elaborate vision?

EVERY SELF-RESPECTING INSTITUTION HAS A VISION STATEMENT THESE DAYS. SUCH statements become highly publicized aspects of what top leaders are expected to do. Much of the time, however, management below the top is not sure exactly what the official vision statement really means—although they are usually reassured by having one.

The best vision statements are like John F. Kennedy's historic declaration in April 1961 that the United States would "put a man on the moon by the end of the decade." Short, memorable, and meaningful to people at all levels, this comment became the core of the vision for NASA's Space Center in Houston, Texas. Even new hires were able to sense the excitement, form an immediate mental image, and make a strong personal commitment to the program's target. While few visions are so immediately compelling, many produce clear mental images that enable people to see where their leaders are taking them. When an overall vision provides an umbrella under which personal and team efforts can fit, it is clearly helpful in creating unity and extra energy within any major change program. People throughout an organization are truly enabled by compelling, slogan-like top visions such as:

- "A Coke within arm's reach of everyone on the planet" (Coca Cola)

- "Encircle Caterpillar" (Komatsu)

- "Become the Premier Company in the World" (Motorola)

Unfortunately, it doesn't always work out that way. Many companies simply do not have clear visions or even compelling vision statements at the top. What statements they do make are little more than generalized phrases in Lucite frames, made primarily to be able to say "we have a vision." Even if more carefully considered, a vision statement is still likely to be stated in such general or abstract terms that it carries little practical meaning, and is certainly not memorable to someone on the front line. In fact, some of the most well-articulated and strategically sound vision statements are virtually unknown down the line.

When a top management vision doesn't exist, is poorly understood, or just is not doing the job, it is invariably the real change leader who fills the gap. The RCL creates a *local vision* as a practical tool for managing change—almost independent of the quality or relevance of the top vision statement. The local vision may come to have company-wide significance, or it may just stay within the province of a single team working on a piece of the change effort. These local visions turn out to be an integral part of what RCLs do that helps at both a personal and a working level—in fact, more so than we would have expected. For that reason, it is worth differentiating them from the corporate or overall enterprise vision, by referring to them as *working visions*. This chapter explores what it takes to make working visions a distinct and effective means of focusing and energizing personal commitment to change:

1. What working visions can accomplish for RCLs;

2. Why the power is in the process of shaping such visions, not in the words; and

3. How RCLs play a critical role in this process.

1. WHAT WORKING VISIONS ACCOMPLISH

A working vision consists of those few words—closer to five than fifty—that enable people to see clearly in their mind's eye where the change will take them, and why it matters. That is a lot to expect of a few well-chosen words. While each person's mental image may differ, each image needs to produce consistent meanings and encourage cohesive actions throughout very diverse groups. For the people in an RCL's change effort, it is their equivalent of "putting a man on the moon," because it must:

- *Give meaning* to the changes expected of people;

- *Evoke clear and positive mental images* of what "it should be like around here";

- *Create pride, energy, and a sense of accomplishment* along the way; and

- *Link change activities and business-performance* results.

Such working visions can relate to a single initiative or to an entire change effort of multiple initiatives. In either case, most RCLs believe that the value of a working vision is entirely practical. Mary Livingston certainly sees it this way, based on her experience with a series of change initiatives spanning several years. These all took place within the sales force of AT&T's Business Communications Services (BCS), the multi-billion-dollar unit that provides businesses of all sizes with everything from long-distance calling to ultra-sophisticated, global data networks.

Mary's easy demeanor and frequent laughter mask a tough, determined spirit stemming from her strong belief that, unless you reach more than the minds of people, you have little chance of influencing them to step out of comfortable, established behavior patterns. Mary is no stranger to facts and logic, and she uses them well. Yet, she is truly a master at building trust, confidence, and risk-taking courage among the people she is trying to influence to change. She also reads all the relevant articles and books on change management, but most of what works for her she has learned the hard way—in the frontline trenches of change.

For two years, Mary headed what was known as CMO (Change Management Organization)—a group of more than fifty people who stepped out of their regular front-line sales jobs to revitalize the performance of the thousands in the BCS sales force.* A veteran of the sales force, Mary had always had an interest in how organizations do and do not change. In fact, she was planning on entering a Ph.D. program in organizational behavior when this change leadership opportunity was offered to her. Mary opted for the real-life experience that several others had already turned down. (The best RCLs are always accepting or volunteering for the tough and/or risky assignments that most good managers seem to avoid.)

In the course of the change program, Mary formed and guided nearly a score of team initiatives that diagnosed current sales performance, designed and implemented sales improvement processes for different customer segments, and reengineered all of the sales force's support processes (compensation, training, etc.). As she looks back now, she sees clear value in working visions—much more than she was expecting at the time.

> The value of vision is making sure you don't get embroiled in activity for activity's sake. I got more mileage out of my time and more quality work out of the teams when we were clear on the vision of each initiative. We could answer the simple question, "What are we trying to do here?"

As Mary implies, without a vision people think in terms of activities only—"my goal here is to lead this task force, to roll out this program, and to train all the branches on this process." They grind through activity after activity until someone decides some other problem is more important, which takes them off into another loop of activities. Unless they tie activities directly to results that matter, their activity loop is endless. As Mary says, "You have no sense of how to measure success."

The modifier *working* is used to distinguish the type of vision to which Mary refers because of its practical value. Good working visions can actually provide extra motivation as well as alignment for making change happen. The label is also appropriate because, as will be illustrated later, RCLs really must work the territory by engaging and reengaging everyone from front-line teams to top executives until a working vision emerges. One seldom results from a blinding flash of individual insight, intellect, or inspiration.

---

* Michael Keith's middle-market initiative and Ray Butkus's Find Waldo effort, described in chapter 1, grew out of this change program.

HOW WORKING VISIONS DIFFER

The best working visions are concise and simple. They could be called slogans, but they are much more than that to the people who use them. At first, like "put a man on the moon," they may not seem very eloquent or insightful—particularly to the outside observer. To those who work with them, however, they gradually take on these attributes.

The working visions of change leaders differ markedly from top corporate visions, which are carefully crafted and finely scripted statements that run for paragraphs, if not pages. RCL visions are not characterized by well-engineered, buy-in processes of interaction, breakout discussions, and flip-chart reporting, although animated discussions and discarded flip charts are often part of the process of developing them. In the end, they come down to a few clear ideas and phrases that convey focus and meaning to the people working the change territory.

What matters most about the words is the images they conjure up in the minds of people—not how they appear in print or even how they sound in conversation. This means that one looks for a working vision in the eyes and expressions of people, not in the memos and speeches of their leaders. *And it looks like enthusiasm, commitment, and trust.*

EXAMPLES THAT WORKED AND WHY

Abstract descriptions are not very helpful to those who have yet to experience working visions. A few examples are worth a thousand words. The following paragraphs illustrate both the simplicity and the range of four change leaders' working visions. As you read them, keep in mind that the words seldom mean much to outsiders. Val Micklus, an RCL at AT&T (who will be introduced later in this chapter), is typical in saying, "I don't think our vision ever struck other people as being that insightful, or even useful. It was like, 'Okay, if you get a charge out of that, fine.'" Nonetheless, these four examples illustrate the words that really mattered to both customers and employees who were involved.

1. **"Eliminate what annoys our bankers and our customers"** **(Texas Commerce Bank [TCB]).**   These words worked at TCB because they got right to the heart of what people really cared about. They super-

seded top management's initial notion of highlighting the $50 million cost reduction that the bank obviously needed to restore its performance to industry leadership, which was a narrow focus that did not motivate most people.

When TCB embarked on a massive redesign of virtually every process and unit within the bank, top management wanted the focus to be a meaningful number. This logic did not help much, however, because change leaders and other TCB bankers found little inspiration in either the $50 million figure or the notions of reengineering, cost cutting, and downsizing. As the effort began to flounder, a small group of change leaders convinced top management to reject the $50 million target in favor of a set of simple words about clearing away and cleaning up all the old procedures that needlessly frustrated their customers and their people. The phrase took hold in wider and wider circles until it soon became engrained in the minds and attitudes of thousands of TCB people. Interestingly (if not surprisingly), it eventually led to economic results of more than the original $50 million vision that it replaced.

2. "The one others copy" (Mobil). This phrase worked for Mobil's U.S. Exploration and Production Division (MEPUS), because it used clear and simple words to revitalize people's pride and competitive spirit. The words came to symbolize people's determination to return MEPUS to their version of the winner's circle.

As already described in chapter 1, this division of Mobil struggled with the disturbing inevitability of downsizing. Stuck in a declining business, it weathered wave after wave of workforce reductions. Yet it continued to rank in the bottom half of its benchmarked competitors in terms of production costs. To bring the division up to first rank, neither "reduce costs" nor "become a high performance organization" was compelling or motivating. Again, through an expanding group of change leaders working the territory, MEPUS hit upon being "the one others copy." This simple phrase not only caught the organization's attention, it helped its members launch a new leadership and organization approach, and make MEPUS the low-cost producer in ways that left others envying its innovation.

3. "No graffiti" (New York City Transit). This statement evoked a clear, desirable image that customers, employees, and politicians alike could witness for themselves.

The transit system was in a shambles in the early 1980s. Subway car and bus breakdowns, track fires, collisions, crime—just name it—were everywhere, not to mention graffiti. Most New Yorkers, particularly the subway riders, assumed the system was out of control, if not beyond hope. Beginning in 1984, fueled by $6.5 billion in new capital, a new management team proved the skeptics wrong. And it all came together around the simple, compelling phrase, "no graffiti," which became the battle cry of subway workers and management alike. This instant recognition made "no graffiti" a powerful, coalescing war cry for the change efforts at New York City Transit.

4. "Be our customer's best sales relationship" (AT&T's Business and Commercial Services [BCS]). This phrase worked for one of Mary Livingston's AT&T teams, because it highlighted the critical personal tie each person had with the customer. It conveyed a very personal meaning and responsibility that people could feel good about and develop a pride in accomplishing.

The BCS sales force change program included the redesign of all support processes to shift accountability to branch offices and cut overhead in half. This team was charged with redesigning the hiring, training, and related human resources processes. Comprising salespeople, the team couldn't relate to what they saw as "staffy work," and was overwhelmed by reams of documents, none of which fit together. As described in more detail later, a group of potential change leaders worked the territory until they came upon a simple phrase to remind them of what these processes were really about: developing the people who could build unique, value-adding customer relationships. This discovery clarified and breathed new life into their effort.

None of these working visions were the result of special visioning exercises that led everyone to endorse a special phrase. "No graffiti" was a challenge that came top-down, directly from David Gunn, then president of NYCT. Each of the other three developed as a group of dedicated, determined RCLs worked the territory, until one or more simple phrases started producing a set of positive reactions from more and more people.

THE MAKINGS OF A GOOD WORKING VISION

An effective working vision is best judged by the looks on the faces of people as they tackle the change task at hand with enthusiasm, commitment, and trust. It is not surprising for groups to experiment with several phrases before arriving at just the right words. Yet the words per se seldom reveal to outsiders the full meaning and implications that employees will see in them. Nonetheless, when insiders do start responding to a working vision, it is because they find the words to be memorable, motivating, and relevant. Change leaders learn to look for those characteristics.

MEMORABLE

An outsider coming into an organization and wandering around for the day hears similar sets of words often enough to sense that they convey an esprit de corps about the place. The exact phrasing may vary, but the message is always clear. Keeping it short helps make it memorable, but expressing a clear theme is more important. The theme conveys a strong central idea or clear image to the minds of both senders and receivers throughout the organization.

The best change leaders believe that a vision can enable hundreds of people to take thousands of actions that are more constant, consistent, and of higher collective impact than they could be otherwise. A "no graffiti" subway car or bus is easy to picture; as a result, people can more readily take consistent actions to achieve one. This simple vision triggered an amazing alignment of people, functions, and communications that did not exist before—transit police, train and bus operators, car cleaners, and even materials management staff (to find new cleaning solvents). The further challenge of 24-hour-removal of any new graffiti provided memorable specifics and zero tolerance to an organization more used to a nonspecific, plodding pace and wide tolerance for error. The presumption that such "Six Sigma"-like efforts to improve quality are possible only within the dynamic Motorolas of the world was proven wrong. (Six Sigma was the term Motorola used for the company-wide quality program that led to its winning the prestigious Baldwin Award for quality in 1988.)

MOTIVATING

People at different levels and in different functions come to attach a very personal set of implications to the right set of words. They are able to develop a personal vision of their own change situation that is compatible with, but not necessarily identical to, the broader organization-change vision. Virtually every employee of TCB had personal experiences they could easily relate to eliminating "what annoys our customers and our bankers [employees]." The level of commitment which that vision produced turned out to be absolutely critical when more than 1,700 people on 176 action teams had to muster the energy for the arduous work of redesigning each and every process in the bank—while keeping up with their regular jobs at the same time. Typically, people do not perform two jobs well for long, unless the extra effort has personal meaning for them.

While people can be motivated by both opportunities and threats, positive motivations are much more likely to carry the day in a change effort that must sustain itself over an extended time period. The human resources design team at AT&T–BCS needed positive motivation badly. They were salespeople who felt they had been relegated to staff work, and they were catching lots of internal flak from their colleagues. They felt bewildered and betrayed until they could relate their work to what sales is all about—satisfied customers! By seeing the fruits of their work as the means of developing salespeople who could give customers their "best sales relationship," they found motivation similar to what they were used to in the field. Moreover, it was an aspiration that gave them pride in what they were trying to do.

Relevant

The words chosen must be relevant and must resonate with both those doing the changing and those affected by the change: shareholders and customers as well as the workforce. Often, the difference between a phrase that works and one that does not is the inclusion of more than one of the three constituencies. For example, until the Mobil effort focused on more than headcount reductions, it could only meet the short-term needs of shareholders. Once the company focused on challenging the competition, the workforce was included in the act—in a positive way. This made a big difference.

The relevance for a working vision also results in the achievement of attractive business performance results—even though the vision may not speak to that objective per se. In each of the successful change efforts we explored, the direct, hard measures of business performance gains were never subordinated to flights of fancy or warm feelings. The primary purpose of any working vision must be to energize and focus people towards clear performance results.

Keeping these attributes in mind can help RCLs understand why a working vision has not yet come together. It can also help reveal why a working vision sometimes loses impact.

WHEN A WORKING VISION LOSES IMPACT

Working visions do not last forever; changing circumstances often call for a fresh vision. Change leaders, with their linkages throughout the organization, are usually in the best position to judge when one working vision may have run its course and the search for a successor needs to begin.

This is where the New York City Transit (NYCT) finds itself today. The once-effective, "no graffiti" working vision of 1984 is no longer so relevant. By the late 1980s, NYCT had largely succeeded in getting the subway and bus systems under control—when no self-respecting New Yorker believed it could. Not only was graffiti virtually gone, many other physical and administrative elements had been improved. From preservation of historical tile work along station platforms to state-of-the-art, "new technology trains" featuring a quiet, smooth ride, automated station announcements, and advanced communications systems, a system near collapse had been turned around. The magnitude of this revitalization, officials contend, is reflected in a key subway-maintenance measure, "mean distance between failure (MDBF)," the distance a subway car travels before breaking down and causing a service delay. MDBF is a common overall measure of how well the transit authority is keeping the system running. In 1994, MDBF was more than 51,000 miles, compared to 5,000 miles in 1984, a tenfold improvement that was a well-earned source of pride.

This change effort to wrest back control of the system was similar to mobilizing for a war. And, like any wartime mobilization, it required both the infusion of new capital dollars and better management direction and control. People received new marching orders along with the resources and command structure to execute effectively. As a result, "no graffiti" was a battle cry well suited to the situation. It identified the enemy and set the objective in clear, visible terms. It also captured the spirit of the wider effort to restore order to a system that was badly out of control.

In the 1990s, however, the subway system is largely in "peace time." The task in this era—that of increasing customer service and ridership—

is very different and in many ways much tougher. There are no clear ene-
mies to rally against or highly visible victories to achieve. And as the challenge has changed, RCLs are seeking new working visions to align and
energize the efforts of the workforce.

SEEKING A NEW WORKING VISION (NYCT)

When Alan Kiepper became the new president of NYCT in 1990, he
began shifting the organization's primary focus from rebuilding infrastructure and restoring basic service to increasing customer service and ridership. Carol O'Neill has thought a lot about why this new challenge is
different and harder. She is an RCL in the newly formed Office of Management and Budget, which Kiepper formed to help ensure that the system's limited resources are invested in those programs most likely to
improve the quality of service.

Carol is one of the few change leaders encountered who graduated
from a major business school—in this case, Stanford. She also left more
lucrative work with an offshoot of the Boston Consulting Group to pursue
her personal passion "to help see that public resources achieve the greatest possible benefit for the public." From an early age, she has sought to
help people in ways that really make a difference. Work with poverty programs and the World Bank convinced her that "there is something
between policy and implementation that is fairly important that organizations just don't manage very well." That realization sparked her interest in
change leadership. Prior to business school, she worked for the New York
City Mayor's Transportation Office, where she developed a deep appreciation for the vital role that public transportation plays in the city, especially
for the many residents who cannot afford anything else. Thus, when Carol
joined NYCT in 1991, she was primed for helping the organization take
on new challenges.

When Carol describes the challenge of this decade, she points with
dismay to the very measure—MDBF—that tells the success of the 1980s:

> A 51,000 MDBF is great, but the customer does not experience
> MDBF, cars do. Customers experience delays. While the mean dis-
> tance between failures has continued to rise steadily in the 90s,
> delays have remained pretty constant. So at some point, who cares
> about MDBF if our service is no more reliable? What you've really

got to do is reduce *everything* that causes delays that a customer experiences, if you are really serious about customer service.

Obviously, Carol is right. But addressing all sources of delay greatly complicates the change effort. Improving MDBF requires heavy spending on new equipment and doing preventive maintenance. Addressing all sources of delays requires operating the trains on schedule, managing passenger loading in peak hours, coordinating cleaning and maintenance activities, dealing with sick passengers, keeping the track clear of trash, accommodating track repairs, and a myriad of other activities. Moreover, victory in addressing all sources is much less instantly visible than "no graffiti" and much harder to measure than MDBF.

Eliminating subway delays is only one part of NYCT's aspiration of providing improved customer service, which also includes providing more frequent service, improving station environments, and reducing crime. Much of this requires new funding, but in this era of shrinking municipal budgets, such efforts must be funded largely by productivity improvements.

Not only is the scope of the effort daunting, but the kind of change required is very different from before. It is not so much about doing things (buying new subway cars, adding management positions, revising procedures) as it is about changing the skills, behaviors, and attitudes of people—in this case more than 44,000 employees. Consequently, each small aspect of improving customer service becomes a major change challenge. Selling tokens with a smile and a courteous response requires a positive attitude from 3,500 clerks who work in cramped bullet- and fireproof booths and must be wary of hoodlums every time they leave the booth to empty tokens from the turnstiles. Since people actually suck tokens one at a time out of the turnstiles, a clerk carrying a whole bucket of them is a lucrative target. Introducing the first-ever customer training in this environment is itself a major change and undertaking, but only a beginning. And that is just one small function. Preventing or minimizing a service delay requires developing agile front-line problem solving and cross-functional cooperation that is extremely difficult to obtain in a hierarchical, function-bound organization. Again, Carol makes a compelling contrast:

> The challenge is to try and change the way we think about what we do. . . . Of course, you could say, "We are a railroad. We run trains. You want to ride them, you ride them when we run

them." With that attitude, you do fix "things" and keep them fixed. But that's about all you do, unless you adopt a completely different mind-set.

To Carol and other change leaders in NYCT, this means you have to infuse the organization with a sense of noble purpose. Thousands of people need to get excited about trying to provide what the customer wants: trains that show up on time, get riders where they want to go quickly, and are reliable, cost effective, and safe. Superior customer service requires thousands of people committed to a transit system that delivers the kind of service the customer wants and deserves. That is a very big order.

While Carol and other RCLs certainly have a personal vision of customer service, a new working vision of this dimension has not yet gelled to take the baton from "no graffiti." Nonetheless, progress has been made. A strategic plan matching service improvements with productivity gains has been developed. Multiple initiatives have been successfully launched—for example, a station-manager program that, for the first time, provides customers with a name and face they can come to with their concerns. Real improvements since 1990 are also evident: crime is down 60 percent, customer satisfaction is up 30 percent, and a twenty-year ridership decline has been reversed, despite the fact that total headcount is down 5 percent.

Still, there is much to do: perception of crime remains high; customer satisfaction is just 6 on a 10-point scale; and service reliability remains a problem. Moreover, the focus and energy that come from a simple working vision like "no graffiti" are lacking. It may be that NYCT's current challenge is too complex to lend itself to a single phrase. In that case, it is incumbent on Carol and other RCLs to fill the gap by working to develop multiple working visions at the local level for the particular initiatives and subgroups with which they work.

It may also be true that a new, overarching working vision for NYCT will yet develop. Official reports refer to having a "world-class transit system for the twenty-first century." Perhaps change leaders scattered through the organization will find a way to wed such high-level official aspirations with the realities of change at the front line to create a working vision that equals "no graffiti" in leading the system to higher levels of service. One way or the other, it is the RCL who must fill the gap.

2. THE POWER IS IN THE PROCESS

The key to crafting a working vision lies in the process, not the wording. Though the phrases and words contain meaning for those who must change, the real power of the working vision comes from the largely informal and opportunistic process of working to find and make meaning from those words. Many change leaders have special stories to tell about how their organization got its vision. Each RCL approaches his or her situation differently in trying to obtain a working vision. As we listened to and explored their stories, however, we noticed a few commonalties.

- The impetus comes from different places. Thus, the process takes many forms, and it is essentially a matter of working the territory until one emerges.

- It takes time. Working the territory is not an overnight task.

- RCLs cannot count on it coming from the top. Any gap between a top vision and what works for their people, or the void of having no top vision, is a hole that only RCLs can fill—because they are the only ones who are in a position to work with people to translate top intentions into workforce meanings.

To help change leaders think about their own process for obtaining a working vision, this section describes actual examples of how it has been done in different situations, specifically those of the Texas Commerce Bank (TCB), Mobil's U.S. Exploration and Production Division (MEPUS), and the AT&T Business Communications Services (BCS) sales force.

"ELIMINATE WHAT ANNOYS" (TCB)

The Texas Commerce Bank is an unusual case of a company whose historic performance record and current performance situation were hardly serious enough to warrant major change. Moreover, the impetus for a working vision for change came from people's initial discomfort with a most logical, yet uninspiring, performance objective. Overall, the bank's leadership aspiration was to return the bank to its rightful top ranking among its competitors in return on assets. It was obvious that TCB's costs were too high relative to those of competitors, so it was natural that CEO Marc Shapiro had cost reduction on his mind when he began thinking about a major change initiative in late 1993. Initially, major change and expense reduction were linked in his mind, since TCB had already tried everything else to regain its historic top ranking.

Marc knew that TCB would need about $50 million to achieve its aspirations—and that it would require some kind of major change to do so. He actually wrote down on a piece of paper, "want to save $50 million through doing this." Next he penciled out what part of the total amount should come from each section of the bank, making sure it all added up to the $50 million. Then he set up six task forces and talked with each one about its share of the total, trying to emphasize that $50 million was not intended to be a quota—just a ballpark figure for which they should shoot. Those discussions seemed to go all right, even though Marc readily admitted to each task force that he did not have a clue as to what the real number for each department should be. Most of the 120 people on the various task forces kept heading down the track toward identifying cost-saving ideas, and seemed to go along with the multiple task force approach. Yet, it was not too long before Marc and his top management team sensed unrest:

> As I began talking more to these people, however, my feeling was this isn't flying. People were really uncomfortable with the number. They didn't know exactly how I got it, and . . . [many] were threatened by it. It didn't seem to be working.

Marc's perception was correct—the effort was not working. And it was the change leaders in this situation who brought this fact to his attention and who eventually shaped a more compelling working vision. Typical of those who recalled their thoughts at the time:

> Having lived through several reengineering processes with other institutions, it was like, oh no! They're not going to make the money mistake, are they? It will fail. The way to get the $50 million was not to paint a sign saying, WANTED: $50 MILLION.

Marc realized that you cannot "capture people's souls for a number." In fact, the question he pondered was almost "what would they die for?"

Then he remembered an earlier effort to improve customer satisfaction, which had worked pretty well. "We got a lot of feedback, and it refocused the organization on that issue . . . so I started thinking, 'let's build on that theme.' " As he talked to more and more people, it became clear in his mind that expense reduction had to be the by-product of something more fundamental. Again, however, Marc's best source of information on this issue was the change leaders who were immersed in the problem, and who had the conviction and courage to speak up and tell him and other top leaders the reality they were facing. Even he admits that without the RCLs' persistent feedback, he might have missed it.

As a result, his RCLs convinced Marc to let them tell the task forces to forget about the money and focus on changing whatever was a *source of frustration to customers and employees*—a simple insight, perhaps, but it made a big difference. It resonated with what task force members already knew and felt:

> We knew people were already working very long hours . . . and what we found was all this stuff tying people's hands. We made money in spite of ourselves in the early eighties and then we had a downturn. In reaction, we jumped in with a policy to cover everything that went wrong. We policy-ed ourselves to death.
>
> My thoughts were to never mention the number. Just say, "Go out there and streamline the way we do business . . . and remove the frustrations and the impediments . . . the dollars will come."

Still, a working vision did not just automatically fall into place. Not everyone agreed with the new emphasis, so the RCLs had to continue working the territory on the other side for a while, as Marc recalls:

> It took a while to get everyone there. Some people really liked the expense targets as a way to prioritize. We had to say, "No, let's just focus on whatever frustrates us and frustrates our customers."

There was no formal process—or even clear intent—to develop a specific working vision. It was a case of simply working the territory of change for several weeks through open dialogue up and down the line. It is this kind of trial and retrial, and testing and retesting, that working visions are made of. The informal process that works is built a step at a time, and is based on multiple dialogues, listening carefully, and learning as you go.

Marc, as CEO, made the environment receptive. He worked in partnership with his task force leaders to understand the concerns of employees all the way down the line. He really listened. He also took time for personal introspection about what motivates people. He was willing to try, learn, and try again. At the same time, change leaders down the line also had to step up to the problem, speak out for a different objective, and take the personal risk associated with objecting to top management's announced target. Change leaders at all levels made sure their people's concerns were heard and interpreted correctly. They knew they had to confront top management, and they did. And when Marc was convinced, it was the RCLs who carried the new message back down the line. Most traditional managers in this kind of situation would simply follow the path of least resistance and support the announced program.

"THE ONE THE OTHERS COPY" (MEPUS)

Chapter 1 described how a special initiative within Mobil's U.S. Exploration and Production Division (MEPUS), worked to get the organization's change program focused on the right performance priorities for surviving in its declining industry. As this effort was under way, a parallel vision effort was taking place that had both formal and informal elements to it. The need was first recognized by Paul Hoenmans and Walt Piontek, the corporate executives who were responsible for all of Mobil's North American exploration and production operations. On several occasions they discussed the need to put the continuing cost reductions in a more positive context. Walt Piontek was convinced that the empowered-downsizing themes of the past would not continue to work. You cannot motivate and energize a workforce, even a proud one, with shrinkage over time as the only performance prospect. Something more was needed, and it could not simply be pronounced from on high.

In meetings with his direct reports, Walt kept insisting on "the vision thing" above all else. He was determined to shape one that would really be positive for the workforce without "spouting more unrealistic pap." While all present would nod their heads, most felt in their hearts that Walt was hoping for a miracle. And when they submitted their next-phase change plan, Walt was disappointed. The plan recommended starting with a brief conference speech on a vision—achieving exploration and production excellence—and then moving on quickly to how to further reduce the cost base—again! This was not what Walt had in mind, but he knew he could not simply pronounce a new vision on his own. Somehow, it would have to emerge out of his troops in a way that even he was not completely clear about. Tom Timmins was given the task of making a second try:

> I had just been put in charge of MEPUS, and all of a sudden, Walt is talking vision. I wasn't sure what I was getting into. My background is in nuclear engineering, so having a line operating job was a big enough change for me without trying to understand what Walt meant by the vision thing.

While neither Walt nor Tom knew exactly how to generate a vision in the first place, they certainly knew how to recognize one when they saw it. More important, they instinctively sensed that unless the vision was shaped and disseminated by respected RCLs and potential change leaders, it had little chance of making a difference.

Timing

Looking for a place to start, Timmins took the leaders of the SO-NAAR team (the initiative team then working on the core and noncore approach to managing their production fields, described on pp. 33–34 of chapter 1) and a few others to a change management workshop, sponsored by a consulting firm. It was attended by a half-dozen other company groups from noncompetitive industries that were also in the middle of what they each thought of as major change. The workshop gave them some ideas and got a discussion going, but no definitive vision emerged. Looking to expand the dialogue, a few of the team members broke off to the side and got together a larger group—"a diagonal slice of people from across the organization"—for a workshop of their own. It was out of this gathering that the MEPUS notion of becoming "the one others copy" first started to emerge.

ARRIVING AT THE WORDS

Greg Cox, one of the original asset team leaders and a participant in the workshop, remembers it as follows:

> We were struggling with coming up with a vision to be the best or number one. . . . But the question we kept asking ourselves was, How would you measure yourself against that? We finally came down to . . . when everyone's copying you, you must be doing the right stuff.

These discussions continued after the workshop, and other formal and informal discussions were initiated with a variety of other people. There were several versions of the main message—"the one the others imitate," "the company that competitors envy," "the one that the rest all follow"—and most commonly, "the one others copy." No one is exactly sure how and when the last one was adopted—and it did not seem to matter. What did matter was more and more people getting the idea.

Clearly, the vision had significant value in both conveying a purpose to the change effort and providing a rallying cry for team leaders to use. Greg believes that it really helped in getting the program going. "It gave us something to focus on." But he also thinks that they did not get as much out of it as they might have.

> A lot of people misunderstood it . . . we didn't do a good enough job explaining what it meant so a lot of people interpreted it to mean different things. We tried, we did do some work on going out explaining it and building a common understanding of it, but we weren't effective enough.

Working visions come and go. Some last a few months, others for years. They are what change leaders make of them, and they require ongoing attention by a critical mass of change leaders. At particular points in a change effort, they can make a big difference.

"CUSTOMER'S BEST SALES RELATIONSHIP" (AT&T–BCS)

Meanwhile, at AT&T, Val Micklus also recognized that the process of developing a working vision cannot just come down from on high. Val was the RCL leading the HAL (Human Assets and Learning) team, which was charged with redesigning all of the hiring, training, evaluation, and other human resource processes for the many thousands in the AT&T–BCS sales force. Hers was only one of four teams redesigning all of the sales support processes as a part of Mary Livingston's overall change program. But Val is keenly attuned to the need for every team and every initiative to have its own working vision. As she recalls, "I learned that the quicker that team members can find ways to know what they are dealing with, and to artic- ulate a vision about it to each other so it comes out the same, the quicker you can get to your goal."

It is clear, however, that her initial team started with little vision. Before they were a month into the effort, they were struggling more than the other three redesign teams. They had a work plan and a time line; they knew when to deliver this and that report. But in reality, Val knew they were just going through the mechanics; something was missing. Then came a Satur- day Val remembers well. Everyone was dutifully working on the charts for their presentation when some informal conversation got started around the table. Val recalls it was "just some loose talk at first, half-joking about 'tell me again why we're doing this.'" Pretty soon the conversation became serious; the charts were pushed aside. As the discussion became more animated, people started to openly question what all this redesign stuff was really sup- posed to do for them, their people, and the company. Val doesn't recall exactly how, but at this point the process really started to come together.

> We said, Okay, everybody think about this environment we're trying to create. Put your ideas down on little Post-Its. We stuck the ideas on foam boards and moved them around into group- ings. People's ideas started to converge around the idea of attempting to be our customer's best sales relationship. At that point we started to get excited. People began saying, that's right, that's it! *Be our customer's best sales relationship!*

The words were simple enough, but they really hit home in terms of emotional meaning—the team knew it was on to something powerful.

Then came the real task—figuring out what the catch phrase really meant. What is "the customer's best sales relationship"? Best in comparison to what or to whom? What would cause a customer to say, that's the best!? What makes it the best? The team members pushed themselves to answer these questions to give further definition to their working vision. Then they started asking themselves, if that's what we're shooting for, how would we hire to do that? What set of skills would we need to develop? They kept going through all the processes they were supposed to be redesigning—hiring, training, promotion, evaluation—testing them against their new working vision. Val sums it all up this way:

> Now, it may seem like no big deal, but just getting our thoughts visually up there on the board, having everyone contributing, and reaching the point of everybody saying the same thing . . . we were creating this vision! Most of all, I remember the following Monday, we were just all so energized. We said, Okay, we've got it! We have this vision. We know what we're doing!

Was it just a matter of good fortune that Val and her team got into the vision thing that Saturday afternoon? Or was it more a matter of readiness and responsiveness to the opportune moment? Val admits that they "probably had to roll around in the stuff" for several weeks before they could have made it work. But as an RCL, Val did one critical thing that day that made the process work. She cleared the time and encouraged the talk, even as a presentation deadline loomed. *"We, in essence, took a giant step backwards in order to move forward."*

MORE THAN SERENDIPITY

The foregoing examples illustrate both the importance of, and the variations in, the processes whereby working visions emerge and take hold. In each case, it is clear that the real value was not in the end product—the handful of words that captured the working vision—but in the understanding and personal conviction that developed within those who participated. While it may not always be possible to directly include everyone in the intense, sometimes extended period of discussion that is the heart of the process, the more people that are involved, the more there will be to communicate the meaning to others.

Some of these stories may make the process sound almost serendipitous. Do not be fooled. In each case, there was plenty of work on the part of one or more change leaders as well as top management. While the process may be unpredictable, RCLs do not leave it to chance. They lay the groundwork and work the territory so that the process of open interaction and dialogue, in whatever form, does occur—and does lead to a simple, motivating image.

3. WORKING THE TERRITORY

The development of working visions is murky and uncertain at best, and the process can vary widely depending upon the performance situation and the people. At the change leader level, it is often necessary to work on more than one approach at a time, probing different ways to stir individuals and groups into shaping ideas and images that will work for them. Among the many ways RCLs work their territory to cultivate a working vision, four are most common:

- *Matching the motivation to the situation,* by considering the individual and collective emotions and desires they can tap to reach different groupings of people.

- *Shaping and sharing their own personal visions* to encourage others and demonstrate how to find personal meaning in the change effort.

- *Encouraging and influencing top-level visioning,* even though it is not always possible to obtain a vision from the top in a form, or with the timing, ideally desired.

- *Keeping vision dialogues alive,* so that others can develop and reshape their own working visions, whether for an entire change program or a single initiative team.

MATCHING THE MOTIVATION TO THE SITUATION

Real change leaders become adept at obtaining the personal commitment of their people to change and perform. They use a range of motivations for that purpose, depending again on both the change circumstances and the people involved. This will be evident in the many change situations described throughout this book. For example, at GE Motors, Rick Tatman points to "a passion for achieving goals that are mutually determined" as the dominant motivating force in his organization. This force is a collective urge to build the business, born out of a competitive spirit, a desire to build a great company, and a strong team-based environment. As Rick says, "Things get done around here because people really want them to happen, not because they personally want to get ahead or make the big bucks." At GE Motors there is more to it than personal financial gain. Skeptics from other environments may question this, but a lot of RCLs make similar claims.

In other companies, the financial results are more dominant. For example, Enron's Operating Corp. (EOC) has a performance focus that rivals that of GE Motors but is driven by somewhat different motivations. Tom White heads this unit of Enron, which manages the parent's gas pipelines, gas processing plants, and electric power generating plants. He keeps a constant, rolling program of change initiatives going at EOC, all aimed at helping to make Enron the first natural gas major (analogous to an oil company major such as Mobil, Shell, or Texaco; historically there have been none in natural gas). Throughout Enron, "meeting your numbers" is what matters. As Tom explains:

> No matter how much we rearrange the deck chairs, no income is going to leak over the side. The monthly requirements for income and cash flow really drive the organization. That never changes. There is a certain rhythm and imperative to the financial side of this thing that I think keeps people focused on the fact that we can make all these organizational changes, but in the end, we still have to move molecules and we still have to make money.

"Meeting your numbers" is not just a clever slogan at Enron; it is the primary basis of personal motivation. It is widely perceived as the way to get ahead, and the way to personal-opportunity growth within the company. Having a personal financial stake in the outcome of change initiatives further affirms this motivation. As Tom also notes, "The fact that we are shareholders of the company in large numbers provides a very powerful argument." A good part of the impetus for Enron employees comes from the pride of accomplishment and the excitement in continued growth that accompanies making the numbers every year. There is little question that growth and profitability are motivating.

While every situation has its own blend of motivations, most draw from a generic set of reasons for undergoing major change. These are the universal appeals that change leaders can consider when first thinking of what basic message they can form that matches people's motivations to the change task at hand. Many are obvious, but the list is worth repeating here:

■ *Fear.* This is the crisis mentality. Many still believe that major change is impossible without it. There is little question that a true crisis clears the mind, particularly when a large number of people are involved. Most major change situations have some degree of fear or anxiety that motivates or intimidates people and helps establish a serious sense of urgency. The best RCLs, however, do not actively promote fear or anxieties. Rather than overplay the tendencies of people toward excessive anxiety that can immobilize rather than energize them, they inject counterbalancing positive incentives that create constructive energy for change.

■ *Competitive spirit.* Most people like to compete and want to win. Like it or not, most people are competitive creatures at heart, and under the right circumstances and encouragement, are energized by healthy competition. RCLs are unusually good at recognizing and exploiting the competitive tendencies in their people, particularly by refocusing attention from internal disputes to external competitors. Many numbers-driven cultures rely heavily on this motivator.

■ *Desire for greatness.* People not only like to compete, they like to think of themselves as the best. As a result, many change leaders at the top espouse aspirations that imply greatness. At the RCL level, this kind of motivation is easy to tap into if top management is credible, very difficult if it is not. Yet there are change leaders who, despite surroundings of relative mediocrity, create a distinct identity for their group and strive to become the best within their area (e.g., by achieving high manufacturing productivity within a company with poor marketing).

■ *Doing the right thing.* It is not surprising to find that many RCLs are strongly driven by the Harry Truman philosophy of simply doing the right thing. They are not always sure where it will lead—just as Truman was never sure where his political fortunes would lead—but they have a secure faith that doing the right thing—for customers, the company, and people—will work.

■ *Personal gain.* Real change leaders sometimes rely on this message, since the possibility of strengthening one's performance record to gain financial rewards is a natural incentive for most people. This is particularly true in aggressive, fast-growing companies in which big personal gains (especially through stock appreciation) are possible. Even in these situations, however, the best RCLs do not rely heavily on the idea of personal gain, simply because it does not have the energizing value of the more intangible appeals previously listed. There is also the difficulty of using this rationale to achieve broad-based change (if those really gaining are only a small minority) and long-term performance improvement (if industry cycles slow the heady growth).

■ *Making a difference.* Increasingly, we find RCLs using this rationale, both for themselves and their people. In some ways it combines several of the others (competitive spirit, doing the right thing, desire for greatness), but it is more pragmatic. People who work hard at difficult tasks take great pride and personal satisfaction when the accomplishment of the task really makes a significant difference in the performance of the enterprise.

Most RCLs who ply their craft over time find themselves relying on all of these messages at one time or another. And in any specific change situation, they will employ more than one. Mary Livingston of the AT&T–BCS sales force (introduced earlier as an advocate of the practical value of working visions) provides a good example of an RCL who, over time and in many change situations, has used multiple appeals in developing her personal vision as well as the vision of others.

SHAPING A PERSONAL VISION

Besides knowing the value of working visions, Mary Livingston also believes strongly in personal vision. She contends, "You have to have a mass of people with personal visions that are aligned, though they don't have to be identical." Mary has always given careful thought to personal motivations, perhaps as a natural outgrowth of a career in sales. The roots of Mary's personal vision go back to when she joined the organization, at a time when the group felt really good about itself.

> In 1982, I started my career with a AT&T sales organization that was really proud of what it had done in the marketplace. . . . As a graduate of that sales force I knew how things could be. . . . I had "skin in the game" and felt the same way you do when you see your alma mater start screwing up its reputation.

Unfortunately, 1982 was the last time the sales force felt good about itself. As competition from deregulation drove AT&T's market share down, internal controversies waged between the sales force and business units (product management) over who was to blame. It reached the point where internal competition superseded the external. Mary's emerging personal vision as she started the sales force's change effort bridged these extremes:

> I wanted a vision of pride based on results the business units recognized. . . . People were still proud of being in the sales force but were unwilling to acknowledge the real performance problems, so anything that business unit people said was discounted. I knew that the sales force had to own the change effort, that it had to be our data, our sins, and our fixes—nobody could do it for us.

Holding to a vision of pride in improving by facing business reality, versus taking false pride in internal standards, proved very difficult for Mary. Rigorous performance analyses—of the sales force by the sales force—revealed real problems in covering customers, identifying opportunities, and delivering an effective sales message. Many in the sales force felt that Mary and her change team were traitors, but she and they persevered.

Several months into the effort, when the change effort was still struggling to build wide support, she wrote out her vision as a "I have a dream" speech, drawing on the mix of motivations she and others in the change effort were feeling, as well as the inspiration of one of her motivational role models, Martin Luther King.

Mary carried a copy of the speech in her purse and found numerous occasions to recite it, usually impromptu at gatherings of branch managers or sales people. Sometimes she gave it to her initiative teams to bolster their own spirit. She remembers the moments after giving the speech as quiet and intense—a moment of renewed conviction for the groups, according to those who came up to her afterward or from comments she heard about later.

Mary's personal vision was deep and lasting; it carried her through some very tough times. She also found many ways to communicate a vision through different images and metaphors. "I even found I could use favorite Broadway musicals to express the struggles and aspirations of the change program." One memorable adaptation came as the change organization was celebrating its own success and dissolution. The band played a reworded song from *Les Misérables* recounting the sales force's once-troubled plight, Mary got up and read her vision once again, and the

MARY LIVINGSTON'S PERSONAL VISION

Primary Motivation

- *I have a dream that one day we will be a sales force that stands tall and commands respect from customers, business units, and competitors.*

  } Pride

- *We will be a benchmark for other sales organizations. Business cases will be written about us.*

  } Desire for greatness

- *I have a dream that we will one day be a sales force that consistently meets commitments and says it can do more (vs. being skilled in defending forecasts we know we can meet).*

  } Competitive spririt

- *We will be a sales force that delights customers, that is, raises the bar for customer satisfaction.*

  } Serving others

- *We will be a sales force that thinks more about the competition and the customer than about turf. In other words, there is an abundance mentality; we intuitively understand there is more for everybody if we do the right things . . . vs. divvying up the same pie in a different way.*

  } Doing the right thing

- *Borrowing from Martin Luther King's dream analogy is no accident. I respect the difficulties and obstacles, but I am not concerned about the obstacles.*

  } Overcoming all odds

"For when people get caught up with that which is right, and they are willing to sacrifice for it, there is no stopping short of victory."—M.L.K.

assembled change leaders of the sales force cheered. The room was filled with well-deserved feelings of pride.

INFLUENCING TOP-LEVEL VISIONS

Despite Mary's burning personal vision and experience with team-level working visions, she still felt the need for a vision from the top to add some emotion to the project plan and official endorsements. For a long time she struggled with Lou Golm, the president of the sales force, to develop a working vision for the overall change program. "I really wanted Lou to say, 'Here's the big picture, here's the vision.' And I tried everything to get Lou to come up with a vision like that."

Lou responded to all of Mary's questions and promptings, but he seemed more amused than moved by her efforts to make him into a visionary. Sometime later there was a meeting of branch managers at which Lou was to speak. Needing something for the event, he took along a copy of the mission and goals statement that had been crafted for the change program itself, in order to get buy-in from senior management. The statement was politically positioned and included expedient language like "satisfying the needs of each business unit." Lou took it anyway and changed the word "mission" to read "vision." Mary figures he was probably thinking, "Okay, you want a vision. Here's a vision."

After he spoke, one branch manager raised her hand and said, "Lou, that is no vision!" and then proceeded to describe the attributes a vision should have. Mary, who was there, sat quietly in agony because, as the ghost writer of the statement, she knew it was not a vision, nor was it ever intended to be one. But:

> It could have been an opportunity for Lou to say, "That is interesting, why don't we try to create something here? What should our vision be?" But no, he did not want to do that.

At that point, Mary gave up pushing the vision thing with Lou. Several months later at a meeting, however, someone asked Lou what he thought the change program would end up accomplishing. Lou got up and, off the top of his head, answered with "the most beautifully articulated vision" Mary had ever heard. Lou drew a picture of the sales force that did away with the centralized, rigid, staff-heavy organization he himself was a part of, and replaced it with a new operating model—one in which the branch offices would have new flexibility, capability, and responsibility to say yes in meeting customer needs. Mary nearly fell off her chair. It was his version of what he was trying to do and, as he said it, everybody knew that he meant it. It came from the heart, "evolved from a thousand trillion discussions"—not from some speechwriter or visioning process.

Mary draws two important lessons from this experience. First, change leaders must work to complement rather than try to force their top leader's visioning approach—different strokes for different folks. Lou was intent on doing the right thing all along and was driven by the competitive need he sensed in the marketplace. Well-articulated, comprehensive vision statements prompted by others just did not make sense to him, but when asked a question that did make sense, like "Where's this all headed?" he knew exactly what to say. Mary now admits:

> That vision isn't something to be forced. Some people will be very hooked in to some visionary thought but not know what kind of steps to take to get there. Others don't seem very visionary but are real clear on things that need to be done. That is where Lou was. He was really good on how you make stuff work. I think we complemented each other that way.

Mary's second lesson is that the process by which visions develop, whether at the top or within some team laboring deep in the organization, is murky and unpredictable. It doesn't start with clarity, nor can it always be made to happen, but the process can be primed by a change leader's own nascent vision.

> You have to start out with a vision that isn't well articulated. You have to sense that it can be gray, it can be murky, but it should have at least the attributes of the things that *you* want. Then I think it is helpful *to talk long and hard to a lot of people.*

This lesson is certainly confirmed in the case stories cited earlier and highlights the RCL's fundamental role in developing working visions. The talking long and hard to lots of people is, in fact, the essence of the process, be it formal or informal. The RCL's role in that process comes back to working the territory of vision: shaping and sharing his or her own vision, listening to the thoughts of others, working with leadership on vision in complementary ways, and talking it all through until the words, phrases, and images resonate with people. It is most important, perhaps, for change leaders to be able to recognize when a set of words from whatever source is capturing the imagination and conviction of their people.

KEEPING VISION DIALOGUES ALIVE

So what works best? The experience of change leaders shows that the actual working visions that prove most effective in focusing and energizing change are not official-sounding treatises or well-crafted strategic statements. Likewise, the actual processes for developing these visions vary greatly and are seldom formal exercises. Consequently, it makes sense to conclude this chapter by looking at the roles that RCLs play in fostering working visions, rather than attempting to prescribe a process. These roles fall into three basic areas: initiating discussion, assuring constructive dialogues, and checking the vital signs to see if and when the process is working.

INITIATING DISCUSSIONS

Because the process is often improvised, timing is critical. Though setting-your-vision is typically espoused as the first step in change management, RCLs usually find that some time to roll around in the situation is needed before people are even ready to consider the idea. Moreover, it is hard to talk vision without a compelling performance context. In this way, it is like trying-to-become-a-team, which almost never works. Trying to accomplish a demanding task that requires a team is what works. Similarly, trying to create a vision seldom works; trying to figure out how to accomplish a demanding performance challenge, however, will usually produce a vision. And it may or may not make sense to even call it a vision.

A certain gestation period is often needed to develop a fact-based market perspective and to identify issues, before any vision-like discussion occurs. But the RCL must be alert for signs that personal commitment may be waning, as the hard problem solving and project planning proceeds. In the cases described earlier, RCLs picked up on such signals—for example, TCB's recognition that "this isn't flying" and the

HAL team's that "we're just going through the mechanics"—and knew it was time to move on to motivational concerns.

Though many others may sense the need to develop a working vision, change leaders are usually the ones in a position to act first and show the way—because of their unique perspective on both top and bottom needs—and their belief in the value of a working vision. Depending on the situation, this initiation may be as simple as having a series of informal one-on-one discussions with others, or perhaps calling together a group session to step back and consider the greater purpose of the work everyone is pursuing. It may also require the RCLs to intervene directly with their own teams, with another team whose leader is not stepping up, or maybe with one or more senior leaders (even the CEO) who are not yet aware of the lack of meaningful direction.

Val Micklus moved on from the HAL team to a line position in AT&T–BCS product management. Coming with a fresh perspective into a group of seasoned product hands, she soon had a feeling of *déjà vu* that "we're badly caught up in an activity mode again." Each day in her new position was the same struggle to get the half dozen or so immediate requests that came down from senior management out the door on time. Meanwhile, the organization was facing fundamental changes and new competitors in developing advanced telecommunications service for large customers. Too little time was being spent on that challenge. Though she was the newest person in the organization, Val soon began discussions with her team about larger objectives, in hopes of their developing a working vision to get themselves out of the endless activity loop.

Sharing a personal vision can sometimes be a good way to initiate the idea of a vision, and sometimes that means the RCL just starts talking. Mary Livingston took this simple approach at a dire moment in the life of another team, a group that was working on developing a new process for uncovering and capturing opportunities in major accounts. They were nearly ready to begin training on the new process (starting with a tough crew of sales vice presidents), and it just wasn't ready. The piece parts were there, but somehow they had not been integrated, and the new process didn't look like much more than the same old account planning. She knew the team was in trouble and thought she might be able to help them by thinking out loud about her own aspirations for their work.

> I brought them in, and just started talking—for about an hour and a half—about all the things I had been thinking about. We

all began to realize that the potential of this was phenomenal if we could just pull it together. It was energizing for me. I don't know if it was energizing for them. All I can tell you is that when they came back with their final work, it knocked my socks off.

Mary could have stepped into that meeting and simply focused on tactics and specific tasks. Instead, she took the time to bounce ideas around with the team on what the big picture could be, and left the group to develop (and own) its vision of the solution.

ASSURING CONSTRUCTIVE DIALOGUE

Forming a working vision inevitably requires one or more periods of intense discussion without a clear resolution as the result. Several people consider a wealth of ideas, facts, and opinions and forge them into early-vision phrases and alternatives, one of which eventually catches on, or gets pieced together over time. The quality of that dialogue and the effectiveness of the resulting working vision can be affected by several factors in which the change leader can play a hand. A noted physicist, David Bohm, defines dialogue as "a more open-ended process in that resolution is not necessarily a goal. Rather it is a free and creative exploration, requiring careful, non-judgmental listening from all parties."* Such a process is obviously very different from formal discussions aimed at vision resolution, and is at the heart of the best vision dialogues.

The process should be inclusive rather than exclusive. Thinking specifically about who to include is helpful. Sometimes this is obvious (the whole team in a situation like that of Val Micklus' team). At other times, especially in the early stages, a new grouping may need to be defined. For example, MEPUS chose to assemble a diagonal slice of the organization separate from the change-initiative team. Some individuals are natural contributors based on their position, perspective, or character. Think too about individuals with special expertise to contribute (e.g., communications), in addition to their thoughts on the vision itself. Finally, give some thought to including the maverick, or irritant member. Just as in chemical

---

* David Bohm, "The Merlin Factor: Leadership and Strategic Intent," *Business Strategy Review,* Vol. 5, No. 1 (Spring 1994):67–84.

change, such elements often stimulate otherwise unrecognized aspects of the change opportunity.

It is nearly impossible to have a meaningful vision dialogue as a stand-alone activity. Calling people together to talk vision for an afternoon is bound to feel contrived and unproductive, if not downright silly, if it is not in the context of the performance objectives that underlie the change program. Those objectives may not be fully defined yet, but there needs to be at least the context of an ongoing strategy or performance review or an actual change project. After all, a working vision is about the real work of making change happen.

Related to context is the need for grounding dialogues in the facts regarding both the organization and its market. A working vision may reshape current reality, but it cannot ignore it. Therefore, it is critical that the dialogues always face reality openly and in ways that build credibility for the process. The value of fresh information in these dialogues is very high. Underpinning the vision must be a clear view of the organization's economics and the dynamics of its market. While TCB's vision focused on people and customers, it was thoroughly grounded in financial analysis supporting the need to lower costs. No one ever disputed the importance of reducing the bank's expense ratio relative to its peers, even though they argued that it not be the primary focus of the change effort. The RCL can play a special role in making sure that the relevant facts are generally known to participants and that they are recalled at critical points in the dialogue.

Finally, there is the need to ensure top management support. As seen in the case examples, not every vision effort begins at the top. However, it is still essential that top leaders at least acknowledge and, hopefully, take an active and visible role in supporting any new working vision at some point in the process. Otherwise, the organization will sense the disconnect, and the energy behind the vision will be dissipated by personal concerns over which direction the winds of change are really blowing. While Walt Piontek of MEPUS did not directly participate in forming the actual working vision, his attention and emphasis was critical, and his presence certainly was felt down the line. The exact role taken by the top leadership can vary, depending on personal preferences. Some will want to be at the front of the room, leading the discussion. Others may want someone else to take the lead, preferring to work in the background providing whatever support is needed along with a few well-placed inputs. Many approaches

can work, provided top management support is signaled to the organization in a way it understands.

CHECKING THE VITAL SIGNS

Putting a working vision to work requires spreading the vision to all
those in the organization who were not involved in the initial crafting. A
really good working vision tends to spread on its own. If it resonates with
people, it is quickly picked up and starts appearing in hallway conversation, on bulletin boards, and in meeting presentations. But this natural dis-
semination process can be furthered by RCLs. They can reinforce it by
making it part of their daily vocabulary. And more than just expressing it,
the change leader needs to talk it through with people so that they have a
chance to test and internalize the images and themes of the vision for themselves. These people can then, in turn, pass their understanding on to others. It is through this process that the working vision takes on consistent
meaning and garners consistent action throughout the organization.

When real dialogues occur, RCLs can see certain indications—or
vital signs—that the vision is working and that more and more people are
becoming committed.

■ *Informal vision dialogues continue.* The vision continues to spark
constructive dialogue, debate, and discussion across organizational
boundaries long after the initial shaping process is over. At TCB you will
hear something about not annoying customers in most gatherings. People
are comfortable talking about the vision with others outside their immediate areas. It enhances their understanding of the vision's implications and
accelerates the pace of change by involving others. People are not afraid to
disagree and learn from the differing views of others. Communication
opens up at all levels and more people contribute.

■ *Many people walk the talk.* Daily actions are more consistent and,
as a result, collective skills develop. The power of the vision to change
behaviors becomes evident. In the golden days of "no graffiti," even the
New York subway passengers took on the graffiti villains. As the individual acts of large numbers of people become more consistent with one
another, they cumulatively begin to effect the delivery of value to customers. Performance results rise, reflecting, as well as reinforcing, the aspirations stated in the vision. Paradoxically, an operating vision both

liberates energy and controls behaviors far more effectively than a rigid set of processes and procedures can do.

■ *Decisions are free of double checks.* Decision making and priority setting do not require elaborate syndication reviews and checker-checking—they are simply guided by the vision. Decisions at MEPUS that used to flow up the line are now made regularly at the asset-team levels. People understand and learn the priorities that support the vision, by trial and error. Thus, they actually experience the importance of making decisions that are consistent with the vision.

■ *Customers know the vision.* Customers, the toughest critics, recognize that the actions and decisions of employees are increasingly consistent. Hewlett-Packard's customers expect to be treated differently—they know their loyalty is highly prized—because of Hewlett-Packard's well-known aspiration of "earning the loyalty of our customers." Customers may never repeat the words, but they know the working vision because they feel its effect. They also often report what they perceive as violations of the vision. The vision builds their respect for the organization and increases their loyalty as buyers.

■ *Employees want to stay.* Perhaps most important of all, employees want to stay with the organization. They may be pressed to the limit, but they are energized as well. Outsiders are attracted to the organization. Recruiting is easy. People sense the energy and direction and want to be part of it. Like a magnet, a working vision not only aligns those already in the organization, it draws in those who pass by.

Once a working vision is showing these effects in an organization, it is probably something that could actually be hung on a wall. But that wouldn't be necessary. After all, working visions work because they are heard in daily conversations and their impact is seen in the eyes and on the faces of people—not because they hang as plaques on the wall.

VISION WRAP-UP

An RCI's work with vision is never done. The task is ongoing, primarily because change is not a matter of one vision but of many aligned visions. Each initiative or project team that is part of the change program may need help in developing its own working vision. And someone needs to be sure that all those visions remain aligned.

There are also always newcomers who need to be inculcated into the change process. These may be individuals just joining a team, or they may be colleagues in staff or line jobs. These people need to understand the meaning of the vision and hear the story of how it came to be. Then they need time and thought of their own to give the words personal meaning.

Finally, a working vision needs constant testing and refining—and sometimes replacement. Market conditions will shift over time. The organization's performance level and performance issues will change. New constituencies may enter the picture. Any of these events may trigger the need to revisit a working vision. Once again, it is the RCL who must step in and start the process anew.

CHAPTER 3

COURAGE

Where do I get the courage to take on this kind of career risk when few others will?

■ *I'm offered the chance to get involved in changing things around here. Do I want to do this? What do I get in return?*

How do I get people to try new ways when jobs are at stake?

■ *So here we go again—reengineering, delayering, restructuring, total quality, major change. Still sounds like more layoffs to me.*

Can I be straight with my people without causing panic?

■ *If I let people know how bad things really are, won't they just be even more discouraged?*

How do I help them find the courage to try again?

■ *Just asking people to change things to make the company better does not deal with their immediate anxieties. What can be done to bolster their confidence and conviction?*

Do we really have any choice if we want to keep our jobs?

ACTS OF PERSONAL COURAGE INVARIABLY INFLUENCE OTHERS. WE ADMIRE THE courageous among us, remember their acts of heroism, and make them role models for our children. It is not surprising, therefore, to find personal courage so evident and essential among RCLs working to bring about major change.

Most often we associate courage with conspicuous heroic acts by seemingly ordinary people. When Air Force Captain Scott O'Grady's plane was shot down over war-torn Bosnia, his escape stirred the spirit of patriotism across the entire country and captured the attention of most of the free world. In World War I, Sergeant Alvin York of the Tennessee Volunteers captured 120 Germans single-handed with only a standard-issue army rifle as his weapon of attack. This dramatic act of bravery became a beacon of pride for all of his comrades in arms. Yet neither of these men claimed any special courage for themselves; they were ordinary people "doing their duty with the help of God" and their military support.

Many equally courageous acts are less conspicuous. At the turn of the century, an ordinary man by the name of Nephi Daniel led a small party of Mormon pioneers across the Great Plains in search of farmable land that would be free from religious persecution. As they camped one night, all of their horses were stolen, presumably by one of the bands of renegade Indians known to pillage small wagon parties in that area. On foot and alone, Nephi Daniel set out to get them back, since without horses, his party was doomed.

He tracked the stolen horses for several days and nights across difficult Wyoming terrain, primarily because he was able to recognize the hoofprints (made by the iron horseshoes he had personally applied before the journey). When he caught up with them, however, he experienced the surprise of his life. Instead of a few straggly renegade Indians that he might bargain with, the perpetrators were none other than the infamous Hole in the Wall Gang of ruthless outlaws and desperadoes. At this point, common sense would argue that Nephi Daniel beat a fast retreat for help, particularly since he was only five foot six inches in height, less than 150 pounds in weight—and completely unarmed.

But retreat was not an option in his mind. He had come this far, the horses were the key to the survival and future well-being of his family and friends, and he knew he "was clearly in the right." To this day, no one knows for sure how he pulled it off, but somehow he entered the outlaw camp, accosted the leaders of the gang, and returned with the horses alive and well. It was an act of personal courage known only to his family and close friends.

Like Scott O'Grady, Alvin York, and Nephi Daniel, most RCLs are ordinary people who summon personal courage when needed to "do their jobs" as they see the need. They do not talk much about their own courageous acts. Unlike O'Grady and York, however, few acts of RCL courage make the history books. More like Nephi Daniel, they are known only to family and colleagues—and their courage is seldom self-acknowledged. Nephi Daniel was too early to be an RCL (although settling a new country is clearly some kind of major change), but he still typifies what most change leaders told us when we asked them why they take significant personal career risks to bring about change for their people:

■ *It was clearly the right thing to do.* Like each of the preceding examples, most RCLs claim to "do what they have to do." Yet, that pragmatism suggests a high degree of character, because doing what they believe is right often opens them up to potential personal sacrifice. Without belaboring the point, Randy Howard, an RCL from UNOCAL (described later in this chapter) says, "I guess I personally never worried about courage. From my standpoint, if you end up doing the right thing— things that you think are right—it works out in the end." This sounds strangely similar to what both Nephi Daniel and Scott O'Grady gave as the rational for their acts of courage.

There is probably no better summary of why RCLs take the personal risks that they do than these words of Harry S Truman: "Always do the right thing. It will gratify some and amaze the rest."*

■ *The status quo was not acceptable.* Nephi Daniel simply could not accept returning to his party without the horses. To him, courage was not the issue, because the horses were essential. Likewise, change leaders today simply become frustrated with the current level of performance or customer satisfaction, or workplace conditions. The best ones believe so strongly that there is a better way, that the pursuit of that better way becomes the core of their effort to improve people's jobs as well as their lives. This notion became the primary motivating force in the Texas Commerce Bank's process improvement effort, which involved close to 4,000 people focused on "eliminating what frustrates our customers and our bankers."

■ *It would build new skills.* If change occurs and succeeds, two kinds of skills will likely be in high demand in the new environment: the skills needed for the new business processes or techniques, and change skills

---

* David McCullogh, *Truman* (New York: Simon & Schuster, 1992).

themselves. RCLs demonstrate keen interest in obtaining the new skills needed to carry out the change challenges they anticipate down the road, and they believe that these same skills will be required again and again in the future. In Nephi Daniel's case, he did not anticipate his confrontation with the Hole in the Wall Gang as a skill-building opportunity, but there is no doubt that it helped to prepare him for many similar confrontations as a pioneer staking his claim in a new land.

■   *There was no other way to preserve my job.* Clearly, Nephi Daniel saw no other way to preserve the future well-being of his pioneer party than to confront the Hole in the Wall Gang; the alternative was aborting his quest for the new land, and perhaps bringing death upon his party. RCLs face less devastating alternatives, but loss of jobs and life-styles can be almost as frightening to contemplate. Sometimes there seems to be no other choice but to leave the company, which may not be a realistic option. When an enterprise is overwhelmed by change, everyone is a part of it almost by default. Top management's request, therefore, is really a requirement—or at least change leaders see it as essential to preserve the job opportunities they and their people need.

The rest of this chapter draws on the experiences of several RCLs to illustrate what they do that works in getting people to step up to the risks of change:

1. **Building their own self-confidence and credibility;**

2. **Instilling courage in others; and**

3. **Influencing top management's conviction, if not courage.**

1. BUILDING CONFIDENCE AND CREDIBILITY

Five people were killed and more than two hundred injured in the worst New York subway disaster in 63 years. [The crash] plunged the city's transit system into chaos . . . and left the Lexington Avenue IRT, the system's second busiest line, so torn up that officials said it could be several days before it is running again.
—*New York Times,* Thursday, August 29, 1991

Workers chopped and sliced mangled subway cars yesterday, while others tried to return cars to their tracks in a repair job in Union Square station that might best be compared to changing tires in a hallway or performing surgery in a sauna.
—*New York Times,* Friday, August 30, 1991

After four days of round-the-clock work to clean up last week's subway derailment, service resumed early today for 500,000 riders of the Lexington Avenue IRT line, when a No. 4 express train rumbled safely through the site of the deadly accident. Transit workers . . . sacrificed Labor Day weekend picnics and activities to restore service on the Lexington Avenue line. Many workers said they had to work for hours under extremely difficult conditions: temperatures in the tunnel often exceeded 100 degrees and the space was very cramped.
—*New York Times,* Tuesday, September 3, 1991

These six days over a Labor Day weekend in 1991 produced plenty of courage and commitment at New York City Transit (NYCT). Throughout the ordeal no one questioned the goals: rescue the injured from the disastrous crash, provide alternative transportation for 500,000 customers, and rebuild the damaged station in time for the post-holiday commuter rush. Regular hours did not matter; hundreds showed up to work around the clock. Functions did not matter: teams from multiple departments quickly formed around specific repair tasks. Hierarchy did not matter: those who could cut, drill, wedge, and weld were assisted by those who could only hold equipment or bring food. Formal procedures did not matter: a charge account was instantly opened at a nearby supermarket to provide food and drink. Customers were not forgotten—120 buses were mustered to provide shuttle service and staff personnel were out greeting commuters and helping them find a way to work and home.

The recovery from the Union Square tragedy dramatically illustrates why RCLs like Carol O'Neill (chapter 2) believe strongly that NYCT contains thousands of people who can be enabled to change. Most individuals do possess the latent personal courage required to change, but they may need someone or something to draw it out. But drawing courage out of people without having something as compelling as a train wreck to provide the inspiration is not so easy.

In fact, RCLs seldom have the benefit of events like subway crashes to draw out people's courage. Perhaps courage is too noble a word to describe the inner drive that enables some people to step out of comfortable, secure behavior patterns in search of an uncertain better way. Maybe faith, fortitude, self-discipline, or boldness are better descriptors. Most RCLs prefer the terms self-confidence and conviction. Regardless, courage seems to be a most apt description—not only of what RCLs must have, but what they must be able to draw out of many others.

A STEP AT A TIME

Change leaders gain the self-confidence—as well as the credibility—they will need for change by taking a series of connected actions that, once started, play out in series. Some may not seem inherently courageous, but each requires additional levels of risk and boldness on their part. These actions do not necessarily represent one big leap of faith, but rather a set of ongoing and interconnected choices that often appear in retrospect to have been one leap. These choices often include: (1) making the initial commitment; (2) building conviction and credibility through actions (walking the talk); (3) speaking out and up on things that matter; and (4) removing obstacles with bold, visible actions. Each step reinforces the RCL's personal self-confidence, making him or her increasingly effective at helping others raise their tolerance for risk. Often, potential change leaders get into this confidence-building chain without realizing it, but more often they do so with their eyes wide open.

MAKING THE INITIAL COMMITMENT

This is a process that is usually straightforward, but seldom without risk. Either RCLs are requested, or at least perceive that they have a choice, to step into a change role that is new to them and probably to the company as well. Accepting the role implies a commitment to see it through, despite the uncertainty, risk, and confusion about the full extent of the responsibilities and the challenges. Moreover, it requires skills that many realize they do not yet possess or at least have not yet honed. Most RCLs readily admit facing this situation with very mixed emotions, if not serious hesitations. For example:

1. Todd Strong at Browning-Ferris Industries (BFI) likes running a local waste (garbage) company, known as a district. To him, this is a local-service business opportunity that requires marketing and sales innovation, operating efficiency, distribution design and execution skill, and profit-generating initiative. It is a demanding, independent management role that he understands and at which he excels. When BFI's then COO, Bruce Ranck, asked him to join fourteen other high-potential managers from across the company in what was to become the Black & Blue task force, Todd had mixed emotions. On the one hand, it was gratifying to learn that he was regarded by top management as among the company's best managers—the criteria that Ranck applied in picking the group.

On the other hand, the request raised a number of legitimate concerns in his mind: for example: the effort might somehow undermine the autonomy of district operations; BFI might not find nearly the kind of opportunity it anticipated; and this effort might not turn out any different from earlier unsuccessful attempts that were viewed in retrospect by Todd as "kind of lofty, goal-setting processes with no meat behind them." While some contend that Todd could hardly have refused Bruce, it was still a difficult decision for him. For that very reason, however, Todd was determined to make the decision into a positive result for the company and the team. He was committed. (The BFI change effort is described later in this chapter.)

2. Cindy Olson is the vice president of Contract Settlement in Enron's newly formed Capital and Trade Commercial Support Group. She is in her late thirties, with an infectious smile that reflects her seemingly endless supply of energy for hard work. If you ask her colleagues at Enron what stands out about Cindy they inevitably say they can always count on her to get the job done. Her colleagues will also tell you that she cares—really cares—about the people who work with and for her. Her assignment pattern over the past few years clearly reflects that perception.

When she was asked to step out of her current job to take on a critical reengineering effort at Enron as one of several project leaders, she had mixed reactions. Her current job was relatively new for her, and she was challenged by the new responsibilities, the people, and the potential. She wanted to get on with doing what she felt she did best—running a service department of mixed skill levels to meet high-performance objectives. Instead, she agreed to put the bulk of that job on the back burner and to sign on with a major back-office reengineering change effort that was viewed with very mixed emotions across the company. Before the effort was completed, Cindy not only carried the responsibility for her project, but had become the informal cross-project coordinator (in Congress, she might be called the whip) for all other projects. All this, in addition to continuing her formal responsibility as vice president of Contract Settlement. It can make you tired just thinking about it.

In making her choice, Cindy had a clear view of the pros and cons. On the one hand, few doubted that there was substantial opportunity to improve the back-office support services to catch up to the growth of Enron capital and trade businesses. On the other hand, everyone anticipated that the reengineering effort would be difficult and somewhat thankless, and would result in job reductions. Cindy had a choice, simply because she was a top performer, had taken on special assignments before, and had recently been given a new job that she needed to master. As expected, however, she put career risks out of her mind and took on the reengineering assignment with her characteristic smile and enthusiasm. She was also fully committed from that point on.

Moreover, as the reengineering effort she coordinated closed in on the implementation phase, Cindy was the first to surface and worry about the impact of the changes on the people at the front line—not only because she is committed to those people, but because she knows that you cannot continue to energize reengineering efforts if all that comes out are headcount reductions. She badgered everyone connected with the effort—internally and externally—to come up with a realistic plan for relocation decisions based on a rigorous assessment of skills as well as performance.

As we move on to our third example, we leave you three of Cindy's more telling comments, which reflect both her RCL attitude and her commitment to both her people and the performance of her company:

We will always make our numbers, but will we always keep our best people?

If we cannot make reengineering mean more than headcount reduction, we will fall way short of its potential.

Too many of us are blowing by the customer. If we do that, we will lose a lot more than the customer.

3. David Mendez of Texas Commerce Bank (TCB) has always liked managing, and he is very good at it. He is a grass-roots leader who has run several different areas at TCB over the last nineteen years. He found out about his assignment as the action (redesign) team leader for commercial loan processing when he got back from vacation and noticed a number of urgent messages from Harriet Wasserstrum, the task force manager overseeing his team. (This change effort is described in chapter 4.)

Initially, he was not too sure exactly what the work or the challenges would be like. He talked "a little bit" with Harriet about process improvement, and received a "book (presentation) that talked about the expectations," but basically, he admits, "I just decided that I was going in blind." He was sure, however, that this change assignment would not be like managing another department. David is a typical example of a very good manager who found himself in an assignment in which he could not rely completely on his past experience. His real concern, however, was how to do his regular job (since he did not give it up for this assignment). This turned out to be a very legitimate concern, since his team logged 2700 person-hours over about four months. Somehow, David found a way, mainly by relying on his staff to fill the gap.

Despite these concerns, he also knew that these types of assignments were "par for the course" at TCB. This knowledge, combined with his high level of trust that the institution would recognize his efforts, made acceptance the only logical choice. And since trust is a two-way street, once he accepted the assignment, David's commitment to see it through was never a question.

Is it self-confidence, personal courage, or a sense of duty that these three typical RCLs demonstrate? It may not be the same kind of personal courage that war heroes like Sergeant Alvin York call to mind, but it is real nonetheless. And, it is a critical factor in most RCLs' decision to step up to the challenges and commit.

BUILDING PERSONAL CONVICTION AND CREDIBILITY

Once committed, RCLs have to work at building the ongoing conviction and credibility they will need as change leaders. Credibility comes from overpreparedness on facts, knowledge about the issues, and personal relationships developed with those whom they must influence. The harder that RCLs work at these three things, the stronger their personal convictions become—and the greater their credibility becomes with those they must convince and lead. Change leaders know they cannot simply push others aside and rush forward to proclaim truth, no matter what their levels of personal conviction and courage may be. Instead, they understand that credibility comes from walking the talk, understanding the signals their actions give, and trying to learn from their people as well as helping them understand. Wherever possible, they also try to get the other guy in the limelight, either by giving credit to the ideas of others or by getting others to take center stage.

Personal courage and/or self-confidence do not magically emerge because someone signs on for change. Mike Vaccaro had been involved in all aspects of process design at Prudential Insurance for more than twenty years, managing and sometimes building the systems and procedures required for processing insurance transactions as well as claims.

When Mike started to emerge as a change leader, his company was having mixed success with a broad-based change effort that included his processing areas. Still, that did not deter him from learning to swim in uncertain waters as an RCL by simply taking the plunge—a leap of faith he might never have taken without having years of preceding efforts that gave him the know-how as well as the experience base to draw upon. In taking the plunge, his actions were a powerful signal of his personal conviction about what was still a very uncertain proposition. Mike's courage was not the product of a subway crash kind of event. Indeed, he found the courage in the middle of a presentation to the president of Prudential's individual insurance business, as he argued for a radical change in the processing of transactions.

> When I met Don Southwell [former president of Prudential's individual insurance business], it was my first real exposure to him. I was aware of the potential [of the redesign], but I hadn't convinced myself. I knew the subject cold, and I convinced myself as I presented it to him. It became clear in my mind and

clear in my projection. It was a great feeling. It was not just a paper exercise. I was saying to him, "This can actually happen."

While Mike may have first recognized a new level of courage during his presentation, it is clear that he had been building his underlying conviction in the months and years before, as well as during the simple hard work of getting ready for the presentation. Conviction is invariably the result of constant hard work and preparation, and credibility is a by-product of the actions and interactions this conviction enables.

SPEAK OUT WHEN IT MATTERS

The best change leaders are seldom arrogant or egocentric. They do, however, develop higher levels of confidence that enable them to speak out when it matters, much more readily and effectively than their counterparts in normal managerial roles. Moreover, they seem to be able to do it without appearing to be impertinent! A fundamental characteristic of RCLs is that they often ask higher management the kind of questions that others don't believe can be asked. In that way, they challenge established traditions and knock down doors thought to be sealed. More important, and visible to those who observe them, they are seldom shot down by management, but instead are actually listened to and appreciated. They build stronger, not weaker, ties to management. As a result, their own and others' confidence and courage are bolstered, and it becomes easier for others to join in the next time around.

Carol O'Neill claims to have been a naturally shy person prior to her NYCT days, but that trait is not really visible today. She is determined, tough, outspoken, and relentless, but she was definitely not born that way. She says that she began emerging from her cocoon when she worked for a small consulting firm prior to joining NYCT president Alan Kiepper's change effort. It is also clear that the NYCT experience greatly accelerated the development of her confidence—and perhaps more important, allowed her to establish credibility among a hardened group of transit regulars. Carol can recall very clearly the anxieties she felt the first few times she needed to deliver disquieting news to the president.

Alan is a tough person to read. He sends a lot of signals that suggest he doesn't want to hear any bad news. He has a reputation of shooting the messenger if he doesn't like the message. But I know he doesn't really mean to do that. He fully expects me to tell him when something really isn't as it seems. You have to tell him with confidence, but you have a responsibility to tell him.

Similarly, Todd Strong remembers how most members of the Black & Blue team at BFI had real concerns about their first progress report to President Bruce Ranck, since much of what they had discovered was contrary to his expectations. Yet, they never thought much about softening the blow.

> From the start we were honest with both Bruce and Bill Ruck-elshaus [BFI's chairman]. We always called it the way we saw it, and when there was no fallout, and when they kept asking us to go further, it reinforced that was the only way to do it.

Moreover, the team had worked very hard—many nights and weekends—away from homes and families. They not only had built strong convictions, but also they were well prepared. Over time, management has continued to foster an open environment that encourages telling it like it is, and that reinforces the responsibility to speak out and be accountable.

Take Bold Actions Against Obstacles

Bold actions often follow speaking out. When experienced change leaders look back, they invariably identify the two or three truly out-of-the-ordinary actions they found necessary to remove obstacles and sustain momentum. Sometimes they even surprised themselves, because those actions often required them to step beyond their formal responsibility, or normal solution space. In most cases, they could easily have taken refuge in some policy, practice, or upper management guideline that would have excused them from taking the risk. And when they had to violate well-established rules, they put their careers at considerable risk. Had they not done so, however, their part of the change effort would have been stalled, or diverted, or would have died. This is an option seldom even acknowledged by true change leaders.

A bold courageous action can be the key to unlocking change or performance potential. When Steve Uthoff decided to confront BFI's top management (described later in this chapter), he changed their attitudes about the relative urgency of their change situation—not a simple matter in a company that has been as successful as BFI. When Sally Beck of Enron (described in the Introduction) confronted her superiors with her plan to shape real teams to drive her change effort, she was flying in the face of strong values of individual accountability. This was not a task for the faint of heart.

While the removal of most obstacles to change may not always require bold actions of this magnitude, it does require actions that are well beyond the normal experience of the RCL involved. They may not always work as the change leader would like or can even predict, but they are worth the risk of finding out.

2. INSTILLING COURAGE IN OTHERS

Change leaders may or may not wish to acknowledge their own personal courage, but they universally acknowledge the need for it in the people who will be involved in making a change effort successful. Major change is always anxiety producing, and is often frightening to a large number of people who see their job security and livelihoods threatened. Surprisingly, research indicates that there is not much less anxiety when the change is perceived as positive. Paradoxically, a reasonable amount of anxiety or sense of urgency is also motivating. RCLs must be able to gauge when the anxieties have become dysfunctional and people need an extra dose of courage. They must also be able to determine if their actions are enough to provide the additional confidence. This may be more art than science, but experience in leading change definitely helps the art along.

Waiting until panic sets in can be a fatal error. Potential remedies should be applied as soon as the symptoms of hesitancy and unhealthy anxiety levels are apparent across a critical mass of the organization. The situation at NYCT, from which several transit workers emerged as heroes of the subway disaster of 1991, illustrates how important it can be to instill courage in a major change effort. On the one hand, NYCT represents the extreme in degree-of-difficulty for major change efforts; on the other, it is where we found some of our most committed and courageous change leaders.

CLARIFYING THE NEED (NYCT)

It used to take as much courage to ride the New York subway system as to work there. Through the late 1970s and early 1980s, many New Yorkers deserted the system to escape its increasing unreliability and constant threats of crime, accident, and unpleasantness, and many never returned. It was premature however to desert the system for good. Subway boycotters who happen to return today—after avoiding the system's perils for several years—have a surprise in store. To their amazement, they will find that not only is graffiti conspicuously absent, but boarding is typically smooth, orderly, and uneventful; seats are readily available; and even normal conversation presents few difficulties. The subway system has changed noticeably—perhaps to the point where the need for courage now is less with the passengers than it is with the change leaders striving for potential improvement.

This is all due to concerted change efforts, chronicled in the last chapter, beginning in the mid-1980s with David Gunn's (Keipper's predecessor) "no graffiti" effort to rebuild the infrastructure and restore order to the system, followed since 1990 by Alan Kiepper's focus on improving customer service. Many battles have been fought and won to revive and remake the system; many more remain, requiring the continued courage of change leaders.

LACK OF COURAGE AS THE BOTTLENECK

At the heart of the effort is a small handful of change leaders who have the courage to keep pursuing what many might see as the impossible dream: superior customer service. Unfortunately, this small contingent of RCLs do not yet constitute the critical mass of change leadership needed to ignite the entire workforce. They have come a long way in a few short years, however, and they are the first to admit how far they still have to go. They agonize over subway crashes much more than the riding public does. In addition to what Carol O'Neill helped us understand about visions at NYCT in chapter 2, she can also offer acute observations of the many insidious ways that a lack of courage manifests itself in the organization. While situation-specific to the Transit system, similar manifestations can be found in other change situations, although they stand out more clearly in the examples Carol cites at NYCT (see the box on the next page).

O'Neil clearly demonstrates the courage of an RCL. And she is very blunt when asked why NYCT has not yet achieved higher aspirations:

> It is from lack of will and lack of gut. You have to go for it. You have to be willing to deal with the consequences and have the courage and confidence that eventually you will be able to pull it off. It is only by setting a high goal and measuring yourself against that goal that you have any chance of helping the organization raise the bar.

People in visible public agencies face difficult issues that can require more conviction and courage than in the corporate world. For example, they know the press is looking to skewer anyone for a misstep, they feel vilified by the public as a thief of tax dollars, they realize that "doing the right thing" may be overridden by politicians' expediency, and they know that any higher performance commitments must be achieved with reduced budgets. As a result, caution and minimal expectations can seem like the only sensible course for survival.

Yet Carol still claims no special courage attribute for herself. Nonetheless, she is probably willing to endure almost anything for the noble purpose of bringing safe, economical transportation to New York citizens—except perhaps the inaction caused by lack of courage among those she believes to be more concerned with maintaining their position than they are in making a difference in passenger service.

COURAGE SHORTFALLS AT NYCT—COMMON MANIFESTATIONS

1. Why not wait them out? They'll be gone soon.

   The doubters . . . just wait it out. When Alan [Kiepper] first got here, many said, "He won't be around for long. Let's just relax and wait it out; he'll be gone long before we are."

2. I cannot afford to worry about getting better tomorrow; I just need to get through today.

   [Referring to a manager who had refused to permit enough time for a better, more accurate answer] *. . . the guy said "I would rather have a C- [answer] today than an A+ one tomorrow." He didn't say I would rather have a C- today than an A+ 6 weeks from now or a year from now—he meant tomorrow.*

3. It's not my problem; you can't do anything about it anyway.

   Take train delays as an example. One source of delay is a sick passenger. Until recently, people would say, "What can I do about that?" You cannot do something about the incidents of sick passengers, but you can do something about how fast you respond to them, how it translates into a service delay. But you have to start saying, "I care about delays, all delays, even if it is not my fault that they occurred."

4. Let's not set our standards too high—we will feel obligated to meet them.

   One of my real peeves is the passenger environment survey. Among the measures is percent of cars on a train without excessive dirt. Excessive? I mean, how do you define excessive? Is nonexcessive dirt okay? No one is willing to establish a standard that says no dirt. We do not have a good way of gauging our quality because we are scared to admit that we are really aiming to be that good.

5. Why measure things that make us look bad? It's not worth the exposure.

    When a measure is so loosely defined that it shows 98+ percent performance, people do not want to tightly and realistically redefine the measure. *No one wants to be in a position where you drop to a 25 percent rating . . . it's an embarrassment.*

6. What's the use anyway? Nobody will follow through on our efforts.

    People deep in the organization have good ideas and are really willing. They may have even tried or have thought about trying. But . . . they've given up and said this place is just too screwed up. If they would put their money where their mouth is and talk to the right people and get the right ideas advanced, they could help straighten out this place.

What Will It Take

Carol believes in the vision of Alan Kiepper. To her, he is a dedicated executive who will generally listen to a well-developed argument or a new set of facts—and who will both change his mind and take action when the case is convincing. He is neither the cause of the courage shortfall in the system, nor is he the answer. History, environment, and inertia are the causes; a critical mass of RCLs is the answer. And the starting point appears to be a few change leaders in the right places.

A critical mass of RCLs within NYCT would appear to be a long way off, but Carol and Kevin Desmond, who is a change leader heading Operations Planning (his story is told in chapter 5), have an interesting perspective on what it will take. While the logjam now exists among more than 40,000 people, they believe it is really anchored in perhaps no more than a half-dozen key-position holders and a handful of potential change leaders who have fallen prey to the entrenched patterns of the past. They have grown up in an environment that did not seem to want or seek out their ideas for improvement. As a result, they believe they are rewarded for keeping the system running day-to-day, and for putting in their time without rocking the boat. Change leaders must be developed who can recognize the need to instill courage in their parts of the organization. That is a difficult, though not impossible, challenge.

It is this non-RCL attitude of throwing up their hands and assuming nothing can be done that deeply frustrates true RCLs like Carol and Kevin. They know that Alan Kiepper at NYCT does listen, and they truly believe that there are a lot of people working in the transit organization who really care, and who have many good ideas for change. Carol and Kevin also recognize, however, that there are too many people in positions of influence who inadvertently prevent this from happening, because they cannot recognize the symptoms in their people that signal a need for help. Some, sadly enough, have permanently closed their minds to the possibility of instilling such courage in their people. They are content to wait it out. If given an option, Kevin and Carol would rather have a double handful of RCLs in key places than millions more dollars to invest to turn things around. These change leaders, they believe, could swing the balance even in the face of impossible odds.

It seems an unlikely premise that a few dozen people could unleash the ideas and change initiatives of more than 40,000 other people. However, if you believe, as many RCLs do, that the right dozen could easily instill enough courage in the next 100 potential change leaders, who could then do the same in the next 2,000—then the premise becomes believable. Far-fetched perhaps, but that is the kind of conviction that keeps RCLs working to instill the courage to change across the front line. In their minds, it is never that far from reach.

MEETING THE NEED

Recognizing the need for courage is one thing, but instilling it in others is another. Harry S Truman is a memorable example of one who instinctively knew how. Throughout his remarkable life, amid success and failure, he found and instilled courage in himself and others time and again by sticking to a very simple philosophy of always trying to do the right thing, never giving up, and setting an incredible example of hard work. In his own words, "I have tried to give it everything that was in me." Could it really be that simple and yet that hard?

To RCLs like Carol and Kevin, it is. Their ability to instill courage comes from the same simple philosophy. In living by these basics, they instill courage by direct example. They also instill courage indirectly by enabling and encouraging others to open their eyes and try new behaviors. This is not the great-man approach of being the model all look up to. It is a more modest, behind-the-scenes approach that requires lots of hard work and determination.

Change leaders, even those in tough environments like NYCT, find that a handful of specific actions seem to work most of the time: forcing reality to the forefront (*tell it like it is*); focusing on early wins (*get something done fast*); appealing to a clear and compelling vision (*reach both their hearts and minds*); creating an infectious environment for courage (*make it contagious*); and expanding leadership capacity (*take risks on people and approaches*). Most of us learned these truths years ago; somehow, RCLs seem better able to recall and apply them.

ALWAYS TELL IT LIKE IT IS

GE Motors holds a quick market research session, which is nothing more complicated than getting a bunch of RCLs together every Monday morning and sharing the latest intelligence about the customers and competitors. It may not be valid market research, but it is a quick and frequent reality check. The RCLs are never far from their customers' reactions and concerns.

At Enron, an important reengineering effort was positioned as "building the infrastructure for future growth." When the first recommendations came in emphasizing headcount reductions as a part of the growth change, there was debate among upper managers about when to announce the bad news. RCLs down the line were never in doubt, however. They knew that they had to get it out as soon as possible if they wanted any hope of preserving the confidence and trust required to carry out the rest of the change. Their view prevailed, but it was clearly a struggle.

On the one hand, it could be said that the bad news always gets better, so why create further anxieties by continually shoving people's faces into bad news? Thus, it might be better to wait until the news is good—and not create advance anxieties in an already nervous group. Change leaders, however, prefer that their people know the blunt truth up front and deal with it head-on rather than find it out through the grapevine. They believe that people gain confidence and trust in management and the change effort when they see that they are not being deceived, and that the realities of the business situation actually often serve as a rallying cry for the troops. Moderating the message is uncommon.

WHAT'S IN IT FOR ME?

Randy Howard was given the challenge of turning around UNOCAL's largest oil refinery in Los Angeles, which had been a chronic underperformer. Adding to his dilemma was the fact that a number of initiatives had been launched, such as business plans and breakthrough teams, that had had some successes, but certainly not enough to really hit the bottom line or significantly improve the plant's performance. He launched a program (more fully covered in chapter 4) that he knew would have long-term benefits. He was struck with the need to focus in on some early short-term wins to help get some quick action and cut through some of the initial fear.

> We took a couple of the things that we did which were successful and communicated the heck out of them across the refinery. . . . Most important, we wanted to clearly and openly attach the success of these early initiatives to individuals and teams who made it happen and to celebrate their success, hopefully . . . to break up some of the initial fear and hesitation in the front line.

As Randy found, there is nothing as comforting to people in situations of uncertainty as seeing some results from their efforts coming to fruition and being appreciated. In and of itself, celebrating some early wins will not only instill courage, but will also give people some assurance that they are working on something that matters and something they can do.

Mike Vaccaro of Prudential made the same point another way: "I knew the endorsement process so well that I knew we couldn't lose— there was too much inefficiency there. It was an easy early win" and an opportunity for Vaccaro and his team to prove their mettle against a lower hurdle. Clearing the first one takes some of the pressure off.

REACH BOTH THEIR HEARTS AND MINDS

Once people gain a clear image of what their effort could accomplish, RCLs keep that image in focus for everybody. They also help people understand the specific implications of their effort for themselves as individuals. Part of this involves having the working vision that was discussed in the preceding chapter; but there's also a personal twist to it. As Tom Timmins of Mobil told us, "You have to be a good communicator along several dimensions"—meaning that the one-on-ones are as important as the small- and large-group interactions. Real change leaders cannot expect to deal with people's anxieties only at the group level—they need to know the people as individuals. As Randy Howard said:

> Really understanding the individuals was the key to me being
> able to exert leadership. And the only way for me to get
> that . . . was to spend a lot of time with them [as individuals].

By spending time with individuals, RCLs are able to make very personal connections with respect to where it is all heading. They can go beyond even the working visions and help individuals see "what's in it for me, and why I will like it better here once we have changed."

Realizing that the key to keeping the positive view in the forefront was a combination of group and individual interactions, Randy also launched a communications effort for the change program that included large-group, rally-the-troops sessions, as well as small-group sessions and one-on-one informal discussions. All of these sessions were built around consistent messages about where the troops were headed, why this mattered, and how they intended to get there.

MAKE IT CONTAGIOUS

Obviously, RCLs do not stop after the early wins. Acknowledging and celebrating the first few hits will not ensure that the hits keep on coming. The ability to cycle through one set of wins to the next is very important and cannot be left to chance. Nothing is worse than a first-quarter splurge followed by a second-quarter lull that sends the team into the locker room behind at the half. Randy describes this challenge as follows:

> The key over time is to create an atmosphere which at first
> encourages a few—perhaps more courageous—people to go and
> do things a bit differently, take some risks. . . . Then you reward
> successes as well as . . . pick people up and dust them off when
> they fail. Over time even the naysayers . . . get caught up in this
> environment.

Sometimes the momentum develops early in the game, and the early scores are enough to keep the momentum going until the next cycle of results appears. In other cases, the early wins are from easily capturable opportunities, and it is much harder to get the next round. The role of the RCL in the latter case is obviously much more difficult. Change leaders are equally adept at differentiating good failures—well-thought-out ideas that just didn't pan out—from failures due to shoddy work, incomplete analysis, or poor execution. Making these distinctions is crucial because, while courage is generated by the individuals themselves, it requires the kind of attention and support that Randy describes. It also requires a tolerance for setbacks, if not failures, that may occur before regaining the high ground.

TAKE RISKS ON PEOPLE AND APPROACHES

Change leaders take two kinds of risks that require courage on their part, as well as on the part of people working with them. The first is taking risks on the people themselves, by encouraging them to take new initiatives and step into new responsibilities. RCLs go well beyond what traditional managers would do in this regard. They do not always pick the most logical person to take the initiative. In chapter 7, for example, Don Tate of Sealed Air describes how the person with one of the worst plant safety records was chosen to head a special company change effort on safety. That kind of decision would seem counterintuitive and overly risky to most managers.

It is equally important for change leaders to take risks by trying new approaches; otherwise, they can not build the diverse and powerful tool kit that most of them rely upon over time. Often, even when people are willing to recognize and step up to the need for change, organizations fall short of their goals because the change leaders do not have access to a diverse set of tools and approaches. Old tools and approaches are seldom enough in demanding change situations.

John Wood of the AT&T Profiles Initiative provides a quick example. This initiative, a part of the sales force change program described in chapter 2, involved creating an entirely new sales organization with the unenviable charge of winning the business of large corporations where AT&T currently had little or no share. One of the key elements of their approach was developing insightful plans for each account. John was convinced that the organization's old approach to account planning was not doing the job.

One of the things we found out very early is—we had to be very clear about what is different in terms of how we work around here. We took fifty account managers, and had them present their plans to their peers—including some real experts. They gave them tough feedback, really ripped them up in a positive way. Now we have high-quality account plans for all accounts.

Open peer review of account plans may not be a groundbreaking idea, but it was clearly a different approach in this situation, and John's willingness to try it led to an important change. AT&T now uses peer reviews regularly, calling them customer-focus sessions, in which everybody learns together.

This search for new tools and approaches is an important part of what change leaders do. Chapters 4 through 7 will explore a broad range of tools and approaches—and how RCLs use and integrate them. Some will be familiar to some readers, but not to all. The state of the art will continue to evolve, but what will not change is that change leaders will continually pursue new tools and approaches, which can help them build up their capability to attack change obstacles in different ways, and in so doing help instill increased commitment and courage in others.

3. INFLUENCING TOP MANAGEMENT

The final aspect of RCL courage and confidence deals with the task of helping to keep top management support consistent with both the overall change requirements and the specific needs of the workforce. This task entails helping members of top management head toward a common aspiration on a common path, without undermining their ability to provide top-level direction and leadership. It can therefore be a difficult balancing act for RCLs, but it can also be very important to the success of a major change situation. Often, change leaders find themselves in situations where the workforce feels that the statements and actions of the senior management group do not appear to be consistent or unified—either with respect to the relative urgency for change, the kind of changes necessary, or how they will be accomplished. When this is the case, RCLs can help to unify top leaders, sometimes just by understanding and ameliorating some of their fears and uncertainties.

More than RCLs realize, their feelings and observations can influence top management's understanding, commitment, and resolve, if not courage. It is important, therefore, that respected change leaders use their influence to help bring top executives together, as well as to help them recognize and acknowledge the needed changes and act more in concert with one another. Several RCLs faced this situation in a difficult, but fairly typical, change effort still under way at Browning-Ferris Industries (BFI).

INSTILLING COURAGE WITHOUT CRISIS

BFI's record of growth and success is enviable, both in terms of stockholder return and market position. Since Tom Fatjo started picking up his neighbor's garbage in 1969 in Houston, Texas, the company has grown to be the second largest waste disposal corporation in the world, through operating excellence and innovative acquisitions. Its growth was temporarily marred by a downturn in the late 1980s, but it has since recovered and advanced its position. The aspiration of BFI's chairman, Bill Ruckelshaus, is to become a truly "superior company."

This aspiration has influenced, if not inspired, a core group of the more insightful potential change leaders in the company to point out the real and urgent need for change if this aspiration is to be met. Many of these RCLs have had previous experience with less than satisfying change initiatives. Steve Uthoff has a chart that lists eleven "previous improvement initiatives" attempted over seven years at BFI. He recounts that some were "just a failure," some "didn't work here," and still others succeeded on their own terms but were "narrow and didn't drive performance." He uses that chart to remind himself and others of all they've been through to finally get on a path leading to real change. Courage is a big part of the story.

The initiative prevalent in 1993 was Customer-Led Quality (CLQ), which Steve describes as "just an effort to bring back the failed TQM [Total Quality Management]." It proved to be one more effort that "didn't work." Late in 1993, Steve made a simple, but difficult admission. It was a well timed act of courage—he calls it frustration—that began to unlock a long-standing struggle at BFI.

> One Saturday Bill [chairman and then CEO], Bruce [then COO], and I were in Bill's conference room, and we started talking about some of these programs—CLQ, the whole long list. I remember being the first one who said, "I don't understand how all of these fit together. I'm not smart enough to figure it out." My heart began to beat faster as I wondered how Bill and Bruce would react. But I was quickly relieved when Bruce said, "I can't figure it out either." And Bill said, "I don't know either."

Thanks to Steve's willingness to speak out and admit to his own uncertainty, they were all beginning to face reality a bit differently than before. And part of this reality to Steve was that he did not perceive a top management team that was clear and confident in the direction that the change should take.

The Struggle Over the Right Thing for BFI

The struggle they embarked on that day was to resolve a fundamental difference of viewpoint about what was needed at BFI: major change versus simply better execution. While it is easy to argue, as the participants often did, that the differences were simply semantic, it was more than that. On one side of the argument was Bill Ruckelshaus, who arrived in 1988 to become chairman and CEO as an outsider and visionary who sensed a huge potential for BFI. His aspiration was to make BFI a "superior company"—not just number one in the garbage business—but few in the company really knew what Bill meant by that. In pursuit of this noble but somewhat abstract goal, he launched numerous programs in the hope that one or more of them would somehow break through and unleash the company's real potential.

The other point of view was held by Bruce, an up-from-the-ranks COO (now president and CEO) who had spent his entire career with BFI and who is a natural leader—namely, a tough, respected, and practical executive, who truly knows how to get results. Through all the special initiatives, including CLQ, it was never quite clear to him why any of the issues addressed by these programs could not be handled by BFI's line organization through better execution. To be sure, he was always looking for improvement, but he thought and talked about it differently, both because of his strong, pragmatic mind-set and because of his knowledge of how best to communicate with BFI's field people.

Most others in the BFI organization were of Ranck's thinking, and for good reason. After all, since its founding from a pickup-truck act in 1969, BFI had grown into a company with more than $4 billion in revenues. It had a winning formula of aggressively acquiring local disposal outfits (over 600 by now) and integrating them into a very successful enterprise based on a strong, decentralized management approach. Most BFI people would have liked to displace WMX Technologies as number one in the industry, and they recognized the importance of sustaining their own growth and profitability. But few really believed that any kind of *major* change was required.

Interestingly to the outside observer, whenever Bill and Bruce were in the same room discussing these issues, it sounded as though they were closer to being of the same mind than most of the organization perceived them to be. The problem for the rest of the organization was that the behaviors and actions of these men did not appear consistent relative to one another, even though the words they used might sound similar. Nonetheless, both executives shared a great deal of mutual respect and could easily relate to each other's viewpoints and actions—which to them seemed very consistent.

In the middle of this situation were people like Steve Uthoff, Todd Strong, and a handful of other change leaders. They had tremendous respect for Ranck and placed great value on BFI's culture and performance record based upon his leadership philosophy of decentralized, pragmatic, results-driven management. Nonetheless, they could also see that the business was changing markedly. Issues such as environmental regulation, recycling, and wastestream segmentation were complicating the picture. Price pressure was rising. The company's earnings were short of the levels that many analysts believed necessary to return BFI to the growth-stock position it had held in the 1980s. The winning formula of growth through acquisitions had been extremely successful, but growth appeared to be slowing. The remaining takeover targets were increasingly good-size public companies looking for hefty price premiums. In addition to these business considerations, the decentralized management model wasn't effectively developing the skills necessary to fit Bill Ruckelshaus's notion of a truly superior company. Combined, these factors had convinced this small band of potential RCLs that major change was necessary, but they also knew they faced a significant challenge communicating this need and aligning management up and down the line against the challenges.

It was the appearance of different viewpoints at the top, however, that stymied the Customer-Led Quality committee. Some members believed they had a charter from Bill to shock the company by getting customers to define how "quality service" should be determined, i.e., what quality specifics they expected. To the committee, that in itself would be major change. Other members were convinced that Bruce had made it clear that all he was looking for were some good ideas for improving customer quality that the existing organization could readily implement. Besides, he was already about to make a significant structural change to strengthen the role of division managers, which he believed would greatly enhance the executional capability of the organization. To those committee members, it clearly sounded like only incremental change was expected of the CLQ effort.

As Steve observed, this conflicting direction led the committee to conclude it "was heading up a charge it couldn't succeed at." In fact, Steve remembers that one of their first actions was to "confront Bill and Bruce, saying the two of you have different objectives for the committee . . . it was quite a meeting." This took considerable courage on the part of the committee but, as previously noted, the initiative ultimately failed. While there wasn't sufficient courage or resolve within the group to buck the organization and push for real change, their pointing out the appearance of disconnect at the top probably helped set the stage for the Saturday morning session of self-disclosure.

GETTING READY UP FRONT

Steve remembers that initial confrontation clearly, and not just because of the anxiety associated with admitting he didn't know what to do.

> I think it was the first time people realized—without saying it at the moment—that we needed some direction, some kind of help to bring all these different efforts together. Bill could see that none of these individual efforts in itself was going to take us to his goal of becoming a superior company.

And Bruce was above all a pragmatist who wanted to see something tangible come of all this effort. Out of that meeting came the impetus for the Black & Blue (B&B) (derived from black for profit improvement and blue for BFI's corporate color) initiative that Steve describes as stepping back to "diagnose the state of our business, assess these many 'envisionments' of what we should be doing, and get focused on some real opportunities." Bruce committed to a three-month effort by a special task force of eighteen of BFI's very best line and staff people. He even accepted using outside consulting help, though he insisted it be a BFI-driven effort. It was a big step for both Bill and Bruce. Moreover, it was seen by many, including Todd Strong, who was a part of the B&B effort, as a potential breakthrough.

> What Bill and Bruce did by putting the Black & Blue team together was say, "we've pulled all the levers that we know to pull here; and yes, we have gotten some improvement, but we see a lot of room to make even more. We've done everything we think we know how to do, we need another set of eyes to tell us what else needs to be done."

The CLQ committee's courage to confront Bill and Bruce, Steve's courage to admit his inability to make sense of their many change efforts, and Bill and Bruce's courage to face facts, admit their failures, and open the organization to real self-examination all worked in combination to get BFI moving forward. But it was just a start. The B&B team would find the need for considerably more courage as it reached further into an often skeptical organization. None of them, of course, admit to courage on their own part, but each clearly saw it in the others—so it is with RCLs and courage.

Taking a Hard Look

The three-month diagnostic conducted by the B&B team proved to be trying. Clearly an ambitious effort with a broad charter, it was described by Todd as "a total review of the company from top to bottom, no holds barred, a look at everything to find $50 to $100 million in sustainable annual profit opportunity." Not surprisingly, because of its scope, there were troubles at the start-up. Some of the team members were reluctant to get involved in yet another analytic exercise that took them away from their real jobs (and families). Others wanted to reduce the scope of the effort so as not to disturb or disrupt the organization. Fortunately, the team had enough emerging change leaders to step past these usual hang-ups. They found the courage to take the initial dive into the organization, and what they uncovered gave them the courage to push further.

As one of the change leaders on the team, Todd knew that finding more than $50 million would require looking into the over 600 district-level operations that constitute the fabric of the company. He had been the assistant district manager for waste collection in New Orleans, one of BFI's largest hauling districts, and then district manager of its Austin, Texas, district. He knew the decentralized districts were the strength of the organization. Thus, he wanted to be careful not to damage or adversely affect them while he completed his investigation.

Black & Blue members started by looking at some models, visiting other companies to see both how they managed similar operations (for example, how UPS handled truck maintenance) and how they were approaching their change initiatives. These visits proved eye-opening, and shaped the team's thinking significantly. For example, the team built an analytic model to assess the per-unit operating costs of each of the districts—factoring in structural variations, such as cost-of-living and distance to landfill, that could explain differences between districts. The model was not perfect, but it was sufficient to reveal large variations in performance that caught everyone's attention.

Almost by itself, the act of getting fresh, compelling facts on the table was a source of courage to probe deeper. Talking extensively with people in the districts, the team developed its own viewpoint on the reasons for the wide variations in performance. Todd recalls three major causes:

1. "We had a very diverse group of district managers." As a result there were wide variations in skills, experience levels, and levels of understanding of the job among individual district managers, which raised issues about BFI's recruiting, training, and career-planning efforts.

2.   "Everyone was doing their own thing; even where you'd think there'd be some uniformity [in something], there'd be fifty ways of doing it out there." The lack of uniform procedures and working processes raised issues relating to BFI's culture of decentralized management.

3.   "The accountability really wasn't there to enforce a desire and demand to get better." This led the team to question its evaluation system, which it had to admit was "driven by budgets that were so manipulated that a district manager could come in and justify a budget that was going backwards."

Many district managers were very skeptical about these findings. However, when the B&B team faced the skeptics with new facts, they would usually acknowledge the issues. For example, despite their natural resistance to centralized functions at headquarters, most readily acknowledged the potential value of more uniform procedures, especially in staff functions such as procurement and purchasing. Most people acknowledged that BFI had "a dog's breakfast of trucks out there," and that the practice of buying tires and lubricants locally did not leverage the company's buying power. In effect, they said, "We're a $4-plus-billion company, we should act like it!" By getting the managers to open up their thinking on such points, the B&B team was helping to create the mind-set that would be required to instill enough courage across the system for district managers to change their personal behaviors.

Putting new facts on the table enabled the team to better sense what was needed to change the culture and the management environment. They were no longer dependent on what senior management thought was required for major change. Through their own work, they were discovering for themselves what was needed, and building their personal conviction and courage in the process.

Of course, they still had to confront senior management. Once that was done, however, the senior leadership group rewarded rather than criticized the B&B team. As a result, more courage began to spread through the organization. It became well known that the team had successfully influenced the thinking of the chairman and the COO regarding the direction of major change, and that there had been no major fallout or personal career damage as a result. To the contrary, management had been overtly appreciative, if not truly enthusiastic.

B&B's final report was a blockbuster, relative to what anybody expected at the outset. The team's recommendations covered almost every part of the company in one way or another. Their degree of commitment convinced even the most skeptical minds that a different kind of implementation and change would be required. Much of the top management team's hesitancy and uncertainty about the need for major change also went away.

A broad-based implementation program (BLUEprint for Improvement) was set up under a new steering committee comprising Bill, Bruce, several other corporate officers, and the regional vice presidents. Three special initiatives were launched: a marketing-planning approach to replace the budgeting system; a major operations-improvement effort with breakthrough teams across the geographic divisions as well as a major purchasing and equipment standardization effort ("Selective Uniformity"); and an effort to transform the sales organization into a world class organization. Steve would lead the overall effort, and Todd would lead the critical operations piece. In leading BLUEprint, Steve has given his own meaning to the words "superior company." In fact, he is working very hard to turn the CEO's personal vision into a more tangible picture for the BFI people, to help instill in them more courage to act.

COURAGE WRAP-UP

Courage is clearly important in addressing major change, and, in its most fundamental form, it remains a very individual trait or act. For RCLs, the challenge is to develop the self-confidence and credibility to be able to effectively generate and foster courage, in those below, aside, and above them, that will be required for success. As a result, most RCLs often share a number of very personal perspectives concerning courage.

They recognize that courage is really about making the connection between what's changing in the business world and what needs to change in their *personal* behaviors. They also recognize that personal change offers far more potential rewards than sticking to the status quo. Steve Uthoff knows that he will need to make personal changes similar to what the business and organization all around him are going through, some of which are seemingly small, but are nonetheless personally significant. As one small but significant example, the COO, who had been a reluctant computer user, is taking the time to learn how to effectively use one because he saw the need from a business point of view. A small step to take, perhaps, but one that still reflects personal courage. Such situations can require as much personal courage as taking a stand against the top management status quo.

Change leaders also learn the need to persist and tolerate rejection while trying to instill courage in others. People seldom change fundamental behaviors or gain new personal characteristics overnight. Consequently, RCLs take a long-term perspective when trying to instill courage for change. They combine patience, perseverance, persistence, and a genuine compassion for their people.

Change leaders typically realize that the cycles of courage they begin ultimately come back to benefit themselves. As RCLs look back on what has been accomplished, and see new teams working away, generating their own courage to keep pressing forward, they feel a renewed sense of commitment and courage themselves. Steve is feeling this now.

> What really keeps me going in this change effort is thinking about the efforts of the Black & Blue teams. When I think about the fact that they came down here and worked very hard for three months to come up with some very good ideas, then I sometimes lose sleep over the fact that those good ideas are not getting implemented at the pace that they envisioned. That is what keeps me coming back to the office even in the middle of the night to work on getting some of these things done a little faster.

When all is said and done, the best RCLs remain the ultimate pragmatists. When change is under way, accelerating, and exciting, they lead the charge. When change is stalled and in trouble, they step up to the challenge. However, those who come to believe that their organizations are not willing or able to continue the battle for change, and that their change-agent role is not valued, will look elsewhere for environments in which their unique skills and attributes are not only tolerated but prized. There are likely to be plenty of those.

PART II

ENGAGING
THE
ORGANIZATION

PEOPLE

How can I "empower the people" without losing control of costs and results?

- *We go to all these meetings about empowering people. I know I'm supposed to get them more involved in everything, but what does that really mean I'm supposed to do?*

How do I convert involvement into results instead of more activity?

- *There must be more to people performance improvement than simply turning the troops loose and getting out of their way.*

How do I sort through the myriad of approaches I keep hearing about?

- *Total quality, reengineering, process management, special task forces, team-based organizations—which ones do I use and in what situations?*

With so many people needing to change, where do I start?

- *If I start with too few people, I fear no impact; if I start with too many, I may create a disaster.*

How do I get the right people, focusing on the right things, in the right way?

DEVIL'S CANYON IS A RUGGED CHASM LOCATED HIGH IN THE BIG HORN MOUN-
tains near Yellowstone National Park. Each spring, the Bischoff Livestock
Company (comprising four families), must move its large herd of cattle
across the canyon to feed on the lush grasses of the higher plateaus on the
other side. It is a tough, precarious journey for both cattle and cowboys—
but an essential one if the cattle are to be ready for market in the fall. High
levels of commitment are required, since the safety and livelihood of cowboys and cattle depends on a successful crossing. The journey requires a
great deal of hard work and resourcefulness.

No two crossings are ever the same, but the ten or so cowboys follow
the same structured pathway and mobilizing approach that has worked for
years. As the effort begins, the cowboys identify the natural lead cows who,
by instinct and experience, seek out the safer and shorter trail options
(there are many choices). The cowboys tend to let the lead cows find their
own trail options, but they also must keep the herd moving at the right
pace to avoid stampede and injury by falling off precarious parts of the
path. Close attention is also paid to stragglers and mavericks who might
otherwise divert the drive, and/or become lost or injured themselves.

Many different obstacles divert and endanger the drive. The toughest
is crossing the river rapids at the bottom of the canyon; both cattle and
cowboys must swim across, landing in unpredictable patterns, which
requires real-time redirection of the drive. Once across, the cattle assume
it is all over, so the team must reenergize them to start up the other side.
This usually requires time to regroup in order to generate new momentum
and reestablish a sense of direction. The pathway the herd follows both
down and up the canyon is familiar, but it varies from year to year. The
cowboys therefore must constantly reenergize and redirect the herd to sustain its momentum and pace. As they reach the grassy plateaus on the
other side, all creatures breath sighs of relief; most had to perform well
above normal expectations to achieve the difficult crossing.

Unleashing latent initiative and ideas within a large workforce also
involves crossing a difficult chasm, requiring workers and management to
come to a common level of belief about direction and approach. While it
may not be analogous to a cattle drive, the challenge of shaping a structured pathway that hundreds can follow safely—as well as being disciplined about the progress and results—is similarly difficult. As a result,
the task poses a vexing issue for RCLs as well as top management. As with
the cattle drive, the appeal of reaching a higher plateau of performance is

obvious, but the realization is elusive. It is tough enough to get a dozen people to work together, and even more so to get hundreds or even thousands turned on to the idea of working harder and differently for yet another top management drive to higher profitability. Yet most RCLs believe that tapping people's hidden reserves is an integral part of successfully navigating major change. Making this happen, however, is inevitably more difficult than just understanding the concept. As Randy Howard of UNOCAL told us:

> I knew we had to get significantly more out of our workforce to be successful. Almost all of our employees wanted to contribute, but there was real frustration and a lack of understanding of what they could do to help out.

Empowerment is the term now commonly associated with such mobilizing efforts. It means "authorization and power to act," but should not be confused with management cop-out or abdication of responsibility. Top management still has considerable responsibilities in an empowered environment. For example, it must provide clear guidelines for people to work within so that the extra energy of an empowered workforce is channeled in the right directions. Without clear directions and pathways, empowerment degrades into chaos. The task of developing an empowered organization is significant. It is naive to believe that empowerment can be declared, preached, or even inspired—and that the latent energy will flow forth. It does not work that way in most organizations.

Instead, a great chasm exists between where employees are now—isolated, confined, caught in rote practices, unquestioning, unenergized, distrustful, and giving only what is required—and where their leaders envision their potential—highly productive, questioning, innovating, enthusiastic, openly sharing, supporting, and giving their best. Crossing the chasm is hindered by all the accumulated practices, policies, attitudes, and beliefs of the organization that block people's progress. Advocating empowerment as a way to tap potential energy is like yelling "charge" to someone at the brink of Devil's Canyon and expecting them to complete the perilous descent, forge the raging river, and climb up the other side. It takes a good deal more experience, skill, and support than that. This chapter describes how RCLs provided that support in three very different kinds of change situations:

1. Energizing a small group.

2. Energizing the workforce in a large plant.

3. Energizing the broad base of people across a large company.

1. ENERGIZING A SMALL GROUP

Fred Smagorinsky of Sealed Air is a special kind of change leader; he gets things done through other people who do not report to him. Like all RCLs, however, he gets things done by energizing people to change in ways that lead directly to performance. He is also enthusiastic, pragmatic, and determined. Because he was basically a staff leader who had recently joined the company after a consulting career, he was not an obvious, natural fit in the world of bubble-wrap manufacturing. In fact, his first reaction to the job possibility was, "I do not think they really need me." Yet, his open mind, problem-solving style, unassuming demeanor, and respect for people enabled him to influence and energize a large number of other potential RCLs to rise to the challenge of change and higher performance. Change leaders like Fred are every bit as critical to successful change as RCLs like Don Tate, Ted Bell, and Randy Gouveia. These RCLs led the early years of Sealed Air's World Class Manufacturing (WCM) program through their traditional line management positions (as described in chapter 1).

The WCM program had been running for three years when Fred accepted what was a fairly amorphous job at first—to move WCM along in whatever way would work—though he had little direct authority. Moreover, the environment he now faced at Sealed Air was a significant contrast to his former consulting career. He soon discovered, however, that by using a simple, structured, performance-improvement process that incorporated a set of simple fundamentals for energizing people, he could at least begin to unleash the latent potential of many people in his new environment. The fundamentals that Fred applied are basic, and common to most successful efforts by RCLs at all levels and in many different kinds of change situations:

1. **Clear performance goals** to help people align diverse activities, focus efforts on what counts, and provide checkpoints to assess progress and alter pace and approach.

2. **A well-defined playing field** so people know what is in play, thereby reducing their uncertainty and anxiety and helping to release their energy and ideas.

3. **The right people in the right situations** to assure focus on areas of greatest value and to assemble complementary skills and perspectives.

4. A clear-cut, flexible involvement process that provides a few common tools for problem solving, a set of work plans with hard delivery dates, and specific end products.

5. A committed leadership group that works together to bolster conviction among themselves and others by resolving impasses, relieving confusion, and encouraging teamwork.

6. Communications that answer key questions—What's going on? Why? How does this fit together?—and address individual concerns at all levels.

There are many examples of structured performance-improvement processes with proven track records. Although they have different names and frameworks, all tend to emphasize the same fundamentals. For example, most quality programs have at their heart some simple multi-step performance-improvement process. Understanding and applying these fundamentals for unlocking the hidden reserve in small groups of people, as Fred did at Sealed Air, can help potential change leaders exploit this understanding in situations of increasing size, scope, and complexity.

A STRUCTURED PROCESS FOR SMALL GROUPS

One of Sealed Air's core products is polyethylene foam (the white, solid-sponge material in which new TV sets are packed). This product is manufactured in a number of Sealed Air plants, including one in Hudson, North Carolina. The Hudson plant was having difficulty because of a critical bottleneck in the converting section of the factory—the area where huge three-by-six-foot rolls of polyethylene foam are slit, perforated, sheeted, and punched into various packaging materials.

The converting process defines the lead time in the plant, and as such, largely determines inventory, quality, and customer service levels. Thus, there were major advantages to be obtained by removing the converting bottleneck. The plant manager knew this and asked Fred for assistance in coming up with solutions. In addition, the manager hoped to expose some of his plant department managers and supervisors to different sets of tools and approaches that might help them increase their ability to solve similar problems in the future.

In advance of his arrival, Fred requested some preliminary diagnostic work by a few of the plant's managers. Those chosen had the best collective perspective on this problem, so it was natural to ask them to collect data about hourly throughput and downtime history for the converting machine. These kinds of facts would be essential in removing the bottleneck, but it was equally important to start the group thinking and engaging on the specific problem to be tackled. Fred wanted them to work this territory as early as possible so they would not only be better prepared for the group sessions to come, but would also develop a firsthand sense of the importance of the problem.

STEP 1: DISAGGREGATE THE PROBLEM AND SET OBJECTIVES

Fred started the working sessions at the plant by setting expectations.

If we are going to be together for three or four hours—and that's going to be a fraction of the total time you spend working on this problem—two things will be crucial: to ensure this is a high-value problem for us to tackle, and to set a worthwhile goal. Based on past experience, this means the problem will require fifteen to twenty-five action steps to solve. If we see this is a five-step solution, we can deal with it quickly and get out of here. If we think it is a sixty-step solution, we will need to break it up a little bit.

But before we go further, let's think seriously about whether this is the kind of problem that we want to tackle in the first place.

The group, helped by the diagnostic work, readily concluded that increasing throughput on the machine was indeed a critical and important problem for it to tackle. Gaining commitment as a team to the problem's importance was a critical first step towards the team-performance capability required for a solution.

"The second thing we have to do," continued Fred, "is make sure that we set a goal that makes this a worthwhile investment of our time." The group discussed this point for a while before deciding on a goal of increasing machine throughput by 25 percent—drawing largely on their past collective experience and judgment. Thus, they had defined the playing field (by explicitly excluding anything that would not lead to significant throughput gains), and they were committed to a clear, demanding goal.

STEP 2: WORK THE PROBLEM-SOLVING PROCESS

Next, the group began working the problem. "People need a road map if they're going to think about problems in new ways," says Fred. "But it's got to be simple or the process becomes more important than the problem." The process encompassed brainstorming, analysis, recommendation, and action planning. The brainstorming involved all of the preliminary work the group had done. Fred played a critical, combination role: first, he was a facilitator, problem-solving contributor, and source of outside knowledge to help the team to brainstorm root causes of the problems; second, he was a key catalyst when the team began to propose solutions. "The trick here was to enable the team to engage in a 'no-down-side, no-risk' session to surface ideas of all kinds." Utilizing open discussion and brainstorming, this session focused on identifying both issues and possible opportunities. It was an informal and simplified way of getting a rich mix of knowledgeable people into the no-idea-is-a-bad-idea mode until the one or two gems that would solve the problem were discovered. The discussion identified twenty-eight subproblems to be dealt with (which Fred will later help them condense into about ten groupings), ranging from bad splices in the material as it moves through the machine to poor interprocess scheduling, to a hypothesis seriously advanced by one particular machine operator that "the machine is just too big."

While that particular idea was not really actionable, it illustrates the value of getting people to work through the problem in logical steps. Fred urged the operator to talk about what kinds of subproblems were caused by the machine's size—for example, how the machine got in the way of being able to reach the material roll to rethread it when it broke. Obviously, if ways could be found to speed up rethreading, downtime could be significantly reduced.

STEP 3: DEVELOP AND ANALYZE ALTERNATIVE SOLUTIONS

Once they agreed on the specific problems they needed to overcome to obtain at least 25 percent more throughput at the converting station, the team proceeded to generate and test alternative solutions. "We started on a relatively easy problem, in order to develop experience and confidence. The first one we tackled was the problem of loose rolls slowing down the converting machine, which was essentially a communication problem," says Fred. The solution was a series of meetings to ensure that the necessary communication occurs among those handling the rolls, thereby making the roll converting easier, more consistent, and faster. With a couple of easy wins like this under their belts, the team members quickly moved on to more complex and difficult issues and problems.

With each successive problem, however, they followed the same performance-improving pattern, by generating ideas, performing cost-benefit analyses for them, recommending which to implement, and establishing clear accountability for both results and timing. They did not, however, view their work as completed with the assignment of action-plan specifics; only when the action steps were carried out and results obtained was their responsibility over.

This type of interaction and thinking can occur in many different types of structured performance-improvement processes—both formal and informal. It does not really matter which type is used as long as it is flexible enough to stimulate out-of-the-box thinking. Even wild ideas are useful as long as the ideas converge to generate solutions to critical problems.

WHY A STRUCTURED PROCESS WORKS

The Sealed Air example demonstrates two things relevant to change-leader roles: first, how a staff RCL can use structured processes to extract more power out of a small group of operating people; and second, how structured processes help potential change leaders in the group learn new skills and approaches they can apply elsewhere. At the beginning of this section, six fundamentals that RCLs use for energizing people in large and small groups were summarized. Fred's experience illustrates four reasons that these elements invariably work:

1. They provide new tools that can be learned by people of distinctly different skills, experiences, and potentials.

2. They introduce new information that stimulates practical insights and solutions that would not otherwise surface.

3. They provide a safe, sponsored environment in which it is all right to question sacred cows and advance different ideas.

4. They provide a goal to unify the efforts.

Most important, such efforts extend the RCI's reach and influence within the organization because several people learn the process quickly and can apply it elsewhere. A number of proven performance-improvement processes are available, most of which can work if used appropriately and guided by experienced change leaders. They usually work best, however, when modified to fit the specific culture and circumstances of each company or organization.

Change leaders have to learn in single applications what makes these processes useful—as well as how to select the right approach for a particular situation—before applying them to more complex, multiple-application situations. The next case illustrates how and why more complex settings require the perspectives of more experienced change leaders. Randy Howard, a plant manager from UNOCAL, had experienced the usefulness of different small-group approaches, as well as their pitfalls, in a number of situations. In the following story, he faces the task of designing a program to meet the challenges in his plant, one requiring a number of different kinds of involvement from most of his six hundred employees.

2. ENERGIZING HUNDREDS IN A LARGE PLANT

Potential change leaders usually recognize the need for a well-marked pathway for their people. The trick here is to mark a pathway that aligns, but does not overly constrain, personal initiative—easier said than done. Such a pathway requires a combination of disciplined structure and process as well as leadership flexibility. This combination differs from an organization's formal structure and management practices. It must provide clear rules and consistent communications to both individuals and the organization as a whole. Yet, it must also provide for adjustments along the way. Well-marked pathways invariably have the same fundamental elements highlighted in the beginning of this chapter and seen in the small-group setting at Sealed Air. However, they become increasingly important and difficult to design as the size, scope, and complexity of the change situation increases.

Nonetheless, RCLs consistently gravitate to these fundamentals because they are simple to understand and because they usually work. They use them to merge some age-old notions about the value of both individuals and teams at the front-line level with some new tools, techniques, and approaches developing at high-performance companies. Integrating the best from the old and the new thinking, they strike an important, albeit difficult, balance. Some see this as the art of good leadership; RCLs seem to learn it on the job because it is the only way they can accomplish the task at hand.

Randy Howard's experience as an RCL at UNOCAL's Los Angeles refinery, where he executed an effort that resulted in a 20 percent reduction in total plant-operating expenses in less than two years, illustrates these fundamentals in action in a large manufacturing-plant environment.

ELIMINATING CONFUSION AT UNOCAL

Randy Howard is a classic RCL. He tolerates little nonsense, speaks clearly and concisely, and listens intensely. His competitive instincts reflect his experience as a starting center on the University of California football team. He is determined to get results, but he is also determined to do so by obtaining the best of most, if not all, of his people. He had been successful at UNOCAL as a refinery engineer, planner, and technical supervisor. Whatever the job, Randy got it done faster and better than expected, and had developed strong loyalty from the people he worked with in the process. As a manager, he developed a uniquely rich understanding of front-line people and a strong conviction that they hold a hidden reserve.

SHAPING A NEW PATHWAY

In this particular case, Randy faced an interesting challenge. He had been installed as general manager of UNOCAL's largest and most important oil refinery, located in the heart of Los Angeles. He was given a simple directive: to turn around an operation that had a history of increasingly out-of-control operating costs and poor revenue generation. Top management picked Randy for the job because of his can-do attitude and history of getting the job done. For the first time, however, he had significant concerns about how to meet his objectives:

> There was a real sense of hopelessness among the employees. Everybody knew we might have to shut the plant down . . . people didn't know what to do or how to help. . . . I felt that turning things around was going to be directly related to my ability to tap the potential of those scared and frustrated people, most of whom wanted to do the right thing.

Adding to his dilemma was a plethora of partial initiatives already under way. On the surface, it was impossible to tell what, if anything, was working. Consider two examples: new business plans and breakthrough teams. Both had been helpful in some ways, but neither added much to the bottom line. Rather than dismiss such efforts as failures, however, Randy worked to learn what he could that might be helpful in constructing a new pathway. In both cases, he discovered good and bad news.

With the business plans, the good news was that by breaking up refinery operations into forty line and staff units, each unit had become responsible for a plan that surfaced useful issues and actions to improve performance. The bad news was that the first plans contained much information, but not much insight, about the true cause of performance shortfalls. While Randy found the plans to be frustrating reading, they helped enhance his understanding of the real problem:

When I tried to put the forty plans together, they did not add up to one overall plan for the refinery. There was no linking measure or structure that gave everyone a sense of how they fit into the overall business of the refinery . . . [so] my marching orders were pretty clear: employees needed some central guiding goal in which to fit their own plans.

The breakthrough teams (groups of front-line workers in pursuit of small, actionable improvement ideas) were also a good news/bad news situation. The good news (they surfaced good ideas) confirmed Randy's beliefs about the importance of front-line involvement and the usefulness of tools and a process for collective problem solving. He saw the same benefits that Fred Smagorinsky had experienced at Sealed Air. The bad news was that the teams' efforts typically focused on noncritical areas, lacked follow-through to sustain results, and were difficult to extend:

They confirmed the power of getting a front-line team together to solve a problem loosely defined by management. However, our challenge at the refinery was so large that I needed to find a way to extend parts of the breakthrough approach—cross-functional teams, hard deadlines and goals, and accountability for results— and apply them more broadly across the refinery.

Randy used what he learned from these experiences to design a program that would capitalize on the positive things and add the missing pieces, such as setting stretch goals, helping each person understand his/her specific piece of the goals, and explaining why it all mattered. To that end, he made early use of available benchmarking data that measured his plant against a number of similar competitor plants on a set of key measures. The measure that mattered most for his plant was total operating expense normalized to volume of oil refined (cost-per-barrel). This measure worked well for Randy because people could readily understand why it mattered, did not want it to remain where it was, and could easily track their progress as they tried to climb from the last to the first quartile:

For the first time ever, I could stand up in front of my employees and say, here's what matters for us, here's where we are today, and here's where we have got to get to.

This goal was important, but not sufficient. Randy needed a process to help—one that would encompass lots of people, utilize new tools and skills, and measure results. To that end, he shaped an approach that he called the Accelerated Performance Improvement Program, or APIP. It included each of the forty units and a large portion of the employees. APIP forced each unit to define its performance target, develop ideas for meeting it, analyze and recommend actions, and measure accountability for results. Randy added one final step to the process to ensure implementation:

> We set it up so that for every idea recommended, approved, and implemented, the budgets were adjusted to reflect the savings identified . . . to send a clear message: Hey, you came up with this idea, your analysis says it will work, so we are going to do it. Oh, by the way, we've already changed your budget in anticipation of [achieving] the results.

Even with this process in place, the added budget discipline, and an overall goal to shoot for, Randy still sensed confusion and hesitancy among the front-line employees who were essential to achieve his target. So he decided to redefine the rules of the game in a way that had both symbolic and motivational value: he made UNOCAL headcount reductions out of bounds! On the surface this was a risky decision, since headcount was a critical factor in moving up on the benchmarked list. It was also clearly out of step with the rules that almost every other company in performance difficulty follows. However, Randy knew that contract labor made up nearly a third of the total personnel costs in the plant. He reasoned that other nonpersonnel-related factors, such as reducing downtime and increasing process yields, were equally, if not much more, important to the overall plant economics.

Thus, he could essentially capture most of the needed improvements by addressing nonlabor expenses and focusing any headcount reductions on contract personnel rather than on UNOCAL employees. This decision freed up key UNOCAL front-line employees to participate and become engaged in the process. It also alleviated much of the confusion and fear that was previously rampant across the front line. Randy might never have come up with this critical insight had he been less convinced—or less determined—that the key to the refinery's long-term success lay in the increased productivity and initiative of its workforce.

Marking the Pathway

Randy now had in place three of the six fundamental elements identified earlier for a well-marked pathway (or structured process) for tapping the potential of his people:

1. A benchmarked performance target—costs per barrel. The target was one that everyone understood and believed in. By tracking closely against competitors, he built up a constructive competitive spirit and could identify both early and continuing achievements that helped energize and sustain people's initiative and productivity.

2. A clearly understood solution space or playing field. This element was one with unique, motivational significance to his people. In declaring UNOCAL personnel out of bounds for headcount reductions, he effectively defined the playing field as including everything else. This allowed APIP teams to take clear ownership of areas without concern for functional or other turf issues, and removed the ambiguity and fear involved with the process.

3. A well-defined problem-solving process. The process was one that he and his RCLs had designed to fit their circumstances. By building on the lessons from earlier business plans and breakthrough teams, that is, forcing all activities to contribute to the overall goal plus hardwiring the projected savings into the budgets, he virtually eliminated the danger of becoming activity-focused.

In short, APIP was simple, consistent, understandable, and relevant to the task at hand. Employees had a process that not only focused their performance-improvement efforts, but one that also gave them the tools they needed to identify, quantify, and implement improvement ideas.

Lighting the Path

Once the key elements of the pathway were in place and clearly marked, Randy, along with Gary Frieburger, the plant operations manager, and Mike Ruehle, a refinery technical supervisor, had to make sure to light it up through effective communications and personal leadership. The key here was for Randy to be heard and believed at the individual level. This led to a combination of group and individual communications that included large-group, rally-the-troops sessions as well as small-group sessions and one-on-one informal interactions. All of these meetings were built around a consistent set of messages tied to the plant's goal, process, and need for involvement, and the importance of success. The many informal interactions were particularly important because of the signal they sent about the support and commitment of Randy and his management team of change leaders. The mere fact that senior people like Randy, Gary, and Mike would visit the night crews at 2:00 A.M. sent powerful, positive messages throughout the workforce.

In Randy's view, leadership and communications challenges were very closely linked. The real leadership challenge for him was to reduce employee fear of doing things differently, take out some of the risks himself, counteract the cynicism left over from earlier efforts, and generate increasing levels of enthusiasm. What Randy did was create a safety zone for his people where they could experiment, change, and take risk without personal fear. Most important, people had to trust that in the end there would be benefits for both the individual and the refinery. Much of the fear of doing things differently came from their prior experience that if they tried something that didn't work, they would pay a price for it. Thus, Randy's individual connections had to mean something different to them.

> Really understanding the individuals was the key, and the only way for me to get that was to spend a lot of time with them. You create an environment which fosters smart risk-taking and involvement only when you have the employees believing that the management has a real desire to understand what their concerns are, what they do in their jobs, and what frustrates them.

Leadership also meant staying close enough to the process to be able to reward success at both team and individual levels. Equally important, change leaders had to recognize the effort and not penalize good failures—those *not* due to shoddy work. Another key element of Randy's leadership was to find those people with the attitude and potential skills to be developed into a cadre of new change leaders, who would help to sustain and institutionalize the process going forward.

> It's like that old shampoo commercial: you tell two people, and they'll tell two people, and so on and so on and so on. We had 800 people in the plant. My realistic goal was to get 200 of them revved up and carrying the rest . . . the only way to keep them revved up was to find the 20 or 30 people whom I could really

develop into change leaders and spend significant amounts of time developing, coaching, and building them up.

Paying close attention to the fundamentals—clear goals, defined playing field, structured involvement process, clear communications, and individual leadership—paid off in results. After two years, the plant had exceeded its initial target, an achievement that most thought to be unattainable at the start. More important for Randy, however, is the performance-for-people results he achieved.

> In terms of my own satisfaction, certainly achieving the expense results was exciting. There is nothing like seeing the numbers going in the right direction. But I probably got more personal rewards from having people come up to me and say "Thanks, this is great. You helped me figure out how to do my job."
>
> Yeah, I guess the biggest thing was in helping make people successful, seeing others succeed.

3. ENERGIZING THOUSANDS OF PEOPLE (TCB)

"What works in Papua, New Guinea, is not likely to work in Thailand," said Anita Ward, senior vice president of Texas Commerce Bank (TCB). Anita is a graduate anthropologist who is one of the key behind-the-scenes architects and movers in TCB's current, major, process-improvement effort, which is mobilizing literally thousands of employees to higher performance aspirations and achievement. She was key in many aspects of the overall initiative design and played an internal consulting role in many aspects of the reengineering effort. She is also convinced that her background in anthropology has shaped her fundamental perspective on managing change and was as critical to her redesign work as were her business and reengineering skills:

> It's the anthropologist in me who says, respect the culture you're in. Go in and learn about it . . . then maximize it and utilize it. If you're in Papua, New Guinea, make the change effective within that social structure. When you are dropped in the middle of the Third World, you are there to preserve culture. [Similarly] I do not want to come into an organization and destroy the culture. I want to leverage the [existing] culture for adaptive change.

> It's the greatest lesson . . . that anybody can learn. All of us pick up a book on reengineering and go, oh, I should organize this like Michael Hammer says, or like . . . so, we place this model over our organization and then can't figure out why it didn't work. It didn't work because it didn't respect the culture and didn't leverage the existing core of the culture that you need to make change effectively happen.

Marc Shapiro, the CEO at TCB, has taken a unique path toward achieving fundamental improvements to the bank's business. Perhaps the most unusual aspect of the approach is that it has mobilized a large portion of TCB's 10,000 people. As energizing efforts expand to include thousands rather than just hundreds of people, they get more complex and messy, blurring some of the components of the structured program that can be seen most clearly in the small group at Sealed Air, and more broadly in the UNOCAL refinery effort. Change leaders must counter this messiness by looking for opportunities to hardwire the critical elements (e.g., build recommendations for change into budgets), while at the same time being both flexible and evolutionary in marking the pathways people follow as the process unfolds. RCLs often find in these situations that success requires a thorough understanding of the organization's culture. The bank's approach is a useful example, even though it is still evolving. Initially, Marc set out to obtain at least $50 million in improvements to TCB's noninterest expense. The effort is on track to produce the targeted savings. It is also now changing the entire leadership and management approach throughout the bank. This is something that no one anticipated at the outset. It is truly an ambitious undertaking in a performance situation that, on the surface at least, would not have indicated an urgent need for major change. It may be too soon to declare complete victory, but it is not too soon to see what RCLs have been doing that works.

THE BASIC PROCESS UNFOLDS

On paper, the project structure appears comprehensive as well as logical, and it all fits neatly into a one-year time frame. The reality of the situation, however, was a bit different from a brilliantly preconceived master plan. As Anita describes it:

> We called the phases discovery, redesign, and implementation—simply because every project life cycle has some kind of data collection and redesign and then implementation. Each of the task forces did something a little different in discovery; it was not all the same. We figured it out as we went. We are just now figuring out how we are going to do implementation.

While Anita may have had the phases clearly in mind from the start, and a formal project organization structure did exist on paper, TCB's program was not master-planned from the outset. Nor did TCB follow some prescribed methodology or proven empowerment template. The pathway structured by the bank was the result of ongoing skillful improvisation, thoughtful tailoring, messy give-and-take, and trial and error—all based on the unique social structure (culture) and circumstances of TCB. As Ward sums up, ". . . my greatest lesson: 'There is no prescription for this.' "

In other words, you may describe it neatly, but you cannot make it neat!

GETTING ORGANIZED TO ENERGIZE

The "getting organized" phase seldom appears on official charts shown at meetings, but any large energizing effort takes a while just to get under way. At TCB, this phase can be summarized in four areas of thought and work:

1. Shaping an objective. The seed of the initiative was Marc's cost-reduction target of $50 million, but early task force discussions pushed well beyond that somewhat painful imperative. As described in chapter 2, Marc's emerging group of change leaders helped him to recognize early on that a narrow focus on costs simply could not work as a meaningful change target at the bank. However, the initial cost target was not without value. Ward's comment was echoed by several others:

> Analytically, the cost numbers drove us into the need for change. And then as we started, a small group of us started talking: Well, you know, there is more reason to change than just the numbers; we need to be competitive; we need to give people opportunities to improve themselves and move forward, or around in the organization. We really went after three targets: an expense target, an employee satisfaction target, and a customer satisfaction target.

The starting group of change leaders at TCB was rediscovering the inevitable: you cannot mobilize people—particularly large numbers of people—if all you can offer is something of value to the stockholders. Instinctively, they were shaping a target that would enable them to provide performance results for customers and employees as well as shareholders. Not only does this make sense logically, it also makes sense emotionally.

2. Establishing structure. In some ways, a structured process is just like a plain old organization chart of lines and boxes: it answers questions of who is doing what, how will it be done, and who will work with whom to those ends. The key difference, however, is that this structure must operate across, around, and outside, as well as within, the formal lines and boxes of the hierarchy. It must enable people to look outside their boxes and across their lines to obtain information and challenge traditional assumptions about how things get done.

From the start, the change leaders at TCB thought in terms of organizing process improvement as a very broad-based effort structured around task forces. Other approaches would have been possible, but in choosing task forces they were respecting and leveraging the bank's unique set of characteristics that are a product of their history, reputation, and leadership philosophy, as well as of their current situation. For them, these qualities pointed to task forces and broad involvement as appropriate for TCB. As one change leader observed, "TCB is a culture that needs all that mass consciousness to make change happen."

Key elements of the TCB culture, which made the choice of task forces and wide involvement appropriate, are summarized in the box on the next page.

3. Providing basic training and tools. Obviously, there was a need for initial orientation, guidance, and just-in-time training (i.e. training provided on-site at the time it is required to do a specific task). Left entirely on their own, the groups would flounder and become discouraged over their lack of progress. Nor would people know where or how to get their groups off on a reasonably productive trail. To a very large degree, these are skills learned on the job, but some initial sensitizing and indoctrination is an essential part of on-the-job training. So Anita and her staff put together a day of process-improvement training for the task force managers as well as all the task force members, which was a combination of change management, team building, and traditional reengineering. According to Anita:

> You can't just give them Hammer's book [*Reengineering the Corporation*] and say, "Go read all this stuff and have fun." . . . How do you do a wall drawing? How do you create a value-added database? How do you even assess value added? How do you create flow charts? . . . But wrapped around those mechanics were issues of functioning within a team and managing change.

4. Communicating to the entire organization. Top management's communication was another essential element to be woven around the bank's existing culture and structure. During the weeks of the getting-started period, word spread that something was up. But exactly what wasn't clear. Some heard it as reengineering, which is increasingly widely

BUILDING ON TCB'S CULTURE

A rich history of pride in the institution, shared by customers and employees, produced a working style that is more participative than autocratic:

1. Comfort with consensus, committees, and task forces.

   One of the things I used to hate about TCB is that management favors consensus . . . but in this process it helped enormously. Historically, we set up a committee for everything. As a result, we know all about task forces, "so it's task forces—yeah, okay, let's go."

2. Confidence from past successes.

   Last year we put together an effort similar to this to improve customer satisfaction . . . multi-disciplinary teams headed by salespeople, so that you got the customer perspective. Half focused on employee satisfaction and half on customer satisfaction. It worked.

3. Trust in each other.

   People have worked here fifteen, eighteen, even thirty years and more, so we have all grown up together, and we don't have much distrust of each other. It would be hard for another bank to do it [this way].

4. Can do/will do culture.

   Our culture recognizes stepping up to a challenge. I felt that I was going to be recognized. We do a good job of remembering who is contributing. . . . As a result, we do not see it as an extra workload as much as extra opportunity.

5. A strong bench.

   TCB bankers have always thought of themselves as better and different . . . the best of what there was to offer. Middle management is very strong, so middle managers who had the opportunities to be leaders jumped on it. The future leaders have really come up in this process. It's obvious to a lot of people here who can lead change and who cannot.

6. Increasing level of discomfort with bureaucracy.

   We saw it through our employee-attitude survey. We had very, very poor scores on bureaucracy, on decision making, on policies, on approval.

A task force structure fits well here.

interpreted (at TCB and elsewhere) as cost cutting and layoffs. To others, the rumors implied something bigger and broader, but very vague. The growing uncertainty and anxiety was evident to Marc, who sensed a need to quell the concerns brewing within TCB's social structure, as described later by one change leader:

> As we progressed, there was a lot of unease about what we were doing and how we were going to do it. We decided we really needed a campaign around this . . . Marc needed to communicate with all the employees that we were about to do this . . . That communication from Marc was critical to what we did. Now we have regular mission updates, and we talk about process improvement within those mission updates.

A series of communications, especially a videotape message from Marc, not only answered immediate questions, but started the signals that process improvement was going to be a big deal, not just another annual improvement push. As one participant remembered it:

> It crossed every business line. There were no sacred cows. I can remember that term: no sacred cows, everything's to be looked at, all the processes. You could tell by the way the organization was laid out, all business lines were affected. I thought, this really is a big deal!

MARKING THE PATHWAY FOR 4,000

At this point, the task force leaders, full-time managers, and team members were largely on their own. Their task was broadly defined as finding opportunities in those areas of the bank to which they were assigned. Each group faced a different set of issues and considered and used different data-gathering processes. While they were ostensibly after opportunities, in reality they were also searching for ways to bring more people into the act—and they needed something to coalesce around.

The dominant approach converged upon by the several task forces was an expanding series of employee focus groups. The task forces weren't quite sure what to expect as they began inviting participants from across the organization and up and down the hierarchy to participate in focus groups on different topics. Shortly into the effort, however, it was clear they had discovered a highly energizing approach. The focus groups were the first to tap into the pent-up energy across the broader base of TCB people. Task force members and focus group participants shared the same reactions to the potential uncovered in the sessions: surprise, delight, even shock. The focus groups gave the bank leadership a real sense of the potential that lay untapped in their organization, as the comments excerpted in this box illustrate.

TYPICAL COMMENTS OF FOCUS GROUPS AT TCB

People really came prepared—all levels. We had senior management all the way down to our clerical staff . . . in these meetings. They all really opened up.

They were given an opportunity to give their input into areas where they hadn't been asked before. And that's been one of the greatest positives.

They realized there were . . . many ideas they could put to immediate use.

It's incredible the number of times you go to a meeting and someone talks about some system or skill or product the bank has, and three or four people at the table go, "I didn't know that, that'll help me. Will you show me how, too?"

We did between 75 and 100 focus groups. I threw together a quick database as we started getting these minutes in from the facilitators at the meetings. There were 3,300 comments or issues that came out of our task force.

RCLs cannot measure results or even progress by counting activities. Nor are Marc and his early change leaders confused on this point. It is important in this example, however, to understand the scope of the effort as well as its results. Literally hundreds of these focus groups were eventually held, involving nearly 4,000 of the bank's 9,000-plus employees. Out of these sessions, more than 11,000 ideas were eventually distilled and documented to become the grist for the redesign phase. The actual outputs from each of the task forces from the discovery phase varied. Focus-group ideas were captured in various forms. Some task forces pushed on with more analysis and documentation; others did not. Before it was close to over, however, change leaders made sure these initial ideas would be tracked relentlessly through to recommendations and real action.

STUMBLES AND FALSE STARTS

The first phase was frustrating and painful at times, but there was no way that early mishaps could be completely avoided. It took a while for task force members to get a feel for their new role and work and, as a result, they made mistakes and false starts. On the one hand, this would certainly argue for clearer structure, direction, and common practices at the beginning. On the other hand, there is nothing like a few stumbles and recoveries to help develop a new set of muscles and skills. Debbie Gibson, one of the task force managers, describes the shaky start:

> We struggled a bit at the start . . . even though we were told what the deliverables were. It was still kind of hard to visualize them. After [a few] meetings things started clicking . . . people's excitement level was what surprised me the most even though . . . we were really tapping in on people's time. . . . It was very positive.

It was something that none of them had ever done before. This was especially true for full-time task force managers on whom the burden of managing the process really fell. They were not sure that they were even asking the right questions. For example, had any of them done it before, they would have known to gather relevant data earlier, because at the eleventh hour it was a pain to get it. Similarly, change leaders learned they cannot simply gather a group of people together and say, "Tell us what doesn't work right." They had to structure meetings, limit subjects, and facilitate discussion; otherwise, mass confusion would result.

Looking back, some believe that the process structure could have been tighter on defining the methods and tools to be employed, thereby reducing the initial disorientation and struggle. This might also have assured more uniform and useful data output from the six task forces. However, it might also have reduced the learning and commitment value.

Even more troublesome was the initial difficulty in coordinating across the six task forces. When the process was first designed, many believed that Marc intended each task force to be fairly autonomous. Because the bank is so integrated, however, it would have been impossible to segregate business units into groupings that did not affect each other materially. One of the task force managers remembers their initial troubles.

> The six of us [task force managers] needed to get together because of the overlap. It started out with a big group meeting every couple

of weeks. Not a whole lot would happen other than you'd go around the table and each of the task forces would tell what they were doing. The group was too large and it wasn't very useful.

A NEED FOR CLEAR LEADERSHIP

Their stumbles helped the group to realize that the effort needed very strong leadership. Their first choice was the CEO, but they weren't at all sure that he would want to devote as much time as they felt would be needed. After all, Marc had set up a structure that appeared to put him primarily in an oversight-only role, with two task forces reporting up to each vice chairman. His change leaders soon convinced him otherwise, however, by confronting the issue directly, hashing it through with him, and forging the critical link to top management that is characteristic of RCLs.

There is no question that Marc Shapiro's role was essential in this effort. It was also very different from the typical CEO role many have come to expect, and it was greatly influenced by the initiative, insights, and behaviors of the change leaders developing around him. It would be inaccurate to say that Marc is a product of the bank's change leaders; it would also be inaccurate to underestimate the influence they have had on his leadership style. It is hard to separate out what was intuitive on his part and what was learned in the process. However it happened, he truly became "the real change leader's change leader." His naturally unassuming style and unique ability to listen to people at all levels helped make people comfortable with him in a wide variety of settings. He instilled courage in people that allowed them to become effective change leaders. He devoted well over half his time to the process improvement effort in all kinds of meetings, personal interactions, and formal and informal communications. While this sounds like a huge sacrifice on his part, it may not have been, since it gave him a new perspective on the bank he could never have obtained otherwise. It also may be that he actually enjoyed it, if one task force manager's observation is true:

> I think he loves it. I think it's the greatest thing he's ever gotten involved in. He has attended a lot of focus groups and a lot of action team meetings, and he thinks it's great. He said there were two things he loves most about attending one of these meetings. One is someone saying, "I do x," and people replying, "I can't believe you do x." The second thing he likes is someone saying, "I do x," and everyone saying, "You do x? That's wonderful!"

Marc (who gives most of the credit for the results to date to change leaders across the bank) is typically circumspect in his own description of his role in the process-improvement effort:

I talk about it. I write about it. And I think about it a lot.

REGROUPING TO STRENGTHEN THE FOCUS

By midyear, the process improvement effort was through the first discovery phase and had crossed the river. Hundreds of people were into the act, offering improvement suggestions at every turn, but they still had to make the difficult ascent to the higher performance plateau beyond. The bank's leadership knew this from their earlier experiences with the customer-service and employee-satisfaction efforts. Real benefits are not captured unless you regroup, take back control, and reenergize the group to move on. In this case, once the focus groups extracted their ideas, it was necessary to restructure the effort by reformulating teams and task forces to get the right people into a different set of right places, and by tightening up on tools and methods.

Reformulating Teams and Task Forces

When the first phase ended around the beginning of July 1994, the task force leadership group decided it was time to narrow the path and reign in the ideas that had been generated. First, they took all the task force recommendations and created a single database in order to cull, consolidate, and sort the recommendations into a well-ordered mother lode of 11,000 ideas. Working from the database and earlier conceptions, the task force leaders then defined what they saw as the core processes of the bank and designated about 170 action teams to begin redesigning various processes and systems across the bank.

The effort had reached the point where incorporating the task force ideas into process redesigns required crossing organizational boundaries in a more formal and logical way. Consequently, the action-team design was what Anita Ward describes as a "very different, very horizontal" approach compared to either the bank's existing functional organization or even the task force structure. The leadership group was "taking a piece from one task force and putting it with another." This did not go unnoticed. The task

forces had developed a pride of ownership and sense of turf about their recommendations. Some had even moved ahead and re-formed into their own
sub-task forces to begin redesign. They were ready to move out on their
own. The resulting chaos was frustrating for everyone involved, as
recounted by task force manager Harriet Wasserstrum.

> It was really hard because we had this whole month where the
> six of us were like bickering. "This action team should report to
> me, no it should report to me . . . We need a business person
> leading, no—we need a back-office person to lead . . . I'm not
> going to lead it, but this person has to be on the team." It was a
> terrible month. But it was a fascinating process to witness . . . it
> was churning up everything in the bank at once.

The various groups had to wrestle with the confusion for a while
themselves. As a result, a sort of negotiating process took place—because
everybody did recognize the need for it—and most people came to virtually the same conclusion. It was now critical to structure action teams that
could take a true process view across the organization.

Marc recognized the consternation this action caused. "While we
did that, a lot of people on the inside got frustrated with it and with me,
and a lot of people on the outside got frustrated because they didn't
know what had happened to the project." Though Anita recognized the
necessity for compromise at the outset (designing the task forces for the
discovery phase more along existing organizational versus true process
lines) she now believes, "If I were to do it all over again, I would force
the process-based design up front to mitigate the argument on the back
end." Not everyone, however, agrees. Many saw real value in working
through these frustrations, even at the expense of having more clarity at
the beginning. At this point, however, the need for different structure
was compelling. So, too, was the need for several other actions to better
define the pathway for the second phase. The actions taken by the
change leaders toward this end are summarized by Anita in the box on
the next page.

Extra support to the new action teams was also provided. Each team
was assigned an internal consultant to help with process design, technology, finance, and human resources. The consultants were all insiders who
took on these roles in addition to their regular staff duties. And of course,
picking the right people—the potential RCLs—was key.

STEPS TO REDEFINE THE PATHWAY

1. Tighter work plans.

   We have tasks, time lines, beginning dates, and completion dates. . . . On a two-week plan it is simply, here is a task list and you're done, but give me some dates because my next project plan and my next assignment of resources depends on your ability to complete.

2. Hard wiring consistent methods across teams.

   We took the methodology and imbedded it in the work plans. It would say things like, do the flow chart of whatever. We provided each action team leader a template that had thirty to forty tasks, predefined. If they did anything on top of that, then great, but this was their minimum. Within that minimum was that methodology.

3. Clearer definitions of the expected deliverables.

   Just describe the problem as it exists today and tell me what you are doing about it. Give me a picture of your before-and-after process design. We also want a preliminary process-benefit analysis: What am I going to save in terms of this change? What is the impact of this change? Are there fewer people? Are there fewer steps? Is there less time required? Does my turnaround speed up in this process?

4. Firm end dates and points of closure.

   We did not change our dates. That's one thing we did learn. You are asking people to do something they have never done before—to work in teams where they do not know each other. Without a light at the end of the tunnel that says, "October 15th, I get to go on vacation, I get a breather," . . . we would not have the same success rate. People need closure here just like they need closure on emotional relationships. Milestones and closure dates help . . . keep the momentum going.

Simple stuff that makes a big difference in results.

Another round of training was also conducted. This time it concentrated on pure redesign methods and took a cascading approach. A day of training with the task force managers, action team leaders, and internal consultants was held. This session was then turned into a videotape (complete with a message on the purpose of process improvement by Marc) that the action team leaders could use with their full teams. If a team needed further help, Anita and her internal crew were available.

The action teams successfully completed the redesign phase, and the results have already exceeded expectations, by including more than the significant cost savings that were the initial impetus for the change effort. TCB is now in the midst of the third phase—implementation of the more complex recommendations.

Results Beyond the Bottom Line at TCB

A full accounting of the process-improvement effort indicates it will capture the full $50 million cost-reduction target within eighteen months. In addition, the bank can already count benefits well beyond the near-term financials, as reflected in the words of several of the change leaders at about the time the second redesign phase was ending, and the implementation phase was being launched:

1. **A big release of new energy and enthusiasm.**

   I'm amazed by the task force leaders and how they have taken an interest in an area that they really had nothing to do with, [and] the kind of leadership those people have given. When a problem comes up in any task force, five or six hands go up for people who are going to run with whatever it is . . . [what] startled me was how all task force members took this to heart as the most important work they've ever done. That attitude is in all of them.

2. **A high degree of ownership to ease the pain of implementation.**

   You at least have some ownership: it wasn't them that did that to us, but us who did that. That is a real strength, as painful as it is.

3. **A growing sense of community and strength in diversity.**

   You're getting outside yourself and realizing we have so many different people bringing different things to the table. We let people use their creativity and be part of the process . . . it gives us tremendous volume.

4. **The beginnings of a fundamental shift in the management culture.**

It has been hard for people. . . . Your reward system until now has been built on your role as a lemming. . . . Now we're saying, "I'm sorry, we're changing the reward system. . . . You're no longer a lemming; think on your own." It's been very difficult. But Marc has . . . [built] consensus among a management team and empowered [them] to truly manage. . . . They've gone from managers as executors to managers as leaders. That's a big change.

5. **Increased credibility of, and trust in, TCB's leadership at all levels.**

It is going to be successful because it's not just something that senior management came up with, gave a title or a buzz word to, and delegated to somebody else. Our management committee personally wanted to spend as much time on it as possible. This is the glue that is holding this whole thing together. . . . I think this defused a lot of one-area thinking and one-sided suggestion and reinforced the need for teamwork.

The TCB story is still in progress, as top management, RCLs, and internal reengineers regroup for implementation and continued development of the new leadership and management approach across the bank. Even though the best is yet to come, the results to date are impressive.

COMMON INSIGHTS FROM DIFFERENT SITUATIONS

It is important to note, in going through the experiences at Sealed Air, UNOCAL, and TCB, that, while every RCL must create a pathway that fits the specifics of his or her organization, culture, and specific change challenge, each must still adhere to six fundamental elements in shaping that pathway. When any of these elements, recapped below, are missing, both change and performance results suffer.

1. **Clear performance goals.**
While this sounds simple enough, many goals are often unclear or off target. Far too many mobilization efforts count their progress by activ-

ities such as the number of teams mobilized, the number of ideas generated, etc. At first glance, it is easy to mistake the TCB effort as one of those, but nothing could be further from the truth; the bank's activities led directly to tangible results for shareholders as well as employees.

Program goals cannot be activities. They must be performance results for customers, employees, or shareholders. Such goals enable people to align their diverse efforts and activities, to sharply focus their part of the organization on objectives that count, and to establish metrics for assessing performance progress and for altering pace and approach. For example:

■ **At TCB:** Broadening the goal to include customer and employee satisfaction, as well as costs, is what turned on the latent energy across the company. Being relentless about tracking results against recommendations and budgets is what made results happen.

■ **At UNOCAL:** Setting an operating cost-reduction target based on compelling competitive benchmarks is what made costs mean more than headcount cuts.

■ **At Sealed Air:** Getting plant managers to agree on what was worth their time is what helped them set a clear stretch target which they then achieved.

2. A well-defined playing field.

People need to know what is in play and what is not. Otherwise, they will either unwittingly concentrate efforts on irrelevant tasks or become overwhelmed by the seemingly unlimited scope. Many a program has fallen victim to a gridlock of fear and confusion caused by poorly defined rules.

A well-defined playing field also goes a long way toward relieving employees' anxieties and uncertainties about change. This knowledge also helps to break down assumed barriers to action and interaction, since people are as likely to assume a smaller playing field as they are a larger site. For example:

■ **At TCB:** Going after every process in the bank ("whatever annoys bankers and customers") opened people's minds, unleashing hundreds of dormant ideas. In addition, the playing field was sharply defined by the one-year time frame.

■ **At UNOCAL:** Making UNOCAL (as opposed to contract) personnel reductions *verboten* reduced anxieties and unfroze thinking as well as initiative.

■ **At Sealed Air:** Focusing on the critical factory bottleneck, the converting machine, made the problem instinctively important to everyone in the room.

3. The right people in the right places.

The key here is for change leaders to figure out where the right places are and to focus on skills, not on personalities or politics or even positions, when determining the right people. First, RCLs must determine, both factually and judgmentally, what actions, decisions, and interactions matter most in improving the performance of their units—not everything is of equal importance or urgency. If left to traditional patterns or chance, performance will suffer.

Second, RCLs must focus on skills. Lasting change depends on redeploying old skills to obtain new ones. Unless change leaders assemble the right set of skills and perspectives to attack high-leverage problems and opportunities, there is little hope of shaping new sets of skills to sustain higher performance. For example:

■ **At TCB:** While not explicitly covered in the case, an extraordinary amount of time and change leader attention was devoted to handpicking both the task forces and the action teams. Change leaders believe that this approach really paid off, both in team results, and also in the new behavior patterns and lasting new skills that have developed.

■ **At UNOCAL:** Randy Howard started with a few, high-visibility breakthrough teams in high-potential areas, which helped to break logjams elsewhere. Breaking the logjams freed up and developed new skills needed for future performance.

■ **At Sealed Air:** Getting the right people in the room is how Fred Smagorinsky set up the effort to begin with.

4. Structured, flexible involvement process.

Both structure and flexibility are critical in the mobilization process. This is not an irreconcilable paradox, but it does require attention to specifics. First, RCLs need a few, simple, common tools for problem solving. Whatever the label or specific form, such tools are crucial in helping guide lots of people to perform in consistent directions. Moreover, RCLs must find them in many different places, such as past quality or reengineering efforts, the efforts of other companies, or internal training and skill-building programs. They must then use them to identify issues, structure problems, discover alternatives, and assess solutions, and try to deliver them just-in-time to solve real problems as they are encountered.

Second, RCLs need to develop a set of tight work plans that give a sense of order amid ambiguity and uncertainty; provide a way to hard wire tools into prescribed activities; and assure coordination across teams. Third, they have to establish a firm set of predetermined delivery dates that can give teams some way stations in which to savor progress and regroup, as well as to help change leaders balance short-term performance needs against the time required to do it right. Finally, RCLs must remember that it is critical to be clear about the end products so that people know where and how it will all end. For example:

■ **At TCB:** Anita Ward and the other change leaders used different involvement processes and tools in different phases (focus groups for the discovery phase, action teams for the redesign phase); they also tightened up on prescribed work plans, tools, and deliverables with the action teams.

■ **At UNOCAL:** Randy Howard established APIP as the integrated involvement- and performance-improvement process.

■ **At Sealed Air:** The structured performance-improvement process that Fred Smagorinsky used was designed to ensure that front-line operating people could learn the approach quickly and apply new information readily.

5. Committed leadership group.

Successful programs require a top group (even if it contains only a few people) that works together to bolster conviction among its members and others—in ways that can help to quickly resolve impasses, relieve confusion, and encourage teamwork and support across the larger group. The notion that empowerment will require less leadership is faulty; it requires different kinds of leadership at different times—more not less leadership capacity is required. For example:

■ **At TCB:** The task forces' perceived need for leadership was translated into Marc Shapiro's stepping into the role of de facto project manager; Marc's specific role and leadership style changed over time as the process unfolded.

■ **At UNOCAL:** Randy Howard used the APIP process to define his active, substantive role, which also changed markedly over the course of the effort. He was often a peer as well as a leader of his people, two roles he shifted between.

■ **At Sealed Air:** Fred Smagorinsky's ability to lead from behind was critical to the application of the process as well as for the learning that was required.

6. Meaningful communications.

Communication is not a one-time event, obviously. Both formal and informal communications provide the oil that lubricates mobilization efforts over time. There is a continual need to answer the questions of What's going on?, Why?, and How does this fit together? In addition, it is essential that the communication efforts be viewed as two-way, interactive approaches. Otherwise, RCLs cannot be assured of staying attuned to the specific concerns of individuals, nor can they be assured that communications are being received as sent. For example:

■ **At TCB:** Providing a continuous stream of communications directly from Marc kept people clear on where they were and where they were headed next during the massive mobilization.

■ **At UNOCAL:** Randy's rally-the-employees sessions kept people focused on accomplishments.

■ **At Sealed Air:** Fred's insightful questions enabled the group to better understand what it needed as well as options it might not have considered.

Most RCLs believe strongly that these six elements are essential in mobilizing large numbers of people toward any lasting change in overall performance capability. While many change programs enhance and add to this list, and every successful mobilizing effort follows its own unique pathway, these basics are still guidelines to live by.

People's hidden reserves are present in all change situations. They constitute the largest potential source of energy any organization has at its disposal. Real change leaders understand this and, by providing a pathway that uses the six basic elements, attempt to tap and constructively channel people's hidden reserves, to improve performance.

PROCESS

How do I know which "processes" really matter?

- *What is a process, anyway? We put a process label on everything from payroll to global logistics!*
- *We are all huddled in team rooms, flow-charting every process imaginable. Miles of chart paper on walls. I'm lost!*

Where does reengineering fit in relation to all our other change efforts?

- *What problems will it address? What happens to our quality and customer service initiatives?*

How do I make all this more than cost-cutting?

- *People are getting more cynical. I need to find ways to grow the business.*

How do I break down the "stove-pipe" functional barriers that are killing us?

- *Sometimes I think all this concern about process management would take care of itself if we could just work well across departments.*

What does all this process stuff really mean for improving performance?

"Process! Wow, what a concept," as Robin Williams might have said in his 1980s television show, *Mork and Mindy*. For real change leaders, *process* is indeed a valuable concept. It can be powerful, perhaps revolutionary, when it helps change leaders to think less about internal functional matters like hierarchy, procedure, and internal goals, and more about how to deliver value directly to the customer—better and faster than the competition. This way of thinking can add as much value at the RCL level as it does at a top management level. The key insight of *process management*— that managers should think of their part of the business as a set of linked activities that deliver value directly to the customer—is an important advance in management thinking.

Let us illustrate the point by comparing an everyday shopping experience at a supermarket in an average community on Long Island, New York, to a Publix store in any similar community in Florida. The average shopper arrives at the Long Island store on a Friday or Saturday morning to stock up for the coming week. The first problem is parking, since the store lot holds no more than fifty cars; there is a larger lot across the way, although it is a bit of a walk. Shopping carts are strewn all across both parking lots, but some are crammed together at an outside storage area near the store—so tightly that the average shopper can barely separate them. Most are damaged, and, after trying three or four carts that do not work for various reasons, the shopper finds one with a stuck wheel. Since it is at least pushable, he takes it into the store.

The store is busy, since most working people have to shop on weekends. The aisles are blocked with store workers and stock dollies piled high with boxes for replenishing the shelves. It would be difficult to get through the narrow aisles even without the stock dollies; it is virtually impossible while the shelves are being restocked. Since the workers and the stock dollies take precedence over the shoppers, the experienced shopper will leave his cart at the end of an aisle and wander down it picking up whatever he can carry back. Why not; the damaged cart is hard to push anyway. Often the items he needs most have not yet been restocked. The door to the stockroom is adjacent to the dairy coolers, so the shopper takes his life in his hands trying to get milk. Workers pushing loaded stock dollies come whisking in and out without warning—again, they take precedence, because they have a job to do: get the shelves loaded up. If the shopper needs something like film or (God forbid!) cigarettes, he must go to a special counter that seldom has anyone behind it (although there are always a few supervisors in an adjacent office chatting, joking, and ignor-

ing customers completely). Waiting five minutes for someone to acknowledge one's presence is par for the course.

Checkout is the most fun of all. Seldom are all of the checkout lines
open, and if the shopper has only a few items, he can be sure that no one
will be working in the express lane. Invariably something stalls the line he
is in: a new checkout person who doesn't know how to accept personal
checks, a coupon-clipper trying to use invalid coupons, or the checkout
person going on break. Name it, and it is bound to happen while he is in
the line. If the shopper gets checked out in twenty minutes, it is a minor
miracle. Should the shopper offer to do his own bagging to speed things
up, the checkout person is often insulted. Afterward, the shopper pushes
his loaded (and broken) cart across the crowded parking area to his car
(remember, it is not nearby), unloads it, and either leaves the cart in the
way of other cars or trudges all the way back to the "cram-'em, jam-'em"
storage area next to the store. It is an experience to be remembered, even
if he does it only once. It is the most dreaded part of the weekend for most
regular shoppers—but there is almost no other choice.

Contrast this with what happens at any Publix supermarket in
Florida. The difference is like night and day. The shopper arrives and
parks next to the store in an ample and convenient lot. Dozens of clean,
virtually new shopping carts (extra large) are at the entrance—and they all
work! Despite a busy morning, all the well-marked aisles are completely
free of stock dollies. Occasionally, an employee can be sighted stocking
shelves, but it is done quickly, and the shopper is always given preference.
Publix prides itself on quick-shelf-stocking rules to ensure that customers
are not inhibited. All items the shopper wants are invariably available in
abundance, and there are no stock-dolly highways to avoid. The film and
cigarette counter is always manned by several people. Checkout rarely
takes more than five minutes, express lanes are always manned, and all the
shopper's items are bagged by pleasant workers who then follow the shopper out to his car and transfer his bags to the car. No tipping is allowed,
and the entire experience takes less than half the time of the Long Island
nonsense. Obviously, Publix has absorbed the customer's point of view,
while the other supermarket has not. Almost everything Publix people do
reflects the customer's point of view. They do not always succeed, but it is
no accident that Publix is highly profitable.

Process management is all about getting the customer's point of view
right up front and center—and making sure the appropriate actions are
taken to satisfy that point of view faster and better than the competition.

Publix gets it right 90 percent of the time. At the RCL level, however, process design and management can easily appear to be a mysterious concept; it sounds great, but nobody really understands what it means. Hence, confusing, often unspoken questions cloud the horizons for potential RCLs: If I do not understand what a process is, how can I redesign one? If reengineering does not mean job loss, what does it mean? If I don't control the process, how can I influence it?

Once again, RCLs find themselves in the middle for those important process redesign efforts. Michael Hammer tells us that reengineering must have top management support and direction to cut across different functional and product line interests, challenge and change old assumptions, and override narrow priorities.* Reengineering must also obtain the workforce alignment, cooperation, and initiative to tap all the hundreds of down-line improvement opportunities.

The RCL is the linchpin that brings these countervailing forces together. For example, top management exhorts the overall company and shareholder benefits of process redesigns, but the workforce fears the probable job eliminations. RCLs must reconcile this conflict if they are to find practical ways to increase results. In addition, RCLs in many parts of large and small organizations alike are succeeding in bringing process thinking and redesign into their particular part of a change effort—with or without top management cover. None of these different kinds of processes can be changed to work differently unless RCLs are involved in both process design and management.

As a way of thinking across functions and structures, "process" is used to imply a sequence of information, action, and work flows that is fast, direct, and efficient. Unfortunately, process has a variety of definitions and uses, which can be confusing to the reader. To help reduce the confusion, the box opposite defines the various process terms used in this book. To clarify the language, we frequently use the term "action flow" in this chapter when referring to a subset of work activities that comprise a larger business process. RCLs are in a unique position to design and use these different kinds of processes to achieve higher performance results. This chapter describes how to:

---

* Michael Hammer and James Champy, *Reengineering the Corporation: A Manifesto for Business Revolution* (New York: Harper Business, 1993).

1. **Absorb the customer point of view,** to discover and convey what "superior value" means to them—both now and in the future.

2. **Cut through the hierarchy,** to deliver superior customer value—faster and better than the competition.

3. **Learn different approaches,** to find what combination works best—as an integrated process to align and mobilize the actions of lots of people.

PROCESS
Common Terminology and Definitions

Process.   A series or sequence of prescribed actions that delivers consistent results over time.

Action flow.   The basic steps or activities that comprise a business process—the actual work that creates incremental value (quality, speed, or cost) to targeted customer segments.

Business process.   Information, activities, decisions, materials, and action flows that result in a major value for customers: e.g., key-account management, new product design, inventory control, product manufacturing, distribution, and delivery.

Management process.   Information, activities, decisions, and action flows that enable a performance-oriented organization: e.g., planning, strategy formulation, performance evaluation, and compensation.

Core processes.   A combination of business and management processes required to deliver a critical value to customers and meet corporate performance objectives—one that is central to a company's competitive advantage, i.e., commercialization of technology (for a computer company) or site selection (for a fast food company).

Performance improvement process.   A set of objectives, structured involvement approaches and tools, leadership, and communications intended to significantly improve performance by permanently changing the basic skills and behaviors of people.

1. ABSORB THE CUSTOMER'S POINT OF VIEW

Process management begins by totally absorbing the customer's point of view. That vantage point provides RCLs a different way of viewing their business. As a result, it yields additional insights about performance-improvement opportunities. The mind-set required has three basic parts: identifying with the customer to define superior value relative to what competitors can offer; eliminating or changing whatever interferes with—and accelerating whatever facilitates—getting superior value to the customer; and adapting in real time to exploit changing marketplace circumstances. It implies thinking and acting across, around, or through the hierarchy to deliver value to the customer (internal or external) as directly and rapidly as possible. This contrasts with normal patterns in most organizations, which require information and interactions to make unnecessary detours up and down the ladder to comply with hierarchical rules and practices. That is really what the process jargon and boilerplate labels are all about—eliminating unneeded detours, diversions, and indirect work that inhibit getting superior products and services directly to customers—better and faster than the competition. Even when all such diversions cannot, for legitimate reasons, be completely eliminated, the value of thinking this way can be very powerful. Thus, it always makes sense to *think process management*"—even if you cannot always "*do process management.*"

Nourishing a customer point of view throughout an organization requires getting people to maintain a customer perspective and then keying organizational priorities and actions on the few things that matter most to the customer.

MAINTAIN A CUSTOMER PERSPECTIVE

Strange as it may seem, too many good managers inadvertently focus much more on internal priorities and efficiency than on external customer needs. Despite the increasing emphasis on the customer in recent years, many managers in the middle still do not instinctively worry about customers, unless they happen to be in sales and marketing—where, of course, the customer has to be the focal point. They are too busy controlling costs, meeting budgets, and designing efficient organizations. Change leaders develop a keener sense of the importance of the customer, regardless of their functional affiliations or managerial responsibilities. At companies like GE Motors, you cannot talk with a manager in any functional discipline on any subject of importance without hearing a direct reference to customers and competitors. At Texas Commerce Bank (TCB), the entire reengineering effort was aimed at removing the frustrations that customers were experiencing. The very best change leaders become the missionaries for customers within such organizations.

In most large companies, however, the bulk of the mid-level managers have little direct customer contact and see no reason to worry much about the customer point of view—"That's what marketing and sales managers are supposed to do. My job is materials management [or accounting or distribution or inventory control]." Not surprisingly, therefore, large companies often lose track of what their customers really want and need.

Losing Customer Perspective at Prudential

The middle management bureaucracies in large companies have become perfect swamplands in which to lose customers. For example, in the over $500 billion insurance industry, there are dozens of large monoliths whose behavior suggests they have not only lost track of what customers want, they seem to prefer that customers go away. Mike Vaccaro, an RCL at Prudential whom you will hear more about in the last section of this chapter, characterizes it this way:

> You can see how it happened. In the insurance business, if you
> insure the wrong person—that is, you do not get his driving
> record right—you can lose a lot of money fast. So we built a con-
> trol culture like the old joke: "We'll give you insurance *only*
> when you prove that you do *not* need it!"

Mike is a quiet man with a ready handshake. He knows everyone in the organization, and people respond to him warmly and seek his counsel often—so much so that the observer wonders when he finds the time to get his work done. He grew up in northern New Jersey and studied marketing at Saint Peter's College. After graduating from college, he spent four years in the army as an operations officer and one year at Blue Cross and Blue Shield. He joined the Pru in 1973 as a methods-and-procedures person. (This was process design, pure and simple, way back then!) In the course of a Prudential career focused on back-office efficiency and effectiveness, he opened new operations centers, managed customer service departments, and built a new organization to manage and measure regional underwriting and claims effectiveness.

Twenty-two years later, Mike has his old job back, but with a new name: he is a process engineer in Prudential's property and casualty insurance business. Process engineers do exactly what their title implies: examine various systems and action flows to improve efficiency and cost effectiveness. Mike has been working this territory for more than twenty years, and he knows it cold. As he walked us down the long, beige, maze-like corridors of the Property and Casualty Division's suburban New Jersey headquarters, we began to appreciate how easily the customer perspective might get lost here. As Mike explained:

> The problem is that while we are checking, double-checking, and triple-checking, our competitors are giving customers a quote over the telephone and sending out paperwork in three days, while it can take us three weeks or longer. We lost sight of . . . the customer.

And why not? Most of the division's work seemed unrelated to the customer, who is seldom seen anyway. If you have little direct contact, you literally do lose sight of the customer, and it is fairly certain that you have no idea what the key sources of customer value are for them. Redesigning a set of action flows to reach someone you cannot find, see, or touch is one sure way to have a reengineering failure.

But just recognizing the obvious (customers are important, even in organizations that overlook the obvious) is only the first step. The next, and perhaps most critical, step in maintaining a customer perspective is developing a true customer focus for all employees, regardless of function. Mike Perez at Compaq has made a religion out of this.

DAILY CUSTOMER DOSAGE AT COMPAQ

In 1991 Compaq's client server products (the computers that connect smaller PCs into local networks) accounted for under $400 million in revenues and were losing money. Less than three years later, they had become a $3 billion business (40 percent of total Compaq revenues) as well as the company's most profitable division. There are many elements to this success story—creation of a separate Systems Division to focus on this market, a clear strategy, good timing, a well-knit and able leadership team—but underlying it all has been a relentless pursuit of the customer perspective by everyone, regardless of function. Mike Perez puts it simply:

> We're not smarter than anybody else, but we are quicker to move when we see a customer need, because of our *attitude: nobody is excluded from the requirement of knowing and dealing with customer issues*. We don't care if you are the engineering guy or the software guy, you don't delegate understanding the customer to marketing. Everyone is out there talking to customers, developing personal relationships, knowing you are going to go back and be accountable for the answers and promises you gave before.

Mike is vice president of engineering of the Systems Division and the lead design engineer for their innovative products, and he practices what he preaches. Most engineering vice presidents are consumed by the technical problems of product design and manufacturing, particularly in companies (like Compaq) with strong cultures of engineering excellence. Staying home and making sure everything is on schedule and under control is the engineering manager's role. That's not what Mike does, however. He doesn't get his insights from poring over specifications sheets or development schedules—he gets them from spending time with customers in the banking centers of New York and London. Banking and financial services is the customer group that Mike has adopted as his own. Why? Certainly, there was no formal assignment by his leader, Gary Stimac—who is also a devotee of customer immersion. Mike simply gravitated to the area, because, as he puts it, he "clicks" with the people: "banking drives some of the key requirements for our products a little harder than other industries," which provides him with early insight into emerging customer needs.

Others in the Systems Division have their chosen customer groups as well—again, however, not by any formal assignment, just by a sorting out personal interests. That is how Gary believes it works best for the customer. His group also holds over 150 comprehensive customer briefings a year, all as part of what Mike refers to as "getting your daily customer dosage." Both Mike and Gary believe that this is what keeps Compaq's Systems Division ahead of the market. Mike elaborates:

You need this ongoing customer dosage because you always have ideas you want to float by a steady stream of people. Once you have those ideas validated by customers, then you have a lot of leverage to make things happen. If word comes back from the field that so and so told me they wanted this and this is why, then we click on instantaneously and we just go do it.

Obviously, as Mike recognizes, this is a process that does not happen easily at many other companies. All too often, managers have to go through some strategic planning process and attendant approval formalities that can delay the customer response by months—if, in fact, there is enough consensus to produce a response at all. In Compaq Systems, the response is immediate because of the widespread common understanding that exists among change leaders of the customer situation. This understanding also protects the group from chasing technical flourishes with no market value. As Mike says:

When we sense something that smells like "foofoo dust" and it looks like "foofoo dust," it usually is, so we very openly rattle people's cages and call them to task.

Interestingly, the Systems Division's organization charts make it appear to be a functional organization, but Mike emphasizes, "customer alignment is not an organizational thing you can see on paper, it is a mental attitude." This attitude overcomes the inhibiting aspects of functional organization while retaining its benefits for career development and technical expertise. Developing this attitude, to Mike, is like learning a foreign language.

It's easy to mouth the words "customer driven," but not think and act that way. It is almost like learning a new language. If you are trying to learn German, you're never going to get it until you go to Germany and live there for a while. If you are living here, you aren't going to learn German.

But living with your customers is only the first step. The next and perhaps most critical step is being disciplined about both providing those few things that really matter to the customer. Believe it or not, the New York City Transit subway system is a good illustration. Few readers have had firsthand exposure to this infamous transportation web, but most will have no trouble visualizing it.

KEYING ON WHAT MATTERS MOST (NYCT)

As with most organizations today, the idea of being customer-focused has certainly floated down through NYCT. Robert Kiley, then president of the Metropolitan Transit Authority (NYCT's parent agency), began in the late 1980s to refer to riders as "customers" rather than "passengers." The politically attuned quickly picked up on this change in language at the top, and "customer" soon became the correct terminology in all communications. When Alan Kiepper became president of NYCT in 1990, he made it known that improving customer service would be the hallmark of his tenure. Dave Winfield, who worked as second in command for five years under Alan, provides his view of what customer-focused should mean for the subways—as he would like you, the customer, to see it:

> You come to a station, well-identified on the street. As you descend, there is no graffiti; the stairs are in good condition; it is well lit; clean; no one blocks your way. You enter the station; it is well lit; there is no trash, no smell of urine. You buy a fare card, get a smile and "thank you" from the clerk. If you need some directions there is a map: big, clear, and current. Nearby is a telephone with automatic free dialing for 911; it works. Above is an electronic signboard that tells you the Yankees score and the time. A clear public address announcement tells you how soon the next train is coming. The train arrives on time, clean, air-conditioned. You step on . . .

Dave goes on, describing every detail of the ride within the set of action flows he envisions a customer experiencing. This way of thinking (the ride is a set of action flows that deliver transportation value) has been, in itself, a breakthrough idea for the function-bound transit authority. But Dave knows NYCT must do a lot more than just describe the various action flows in customer terms. Change leaders within the organization must figure out what really matters to customers and then redesign the core processes to deliver it. Until customers actually experience the service that matters to them, they receive no value.

Kevin Desmond, chief of Operations Planning, leads a discrete, largely analytic function that checks on both bus and subway passenger loads and travel times. In the past, the data from these routine checks was used only to make service changes, for example, tweaks to schedules or adjustments in the number of trains on a line. If a train wasn't running on schedule, no one necessarily called to find out why. It was enough just to change the schedule. After all, with such a big system (more than 230 bus routes alone), there was plenty to do just checking each route every few years.

Kevin does not look or act like he even belongs in this setting. He is anything but public-service-establishment in attitude, appearance, or behavior. If you were to guess his occupation, you might choose Manhattan lawyer—and you would be close, since he is from a family of five lawyers. Sometimes he reminds you of one of the younger Kennedys, but more often his determination and obsession bring to mind a freedom fighter in action. Kevin got to his current position almost by default.

After taking time off following college to "basically have some fun," he earned a master of public administration from New York University (N.Y.U.). After N.Y.U., he took a job as assistant to the head of New York City's Office of Operations. In a short three years, he learned the ropes of city-management politics, no small task in itself. From there, he followed his boss to the Taxi and Limousine Commission and then to NYCT. He joined the transit authority at the time Alan Kiepper took Operations Planning out of Operations, where it had been conveniently buried, and moved it into a new Customer Services/Operations Planning organization. Kiepper's reorganization move was a clear message about who Operations Planning should really be serving. It was also a direction that suited Kevin.

What marks Kevin most clearly as an RCL is the very different and clear perspective for change that he brings to the job:

> My job, first and foremost, is to find ways to increase ridership. In the bus system that means taking a losing proposition and turning it around. In the subway system it means trying to break away from the business cycle [i.e., increasing ridership in economic downturns as well as upturns].

These are not easy tasks. Bus ridership has dropped by half since 1950. Subway ridership had also significantly declined in this period.

There was a small gain in the late 1980s attributable to the system improvements and a healthy economy, but historic declines resumed in the early 1990s as the New York economy soured. Conventional wisdom says daily subway ridership is so closely linked to the city's employment rate that it is probably the best leading indicator of job growth or loss. In other words, people take the subway only if they have to get to work. This implies that there is little NYCT can do to increase ridership; it simply depends on the rise and fall of employment. As for those who might ride on weekends or choose to ride though they could afford a cab or car, conventional wisdom again says that the negative perceptions of the system from the late 1970s and early 1980s are just too hard to overcome. But such wisdom does not daunt Kevin, who like most change leaders ignores the odds of accomplishing the impossible.

Kevin and the people who work with him in Operations Planning have made it their mission to prove that ridership can be increased if everyone will just keep what is important to the customer foremost in mind. They pursue this mission in four ways:

1. *Figuring out how customers decide.* Kevin gives serious attention to understanding what he calls the "customer's calculus" in deciding whether or not to ride the subway. He explains this notion by first posing these questions:

> Do you use the system at all? Is there any one element of the subway system that most affects your choice versus using a cab or something else? Typically there is not. A lot of things go into your decision equation, such as travel time, your sense of security, who you are riding with, your sense of whether the station is orderly, and so on.

To decipher the customer's calculation, Kevin and his staff work closely with the marketing people in the Customer Services department. Working jointly, they develop and refine customer surveys to determine what factors are most important in a person's decision to ride the subway. Three elements consistently stand out: personal safety, service reliability, and the comfort of the station environment. Obviously, they had to take their analysis to a more detailed level to understand the actionable sub-elements that determine customers' perceptions of these broad elements. For example, a rider's perception of personal safety is seldom a function of the actual crime rate at a particular station—a figure unknown to most riders. Instead, it is set by many details she senses in her local station environment—a newsstand on the platform with the vendor in sight, a working telephone, no boom boxes blaring. Once these details are understood, useful relationships become apparent; for example, an open newsstand can improve perception of both personal safety and the comfort and convenience of the station environment.

NYCT is also continuing to understand better what level of quality or service it takes to effect customer reaction. This is important in making sure that scarce resources go where they will make the most difference. For example, at some stations, spending $100,000 to spruce up appearances made no real difference in customers' perceptions, because the money was either spent on the wrong things or was simply not enough to change conditions sufficiently to matter to the customer. The point is that by closely examining what really matters, station by station, the renovation program has been redirected from uniform renovations of every station to concentrating on places and improvements that new information indicates will help attract additional riders.

2. *Measuring those things that customers care most about.* There are literally dozens of operating-performance measures to chose from at NYCT. Unfortunately, most measure functional excellence, and tend to focus on "things" (subway-car breakdowns) rather than customers (service delays from all sources). For example, "on time" was measured by when a train arrived at its final destination (within five minutes of schedule)—yet another noncustomer-oriented measure. And reporting even on this measure is "charitably a lie," in Kevin's view, because operations personnel simply adjust the schedule if something beyond their direct control (for example, police action) causes a delay. He has been working on indicators that "reflect the public's perception of reliable service, and will also be useful for operating people." These new measures take the perspective of the customer waiting on a station platform. During frequent-service periods (a train every three minutes at rush hour), the standard is that trains reliably arrive at the specified interval. During less-frequent-service periods (trains every twelve minutes), the standard is that trains arrive at the time shown on the published schedule. Changing such measures may appear obvious, but they were being overlooked—and their importance in reorienting the perspective of large numbers of operating people is very significant.

3. *Highlighting the obvious, that is, just how bad the ride has become.* Kevin has found that just sharing the routine data on ride conditions with

operating people is surprisingly effective. He frequently boards the bus from his home and, route-performance data in hand, makes the long ride across two bus routes to a depot in the Bronx. "It's a very long ride, but I do it to remind myself, firsthand, just how bad riding the bus can be." He also notes that "you don't even have to use buses to know the service stinks . . . you can just look down the street and see them bunching up." Even Kevin was surprised by the reactions he received from his first such data-sharing experience.

> When I presented the data to management at the depots, I got this shocked look on everyone's face like, "I had no idea we were *that* bad." But they didn't get mad at me like some might. They said, "Man, what are we going to do about it?" They looked at me, and I said, "Well, we have got to work on this together." Then I presented it to the union, and, believe it or not, they said, "We had no idea the buses were that bad"—a very positive response.

Surprisingly, this was the very first time such detailed performance data had been shared with the people who could do something about it. It may seem a simple first step to pull people away from their focus on internal issues, but function-bound organizations seldom do it. Kevin's courage in sharing tough numbers directly with people also served to galvanize them. The numbers released a pent-up frustration and set in motion a will to act and change.

4. *Going after specific bus and subway lines—one at a time.* The prevailing mind-set at the transit authority is to think of functional problems on a systemwide or geographic-area basis. Customers, however, do not think about an individual problem involving the entire transit system. They think about *all* the problems that exist on the one or two bus routes or subway lines that they use. Adopting this mind-set helps transit managers think of ride problems differently. They now see them as local issues to be addressed collectively, rather than symptoms of systemwide needs that must fit within huge, systemwide, functional-priority schemes.

Taking an individual route and line perspective is also a highly motivating way to get various parties to pursue improved performance. The people at the front line who literally control the service (the bus drivers and train operators) already identify with specific routes and lines—that is the territory they work everyday. Taking a specific perspective also helps break the problem into meaningful chunks, or manageable pieces, that people can rally around. Kevin sometimes actually sounds like a freedom fighter taking the enemy's hill as he says excitedly, "We're going in on the M86 route; we're going to win that back! We're going to take the B41!"

He and his operations planning group, working with field operations and whoever else is needed, have been doing just that. Bus route by bus route, the group is figuring out what sets of actions are necessary to make the ride (the transportation action flows as seen through the customers' eyes) more attractive to existing and potential riders. The group still has many routes yet to go, but it is rolling out a working model for action-flow improvement that keeps the customer foremost in mind.

These actions and others borne of the same mind-set are, believe it or not, resulting in more riders! Over the past two years ridership has turned up, diverging from the employment cycle with the greatest increases in discretionary weekend ridership. Much of what Kevin and his group do is not cutting-edge thinking. But that's the point. If a monolithic structure like NYCT and its 40,000 people can change what is of most value to its customers, then how much more useful might similar changes be in organizations whose points of resistance are less overwhelming?

2. CUT THROUGH FUNCTIONAL BARRIERS

Understanding what matters to customers is one thing; acting on that understanding is another. Process management is all about working through, around, and over whatever gets in the way of getting the right products and services to customers faster and better than competitors. This means breaking through (or sneaking around) the virtual barriers of the hierarchy that most often take the form of walled off departments (marketing, operations, finance, engineering, etc.) or hierarchical ceilings. Most managers are uncomfortable with this kind of thinking. It's safer to follow formal channels, procedures, and lines of authority.

There is nothing wrong with sticking with the safer option, unless behavior change is the primary objective. The problem is that seldom is any formal structure of reporting relationships, however brilliantly conceived, the primary factor in changing people's behaviors. Sure, it helps to redefine job descriptions to indicate more clearly what people are expected to do. It also helps to change lines of authority and individual accountability to better reflect business priorities. For example, if a company's products are sold through both retail and wholesale outlets, it makes sense to have someone in charge of retail sales and someone in charge of wholesale sales. But it may also make sense to be sure that the company's pricing and purchasing efforts take account of customer needs across both kinds of outlets.

Structure alone, no matter how elegantly designed or enforced, cannot align and ensure complicated, dynamic behavior changes—because most people don't like to follow the lines! Moreover, every structure has a hierarchy of jobs and roles that will get in the way of people interactions that do not follow the lines of the structure but are essential to delivering superior value to the customer. Yet, most managers seek to stay within a hierarchy controlled along functional dimensions (or else change it by reorganizing, again and again), because they believe structure is the primary answer to aligning people's behaviors.

Conversely, change leaders continually seek ways to work around and break through the functional barriers in the hierarchy. They realize such barriers are necessary evils that often inhibit the flow of products and services to the customer, particularly when a change of behaviors and skills is required. Rather than destroy the formal structure, however (since it would inevitably be replaced by another, not necessarily better, one),

RCLs rely on streamlined processes and teams to expedite value delivery across whatever functional barriers exist. To that end, they:

- Get rid of obvious obstacles to core processes (unnecessary road-blocks, detours, and diversions); and

- Connect all the necessary pieces.

DETOURS AND DIVERSIONS AT NYCT

A big day-to-day challenge of process management is in working across and through the functional organization. This is certainly the big task for Kevin Desmond at NYCT. It is one thing for Kevin and Operations Planning to get people to focus on what matters in terms of serving customers; it is another to get them acting in unison as part of an action flow to deliver that value to customers.

NYCT is a particularly function-bound organization. The reasons are understandable, most of them having to do with control. Dave Winfield points to the hard, even hostile, operating environment as the reason for this concern with control.

> We have high levels of customer activity, an old, aging infrastructure, and people always trying to vandalize the system and obstruct operations. It puts tremendous pressure on people just to get through the day. There is a real fear of losing control over day-to-day operations, because the penalties for that are so severe and so much in the public eye.

In fact, during the mid-1980s, when the priority was just getting the system under control and in working order, the functional organization was greatly strengthened and any cross-functional oversight was diminished. Division and district managers were given a lot of autonomy and accountability to fix their functions.

Yet Dave also recognizes that this legacy of a "real stovepipe mentality" (functional controls running up and down the hierarchy) greatly encumbers the organization today when it tries to focus on specific customer-oriented processes, such as "the ride" that customers should experience. At least a dozen functional groups can be involved just in the quality of a subway station's environment (let alone all the functions involved in running the trains). Dave says:

> It is simply very difficult to make all the improvements needed at this location or that location . . . one group manages signage, another turnstile maintenance, another replaces light bulbs, another does cleaning.

The behaviors of literally thousands of people are constrained by functional barriers. A given function may earnestly try improving the one small part of some action flow that it does control, but even a dramatic improvement will have little effect on the whole. More important, the right behaviors are often inhibited by cross-checking detours and diversions caused by ingrained attitudes that are far removed from the customer's key sources of value. These attitudes constitute huge hurdles that block people from thinking clearly about what superior customer service aspirations really imply. Every day, a myriad of functional issues and procedures pull thinking, discussion, and action away from a customer point of view. While they have some merit, their unfortunate effect is to sidetrack people from their real mission of serving customers. This is what led Kevin to start people thinking about the ride (or a single route) as a unified action flow.

CONNECT THE ACTIONS (ON THE "A" LINE)

In late 1992, Kevin and Operations Planning began looking for a subway line to showcase what could be done to improve customer service and ridership (his ultimate goal), if all functions really focused on alleviating the concerns of customers. He decided on the "A" line because:

> It's a very difficult line to run and it's plagued with reliability problems. It had falling ridership, and most important, it was the route that caused the greatest outrage when we once tried to make service cuts. You can't cut the "A" line! There is even a song about the A line! And the line is covered by a number of legislators—it can't hurt to put a smile on their face.

Said to be the world's longest subway line, the A train runs from the very northern tip of Manhattan Island all the way down to the World

Trade Center, where it then turns east through Brooklyn to Far Rockaway beach. Though the entire line was included in the effort, special attention was given to riders using the ten stations from 207th Street (the northern terminal) to 125th Street in the center of Harlem.

In developing the "A" Showcase initiative, Kevin made it clear to all that this effort meant considering all the pieces of the ride that a customer experiences that affect his perception of safety, reliability, and the station environment. "We were not going to fix one thing and wait twenty years to see if people would notice. . . . We were going to do it all at once; we said let's try it all and see what works." In describing the effort, Kevin emphasizes that "a lot of different people brought a lot of different pieces" to developing the "A" Showcase. For example:

1. *Refocusing and increasing dispatching to improve reliability.* It is irritating to wait fifteen minutes for a train when you expected one in no more than five minutes. What is even more upsetting is waiting fifteen minutes for a train that arrives so packed that you cannot squeeze in—and then witnessing two more almost empty trains arrive in immediate succession. Customers want trains to arrive at stations at even intervals without the bunching. The dispatchers are supposed to assure this even spacing of as many as twenty trains traversing the A line during rush hour, but they were poorly positioned to do that job. Most were working with turn-of-the-century technology which showed train positions on only a small segment of the line, leaving them blind to the flow before and behind them. In addition, previous downsizings had left some areas too thinly covered and little training and feedback were being provided. Consequently, dispatchers tended to simply report and record train movements.

Problems like the antiquated technology would obviously take time and big money to fix. But Operations Planning could and did team up with Rapid Transit Operations to quickly give the dispatchers other things they needed to do their job right:

- Refresher training emphasizing basic service control principles and techniques;

- New measurements focused on even train flows;

- Added dispatchers to assure a complete view of the A-line flow; and

- "Gap trains" placed in waiting at key locations to be called into service as needed.

And, most important, feedback was given encouraging dispatchers to take corrective action and showing how their work could improve on-time performance, customer satisfaction and, ultimately, ridership.

2. *Publishing service schedules.* Passengers entered the subway not knowing when the next train was scheduled to arrive. Schedules have always existed, but they were not posted or otherwise made known to passengers. During rush hour, when trains are frequent, this isn't a problem. But at 1:00 A.M., when it may be twenty minutes between trains, it is a big time and safety consideration. The "A" Showcase included the rather obvious idea of printing and distributing schedules to customers. Kevin explains the obvious:

> Most people feel a little more comfortable and confident going into the system because they can say, my schedule says a train is supposed to be coming at 7:45, so I'll arrive at 7:43 and there ought to be a train there. That improves their comfort zone and sense of security. It also applies pressure on the operating people—"Oh my God, they've got schedules now and will be expecting the train to arrive on time. I better do something!"

3. *Increasing service frequency.* On weekends the number of riders drops, and service is less frequent. This has a big influence on people deciding whether it is faster to take the subway or a cab. By cutting train lengths in half, the number of trains and frequency of service was increased by more than 50 percent. This change complicated life for the crews in the switchyards (it is easier to leave trains hooked together in the same lengths at all times), but Kevin convinced them to make the extra effort as part of the "A" Showcase.

4. *Adding station managers as a point of customer contact.* Most of the time, riders who approach a NYCT employee find that the employee cannot help because "that's not my job." The relevant supervisor is off in some central office or out elsewhere on the system. And that supervisor, even if reachable, is only responsible for one function, invariably the wrong one.

Again, the solution was obvious, once the problem was clear: give customers someone they could actually talk to by adding a few station managers to walk the stations, help customers with directions, ask for comments, and handle complaints. Since station managers cannot always physically be at the station (most are assigned to more than one station), big color pictures of them were hung at the entrances, with a direct-phone number to call. No matter what the customer concern, the station manager takes responsibility for it, e.g.:

■ Making sure that everything in the station is in good order;

■ Assuring the courtesy of the token clerks;

■ Seeing that small repairs are made quickly; and

■ Working across departments to transmit and enforce a customer's point of view.

5. *Increasing station-sergeant visibility.* Seeing uniformed security increases the rider's perception of safety. The Transit Police (now part of the New York Police Department) have succeeded in reducing subway crime by 50 percent since 1990. Many good passenger-security initiatives were already in place when the "A" Showcase was formed, actions that Kevin did not want to upset. However, improved perception of personal safety lagged the actual drop in crime. To help address this gap, a station sergeant was designated for each station, and his or her picture, name, and number was prominently displayed in the station (right along with the picture of station manager). This move didn't involve any new staffing, since the station was already part of the sergeant's beat. Now, however, as Kevin notes, a passenger could know, "I'm covered. I got a cop here who's taking care of me. It's Sergeant Gonzalez."

6. *Improving in-station customer information.* New York's subways are infamous for their twisting passageways, multiple levels, and poor directions. The system presents an unsolvable puzzle for new passengers: the only way they can feel confident using it is to be very experienced with it. But trying to use the system is bound to reduce their confidence the first few times as they find themselves headed the wrong direction on the wrong train. To improve this situation:

■ More and clearer signs were added to stations;

■ New, more helpful station announcements were scripted and given with more frequency and clarity;

■ Marketing information was developed and distributed; and

■ Information was customized to the particular transportation needs of the neighborhoods of the target stations, including translation into Spanish.

Any one of the above solutions is simple enough—and by itself, makes only a small impact on the customer. When the solutions are integrated, however, the result is faster, better service that has a big impact. In basic terms, that is what process management boils down to: putting dozens of small, useful improvement actions together for high customer impact—and doing it again and again.

An initiative like the "A" Showcase requires that Kevin and his team learn more than anyone else about whatever action flow they intend to focus on. It is the RCLs' way of inserting themselves into the game. Even with a passport into foreign functional territory (for example, top management tells an RCL to integrate inventory management with purchasing), change leaders are rarely welcomed on another's turf until they earn their way in. They can be masters of the customer view, but they cannot operate on foreign turf until they demonstrate more than superior customer knowledge. That, invariably, turns out to be unique expertise about a key action flow in terms of its end-to-end (customer needs to customer-value-delivery) characteristics. By mastering the details of the action flow, RCLs are in a position to help and influence others who might otherwise become discouraged or resistant.

Process management is not about the elimination of people; it is about the ultimate connection between people and customer value. It is up to the RCLs to make the innumerable connections between the ideas and initiatives of dozens, if not hundreds, of people. Unless they can transfer these ideas to others to implement, they cannot obtain the performance promise of process management. RCLs do not eliminate or even break up the hierarchy; they work with it, through it, and around it. Sometimes that means using it, and sometimes it means losing it. RCLs' relentless focus on getting superior value to the customer enables them to see and find ways through or around unwarranted rules and constraints. If breaking down virtual walls at NYCT is required, they do it; if hanging all kinds of teams on the existing structure is the quickest way to get products designed and out the door, change leaders do it. The secret lies in connecting all sorts of unlikely bedfellows into a unified effort with one common objective: superior customer value.

3. LEARN TO USE DIFFERENT APPROACHES

There is no one best way to manage or redesign a particular process or action flow. Nor is there any one best combination of tools and approaches that RCLs must follow to produce an integrated process management result. Obviously, RCLs act on marketplace facts, and they must use whatever combination of alignment, measurement, and motivational elements accommodates their opportunities and constraints. Anita Ward at Texas Commerce Bank (TCB) reminds us to "respect your culture," while Rick Tatman at GE Motors says to "play the hand you are dealt," and Cindy Olson at Enron believes in "giving your people something to work for beyond the numbers." Yet, each one conveys the same message about process management: design action flows to deliver superior value by exploiting existing strengths—and use whatever combination of tools and approaches is most likely to get all members of the workforce doing what matters to customers.

There are almost as many process management tools and approaches as there are process definitions. Anita is a disciple of Hammer's reengineering principles, but she emphasizes the need to design action flows that fit the organization's culture, values, and people skills. Change leaders cannot simply apply the same sets of tools that worked at TCB or at UNOCAL. As described in the last chapter, Randy Howard of UNOCAL decided to use breakthrough teams, but he first redesigned them to reflect what he was able to learn from an earlier attempt that did not work as well as anticipated. Combining whatever elements make sense relative to the specific needs of his plant and people is precisely what we observed RCLs like Randy doing with process issues. Unfortunately, it is precisely what most good managers seldom do, because they see this open-ended approach as less efficient and too uncontrollable.

While we cannot provide a complete starter tool kit for process management, we can describe four different ways of combining different tools and approaches to accomplish a process management task: integrating quality and reengineering; converting early results to broad-based improvements; assuring the right scope of redesign; and relying on basic principles and people. Each of the next sections describes how change leaders combined different sets of change approaches, tools, and techniques to make process management work.

INTEGRATING QUALITY AND REENGINEERING

Edwards Deming's fundamental principles of quality management have clearly stood the test of time. At the same time, more than half of total-quality programs fall short of expectations, and many have failed completely. The problem is not, however, in Deming's principles; it is in the flawed, sometimes careless, execution of what his writings advocate.*

Reengineering principles are encountering a similar problem these days. Hammer and Champy's work reopened the eyes of many to some of Deming's original notions of quality, while adding important new dimensions and ways of thinking about quality management, which they called reengineering. Nonetheless, Champy now tells us that many reengineering efforts have not lived up to their promise. The problem, he says, is with the management, not the concepts.†

At a fundamental level, quality and reengineering are really about the same thing: getting people to do things to meet market needs better and faster than the competition. They are complementary and overlapping concepts, which represent different approaches and alternatives to the same end. However, potential change leaders need not be confused by their similarity; it is not difficult to become skilled at adapting and adopting elements of both.

At first Fred Smagorinsky was very concerned about the reengineering fad sweeping over corporate America and reaching into Sealed Air. World-Class Manufacturing (WCM), based on many quality principles, was working, and he didn't want people to become distracted by some new process or set of tools. He wrestled with several issues: should Sealed Air put WCM under a new reengineering banner? Should it scrap WCM in favor of a new program? This dilemma was resolved when he realized that reengineering is a tool—and a good one at that—but not an entirely new managerial paradigm:

> I don't see reengineering as a separate beast at all. . . . Don't get confused by all the buzzwords. . . . It's all about getting people to do things more effectively. It's all the same stuff; it's just a matter

---

* Edwards Deming, *Out of the Crisis.*
† James Champy, *Reengineering Management* (New York: Harper Business, 1995).

of scale and scope. There's always objective setting, problem solving, action planning, etc.

While the basics of any performance-improvement process remain the same, Fred now sees how the types of analysis, range of possible solutions, time lines, and ways of managing the team can vary a lot. He sees his role as a change leader to be that of framing the problem and adjusting the improvement process for the team. The work itself can be labeled either quality or reengineering; it is still all a part of Sealed Air's overall WCM approach to performance improvement. Sometimes the focus is narrow (a bottleneck at a single machine), sometimes it is wide (the redesign of the company's entire order-to-delivery process); Fred modifies the approach accordingly.

Knowing how to adjust for differences in scale and scope of the problem didn't come automatically for Fred. His "personal breakthrough" came after struggling with a team redesigning the order-to-delivery process. At first his usual techniques for providing a structured process, creating a sense of urgency, and making sure the team heard for themselves the endorsements of senior executives, produced little progress and he sensed some resistance. It was not like his experience working on plant problem solving where action comes quickly. It took about three months before they finally did start progressing. Fred now views the slow start as a function of absorption time. Redesigning that process required a perspective spanning the entire breadth of the business, but individual team members knew only their slices of the action flow. They simply needed the time to become familiar with the details and comfortable with thinking across the entire process.

In retrospect, Fred would have adjusted his time lines and thought more about how to provide the orientation required to get people's heads around the problem. He also learned that it is much more important to be aware of and manage the complex political issues that arise in redesign efforts as you cross the boundary of existing departments and policies. He is now much better able to incorporate the approaches of reengineering into the overall WCM effort.

CONVERTING EARLY RESULTS AT PRUDENTIAL

You heard briefly from Mike Vaccaro earlier. After twenty years at Prudential, he assumed a central RCL role in the midst of a major reengineering battle.

His story illustrates how RCLs rise to the occasion and learn from failures, as well as how they combine a variety of process management tools and approaches to create both change and performance gains. Today Mike heads the reengineering project in the Property and Casualty Division of Prudential Insurance, the largest insurance company in the country. His team has been in the design phase of the reengineering project for three years now. When we first met Mike, he was working for the Quality Department as its day-to-day manager. But, this was only one of his two full-time jobs—the other was a member of Prudential's Service Design Team.

THE SERVICE DESIGN TEAM

In 1992, Don Southwell, then president of Prudential Insurance, faced considerable performance problems in the Property and Casualty Insurance Division after Hurricane Andrew struck and wiped out many Prudential-insured properties in Florida. Customers were not getting claims paid in a timely manner, because of the extra processing workloads. Customer satisfaction, which had been low before, was now much worse. Hurricane Andrew exposed long-standing problems that now became intolerable.

Don believed the root cause of these problems, however, was less about internal control and more about losing sight of the customer. Don had, therefore, chartered two teams: one to reengineer marketing and the other to redesign the delivery of customer service. Southwell was convinced that the entire sales force had to be able to deliver service directly in the field (without hand-off to a central service unit). The second team, the Service Design team (SDT), of which Vaccaro was a member, was chartered both to test that approach and to save $15 to $35 million regardless of where service was eventually delivered.

The SDT spent a year developing a pilot program that gave local field offices the tools to deliver customer service directly. Mike was concerned. He believed that the team misunderstood what the customer wanted. SDT assumed the customer wanted *personal* service. Vaccaro believed that the customer wanted *good* service. As a result, the team's solution left unchanged the large quantities of work that led to customer dissatisfaction in the first place.

Look, no matter how trained, how cordial, or even how ingratiating our new customer service agents are, no customer is going to

say, "Don't worry about taking three weeks to reject my application; I realize you are in business to make money." . . . We were
doing work which was of no value to the customer. Unless we
blew that work up, no amount of personal hand-holding would
solve our customer problem.

The SDT pilots confirmed Mike's fears: although there was some
improvement in customer satisfaction, other key measures of success like
accuracy or response cycle times showed only minor improvements.
Worse, these incremental gains came without any cost reduction and Prudential had a large cost gap to close. Mike Plesko, SDT's leader, was now
also worried. The pilot results were not good enough, and he had to show
performance results. Others would have declared failure at this point.
Indeed, to outsiders, SDT was clearly failing to achieve its cost-saving
objective and, in fact, surfaced some solutions that actually *added* cost.
Vaccaro and Plesko were undeterred. In fact, they found the failure useful,
"because it cleared the ground to do the right thing and finally disproved
a bad idea, popular for years, that would not go away." At that point, they
realized SDT had to go to where the real bottleneck to customer value lay:
the back-office bureaucracy.

Plesko still had a formal agreement (actually, a performance contract)
with Southwell to deliver at least $15 million in savings. So far they had
somewhere between zero and $7 million, way short of the goal. When
Plesko decided to expand the scope to include back-office reengineering,
he turned to Vaccaro for help:

Mike [Vaccaro] knew the guts of the place inside and out. He has
been in underwriting, field management, claims, and now quality. No one was in a better position to reengineer our back office.

Vaccaro saw it as a great opportunity—the chance to do the things he
and his people had wanted to do for years. He knew that the back-office
was complex, filled with redundancy and unclear accountability, and that
most of the people were not fully trained.

This was not because of people's inability to do their jobs, but
because of silly controls. Here was the opportunity to undo that
stuff. We couldn't reengineer everything at once, or we would
have mass confusion and possible breakdown. Plesko and I got

together, and we decided to focus on the policy-change process—what we call endorsements.

Vaccaro and Plesko knew there was significant redundancy in the handling of policy changes, making this area an easy target. They anticipated getting quick results, and they did. Also, this action flow was fairly insulated from the rest of the back office, so they believed they could change it without changing the whole system. They were right again.

> When we got in to the endorsement process, we found early on that very little of what we were doing was for the benefit of the customer; it was all for our own need to control everything.

Vaccaro put together a small team "of folks who know the nitty-gritty details of the business" and in three short months identified $12 million in savings out of a $35 million total-cost-base. The work—and especially the percentage of savings—caught the attention of Don Southwell. In a formal meeting, Vaccaro presented his work to Don and his top executive staff. "Vaccaro was like [General] Schwarzkopf," one participant recalled. "He was on fire. There was no way you could leave that room and doubt that he knew what he was doing was right." For example, Vaccaro brought to the meeting a series of two-inch-thick documents that he held up for all to see as he told the president:

> These procedure and rule books are going to be replaced with ten-page pamphlets. We are examining everything we do: every rule, every policy, every hand-off, every action. *Either it delivers value to our customers, or we don't do it.*

Radical, yes—easy, no. Vaccaro clearly needed Don's support to make the overall company-wide process connections necessary to convert his aspirations into reality—and his degree of personal commitment and conviction was no small factor in getting Don on board.

EXTENDING THE EFFORT

However, Don was left with one concern—why wasn't the Property and Casulty Division reengineering all back-office processes? He told Jeff Lewis, the senior vice president at the time, "Reengineer everything." Jeff asked Vaccaro to lead the effort, saying, "We've got new-business reengineering. We've got claims reengineering. We've got endorsements reengineering. Too many disjointed efforts. We need to reengineer all core processes end-to-end."

Jeff commissioned a reengineering design team. It was to be a self-managed team, but Vaccaro was soon voted in as the leader because he knew what to do, and speed was of the essence. (As we will see in the next chapter, single-leader groups can be faster than teams when the leaders know best what needs to be done.)

> We brought everything in. New business, claims, endorsements. New business reengineering was implemented right away because it was mostly structural. We combined jobs, we created accountability. . . . There were certain things, like underwriting, rate integrity, that we coupled with claims . . . and we focused on the back office, not sales, so we could fix the problem *before* it got to the field.

The team also looked back into the composition and characteristics of the product line, not normally considered part of back-office problems. However, it recognized that product complexity was a root cause of application- and claims-processing complexity at the back office. So they looked at the entire product array to understand the utilization, loss ratios, and premium for each product. And then they figured out the back-office expense for each product feature. Armed with that information, the team went to the marketing people, and it quickly became clear that many of those products were not worth the cost. Those products were scrapped for considerable savings. But other products were too valuable to marketing, and so the team looked at back-office solutions. Where back-office processing skills were lacking, they outsourced the work while still satisfying marketing's need for the product.

IMPRESSIVE RESULTS

Mike Vaccaro says the team identified $75 million in savings from three main areas. First, they discovered the importance of product redesign, by looking at their business from a horizontal view for the first time. As a result, they discovered that the product design and marketing people were producing overly complicated products that made back-office application and claims work a nightmare. Thus the biggest impact on their cost base was also the most unexpected, as they realized their need to simplify products through changes in functions that were far from those on which they originally focused. Second, they separated work flows; important and hard issues were flowed in one way, easy tasks in another. Third, they invested in technology in a targeted way to automate highly repetitive tasks.

> Once we did this, redesigning each of our core processes was relatively straightforward. We did a number of things. We channeled claims in the most cost-effective way. We've changed the structure. . . . We set up a lab. It's up and running in New Jersey with exceptional results. In just a few months, claimant satisfaction is up four points, whereas it had moved only two points in the previous four years.

Last, but not least, Mike Vaccaro and his change leaders brought senior management along every step of the way, showing them the potential and the design recommendations. They had seen all the elements. They were prepared for major change. However, there was still a credibility problem.

> "Can you really save that much money?" they kept asking. So we laid out process by process how you would change and save money in a very believable fashion. The savings will be $75 million on a $200 million base—over 30 percent. Loss control is in good shape. Clients love it. Employees are very happy with the process change.

ASSURING THE RIGHT SCOPE OF REDESIGN

RCLs sometimes focus on redesigning one or two relatively small action flows of the many that comprise a core process. This may be a tactical choice, as when Mike Vaccaro decided to first tackle only Prudential's policy change process. Mike saw this as a way of getting some early gains as well as a way to develop a better focus for the wider back-office reengineering effort he knew would eventually be required. Often, however, the scope is not a matter of choice; a developing change leader simply may find him- or herself assigned to a limited area or constrained by his or her formal position from taking on more. The Black and Blue team at BFI in chapter 3 is a good example. They initially believed that such well-established processes as decentralized purchasing and annual budgeting were off limits until they tested their assumed constraints against top management's desire for significant performance improvement. Bruce Ranck quickly dispelled the constraint. As in this case, most RCLs eventually find a way to assure that redesign efforts have sufficient breadth and depth for major performance gains.

Obtaining the appropriate scope is an art, not a science. Most RCLs must operate within constraints they would not set themselves. And most find they must push against—not always successfully—and work around such constraints to squeeze out enough scope to meet their fundamental commitment to the real performance improvement discussed in chapter 1. Reengineering efforts, like other performance improvement approaches, can fall into the trap of generating activities with little commensurate performance gain. A recent in-depth study of reengineering projects revealed eleven of twenty efforts examined produced less than a 5 percent improvement in costs or earnings for the business units involved. Yet many of these cases also showed impressive cost reductions of 15 to 50 percent for the particular action flows redesigned. The reason for this disparity is a matter of scope—i.e., the breadth and depth of the redesign effort. Another six of the cases studied in this same project, judged to be much deeper and broader in scope, showed an average of 18 percent reduction in overall business-unit expense.*

Breadth means including in the redesign all activities that are essential in creating value for the customer and the business as a whole. If a redesign effort is narrowly defined to include only certain activities and functions, the potential for improvement can be greatly limited.

The types of changes that result from effective process redesign require working across and rationalizing *all* the activities and functions required to get value to the customer better and faster than the competition. This implies the following:

1. *Eliminating unnecessary steps* which are often added to action flows over time. Usually this happens because of a lack of cross-functional

---

* Gene Hall, Jim Rosenthal, and Judy Wade, "How to Make Reengineering Really Work," *Harvard Business Review,* November/December 1993.

perspective that results in duplication of effort, double-checking of others' work, and perpetuation of unneeded activities. For example, the AT&T sales force took many steps and loops out of management processes such as compensation and business planning by shifting greater responsibility to the branches and eliminating the myriad of reports, reviews, and approvals previously performed by multiple layers of staff.

2. *Combining steps* which have become over fragmented and specialized across and within functions. For example, when Compaq's Scottish operations converted to cell manufacturing, the long assembly line of individual workers doing discrete tasks was replaced by small groups with each member doing multiple assembly steps.

3. *Reducing, speeding, and smoothing hand-offs* between functions which have become the primary sources of delay, errors, and lack of overall accountability. The "quick market intelligence" approach that GE Motors RCLs describe in chapter 1 is an excellent case of a creative way to get cross-functional action almost immediately upon recognition of a customer or competitor issue.

4. *Identifying and fixing problems further upstream* when errors that consume time and resources in one function at one end of the process are caused by mistakes in another function earlier in the process. The Vaccaro team's discovery at Prudential that the upstream product design issues were causing extra, unnecessary work downstream illustrates this well.

RCLs' ability to think and work across functions, both formally and informally—always with the objective of superior performance for the customer—leads them to seek broader involvement to obtain critical cross-functional improvements.

Reengineering can also fall short on the breadth dimension by giving undue attention to an area of little relative value to customers or business economics. The RCLs' clear customer view as well as their mastery of end-to-end details of all relevant action flows helps ensure they focus efforts and resources on the areas of greatest value. For example, when Harriet Wasserstrum of TCB in chapter 4 consciously decided not to spend more time with a stalled team working on a process of lesser importance, she was exercising that kind of judgment, i.e., focusing on what matters most for results.

Depth of redesign is a matter of working on all factors that contribute to effective action flows, not simply changing the obvious activity steps. These factors can include measurements, information systems, organization, incentives, and skills. Working on these added dimensions comes naturally to RCLs. They know that lasting change is a matter of building new skills and attitudes within their people and supporting them with whatever tools, information, and training they need. A reengineering effort that failed to address such concerns would hardly be considered real change. Because they are the basics of both performance and change, RCLs think of them first and foremost, leaving the fine points of reengineering or other methodologies for later.

RELYING ON BASIC PRINCIPLES AND PEOPLE

George Devlin of Compaq (see the Introduction) has not been to a course on reengineering. He uses none of today's popular reengineering terminology. In fact, in all of our discussions with him, the only time he mentioned the word was to describe his activities in a former job as "re-engineering without even knowing it!"

His efforts at Compaq, however, epitomize the reengineering ideals that many gurus advocate. First, the actions were radical. By ripping out the plant's central conveyor belt—the core of the production system—George struck at the heart of the old manufacturing process. Second, by replacing the automated assembly line with teams of people chartered to assemble the whole machine, start to finish, and test it themselves, he was able to obtain dramatic performance improvement from the people he needs the most from: the assemblers. Third, he is there, every step of the way, personally guiding the assembly teams—to help and encourage, and to make sure the new approach works.

Rather than taking books off a shelf, Devlin reengineers by applying basic principles, many of which have been described in earlier chapters. In fact, his reengineering tool kit—which has produced dramatic results—constitutes an excellent example of the principles that many ascribe to successful change:

■ **Vision.** George has a clear, unifying vision that is simple and compelling to all his people: "Help this company be the PC leader in the world. Period. More market share than IBM or Apple. Period."

■ **Courage.** If George doesn't talk much about reengineering, he talks a lot about courage. "The key to change is courage—it is the ingredient you need for success." He supervised the removal of the plant's conveyor belt, bucking the advice not only of his own engineers, but of Houston headquarters as well in the early stages of the change process.

■ **Performance Measurement.** George introduced performance goals that were more ambitious and more focused than anything that came from corporate. Top brass at corporate headquarters seemed satisfied with Scotland's cost position because it was falling relative to rising volumes. But George said that was not good enough—even if unit costs are falling, he reasoned, total costs are rising, and sooner or later that equation does not compute. He did not merely demand that costs be held flat as volume rose—he demanded that they fall, even in the face of enormous volume gains.

■ **Team Performance.** Through a belief in, and a willingness to rely on, assembly teams, George redesigned the entire assembly process at the plant. Teams became responsible for ordering parts, assembly, and testing. To hear George describe his teams is compelling team testimony. "Eventually, I want customers to place orders directly with the assembly teams. Wouldn't that be wonderful? Could you imagine if our teams on the shop floor could talk routinely and directly to their customers?" Clearly George has his sights tightly focused on his customers; he sees the world through their eyes.

■ **Discipline.** "The engineers questioned me—I told them that we are not about engineering computers but about screwing components into metal boxes. All the energy that was spent in reengineering of the already engineered computer designs was redirected into what we desperately need—engineering the assembly action flows. The benefits have been unbelievable, even to me. Rather than focus on the machines themselves, or more uselessly, the conveyor belt—engineers now assist assembly teams."

George and his teams have combined these basic elements, tools, and values into a set of business processes that delivers truly superior value to the customer. And he is able to energize and align the efforts of all of his people by virtue of his total immersion in the plant operations. To George, you can call it reengineering, process redesign, or teams: names never get in his way. Whatever works and will get his people energized to make the right things happen is all right with him. When we asked him about structure, he talked about it in typical RCL get-the-results-you-need fashion, that is, structure must not get in the way. It has to be flexible enough to avoid turf wars. It plays an important aligning role, but it is never the answer to skills and behavior change. "Keep the structure, lose the functional hierarchy," says George.

Finally, George reminds us that process management is really about people. All he wants is "people that care"; if he gets them, he knows they will be successful. And he treats his people as though each and every one matters to him and to the success of the Compaq effort.

PROCESS MANAGEMENT WRAP-UP

From the RCL's vantage point, process redesign and reengineering are neither magic solutions nor abstract notions. Process management is a way to get through and around the functional barriers to obtain better and faster results for customers than is possible through normal top-down management. It represents a different way of viewing and thinking about the customer, the business, and the RCL's particular part of it. It provides a range of tools and approaches for streamlining the delivery of what matters most to target customers. Finally, it constitutes an essential element of future leadership capability by focusing on the basic elements of customer value, breaking through the hierarchy, and using a variety of tools and approaches. Indeed, the more we think about it, horizontal organization is really about adjusting the manager's line of sight, away from up (to the boss) and down (to subordinates), and toward the customer.

SPEED ORGANIZING SKILLS

FOR FLEXIBILITY

How can I "organize" to change people's behavior if I cannot change the structure?

■ *Structure is a big lever for change in this company, but it always creates such a political upheaval. Besides, I have no formal authority to do it.*

Is changing job descriptions and reporting relationships enough to change behavior?

■ *We have done a lot of this in the past and performance continues to decline.*

When is the best time to rearrange the boxes and lines?

■ *We eventually need to realign our organization structure, and I'm pretty sure what the change should be. Should we do it before we start other change initiatives or later?*

Do we need a "team-based" organization? What does that mean?

■ *Everyone espouses teams as the new way to get things done, but I've seen lots of team efforts fail. And they seem to take up so much valuable time. Are they the only way to go?*

Why isn't changing the boxes and changing the people enough?

IN MANY WAYS, JAMES ROBINSON, FORMER CEO OF AMERICAN EXPRESS, WAS THE classic CEO of the 1980s—he even earned a role in *Barbarians at the Gate* (both the book and the movie!).* Robinson had earned a reputation as a strong leader, and when the New York City Partnership (NYCP) needed an executive with strong general management capability to fill the shoes of David Rockefeller it turned to Jim. Virtually everybody on the board (comprising the leading CEOs in New York City) agreed he was an outstanding choice, and just what NYCP needed for the next phase of its development.

Jim was taking over an organization that had lost some of its focus and vitality. The partnership, born in the 1970s with the New York City fiscal crisis and the need, quite literally, to save the city, appeared to be losing some of its noble purpose and sharp mission. Ten-plus years later, the environment had changed, and the organization seemed to be just going through the motions. It was clearly in need of major change and revitalization. Like most boards, the NYCP board believed that a new top leader would do the job.

Jim's first instinct on taking over was to do what any self-respecting CEO of that period would under similar circumstances—reorganize, or, revise the formal structure of job descriptions and lines of authority. Since he would have scarce time available outside his CEO role at Amex, he also knew that the best way to leverage his time was with a comprehensive organization structure where individual roles and responsibilities were clearly defined.

Two of us had the opportunity to work with Jim on this challenge in his personal conference room. We were providing pro bono consulting assistance to NYCP at the time. We, too, believed that getting the structure right was the first essential step on the road to change. Jim's conference room was the perfect setting for high-level organizing work, with beautiful wood paneling and a view overlooking New York Harbor and the Statue of Liberty. As top management consultants who loved to design organization charts ourselves, we found Jim's work with charts to be masterly—what we would have expected of a leading chief executive. In fact, all three of us at the time believed, along with most top executives, that the organization structure was all important in controlling and aligning behaviors. That's the way it was supposed to be.

---

* Bryan Burrough, *Barbarians at the Gate: The Fall of RJR Nabisco* (New York: Harper & Row, 1990).

The focus of our work was an elaborate chart of different-size boxes connected by a variety of solid and dotted lines. We focused on the classic issues of organization design:

1. *Individual responsibilities.* What are the duties of each position?

2. *Spans of control.* How many people should report to each executive?

3. *Levels and status.* Which people and boxes should be closest to the CEO?

4. *Balance.* Was the mix of line and staff appropriate, and was the role of staff clear?

5. *Relationships.* Which functions should be grouped to ensure proper coordination?

Our fixation on the organization diagram was like some sort of high-level chess game. We truly believed that if you could reposition people clearly in boxes that circumscribed their roles and authorities, lined up their duties with strategic priorities, and controlled their actions within clear lines of authority, you could expect their behaviors and interactions to follow. To some extent, this was true, but only if maximizing the initiative of lots of people was irrelevant to performance results. We have since learned the hard way that when individual behaviors are determined by job descriptions and lines drawn by others, individual initiative and innovation are often sapped. Even if they should actually follow the descriptions and lines (which is usually not the case), that is virtually all they will do. Anything else is simply "not my job."

Obviously, times have changed. RCLs seldom attack change with a set of charts. Performance today is on a much steeper and faster track, and using people as pawns in a chess game is a sure formula for mediocre results. Moreover, most RCLs do not have full chart-change authority, because that usually resides at higher levels in the organization. As a result, organization to RCLs seldom implies drawing a new set of lines and boxes, even though they may do some of that. Organization means aligning the behaviors of people with whatever set of tools and approaches will produce a rapid response to change needs. Organization may include structure, but it includes much more as well. Most important, it means focusing as much leadership capacity as possible on the elements most critical for performance improvement.

Change leaders concentrate on getting more initiative and leadership contributions from all their people. Hence, they rely on teams, working groups, champions, and informal networks much more than they do on formal lines and boxes. In marked contrast, the more typical mid-level managers worry about optimizing their own personal time—by lining people up in controlled hierarchies. Obviously, these are two very different mind-sets. This chapter explores what RCLs do that differs from the typical manager in organizing the efforts of their people:

1. **Clarify and simplify the charts and move on to other things.**

2. **Exploit the flexible units: teams, working groups, champions, and mavericks.**

3. **Restructure less flexible elements later as the needs become clear.**

1. CLARIFY THE CHARTS AND MOVE ON

The chart masters no longer run the world. Organizing for change is important, no doubt about it, but *reorganization* does not mean the same thing to RCLs as it does to traditional managers. Organization charts are not irrelevant, but they seldom make a big difference in anything other than signaling a change: who is moving up and who is not. Since most people like to think that a fresh set of reporting relationships will open things up in their own career advancement, it is often viewed as the place to start; it gets people's attention. While RCLs sometimes start there, they do not waste much time there.

LIKE A SCAFFOLDING

Changing the lines and the boxes of the organizational chart seldom produces much real change. What it does do, however, is communicate a set of job-scope-and-duty descriptions, along with reporting relationships, that help people understand where their job fits with respect to other jobs. Most managers immediately attach individual objectives, budgets, compensation, and advancements to the structure and assume that desired behavior changes will take place. They see the structure as the answer because it seems to clearly define what people should do. Unfortunately, it does not define how.

Real change leaders do use the formal structure to communicate priorities, but rely heavily on other ways (problem-solving processes, customer action flows, informal networks, and teams) to achieve their goals. The formal structure is like a scaffolding that construction workers use while building a house. But the construction workers take the scaffolding down, while, in most organizations, some kind of formal box and line structure remains in use even when other tools and groupings become more important in guiding behaviors. One way of picturing it is that, as the more flexible and powerful alignment guides come into play, the scaffolding becomes more of a fail-safe set of relationships that is used only occasionally. The problem with formal structure (the scaffolding) is its inflexibility; you can add on to it, but you cannot realign it without taking it down and reassembling it.

If you already have a workable scaffolding in place, it is usually not a good idea to change it. When you reorganize a formal structure, you also inadvertently break the informal relationships that make things work. Tom Timmins, who lived through the MEPUS reorganization into asset teams (described in chapter 1) as the producing manager, remembers the problems of changing the formal structure:

> We learned the hard way that if you restructure first, you destroy the networks in which people operate. People do not live in organizational boxes or within reporting lines—they live in networks. Destroy those and then try to overlay a process management approach, and you have implementation hell!

To Tom, the broken people-networks explain why restructuring takes as long as it does and why organizations lose productivity and performance when it happens—at least at first. This is why most change leaders are skeptics about reorganizing. They recognize the power that structural change can have in breaking old patterns and signaling change, but they also know from experience that simply breaking apart an existing structure will not do much for performance unless and until the new structure is in place—and is fully supported by whatever informal networks are needed to make it work. This always takes time. Consequently, RCLs follow what to many good managers is a counterintuitive pattern of waiting as long as possible before altering the formal organization. They focus first on obtaining higher performance results and let organization structure change follow as further improvements require. They may clarify and simplify the structure for people by encouraging them to ignore formal reporting rules or by working around the hierarchy themselves. But since their mid-level authority seldom allows them to officially change many of the boxes and lines, they look elsewhere for more flexible ways to organize people for performance.

LEAPFROG LEVELS AND BOUNDARIES (NYCT)

New York City Transit (NYCT), as we saw in chapter 5, is a classic functional organization; everything is segregated into departments which hold long-established places in the hierarchy. Subway and bus operations are separate, and their organizations basically follow the structure developed by railroads in the mid-to-late 1800s, a model that was itself derived from the military (NYCT still uses titles such as chief stations officer). In the formal structure, the person repairing a turnstile does not connect on the organization chart with the person ten feet away selling tokens until he proceeds up the hierarchy to the person in charge of all subway operations, who is a direct report to the president. This structure does provide deep functional expertise and a clear control structure in an environment where the risk of life-threatening accidents is ever present. But the functional silos make it difficult for someone trying to work on cross-functional issues of customer service or process redesign for greater productivity. Though change leaders in the organization like Kevin Desmond and Carol O'Neill sit in departmental boxes like everyone else, they are hardly constrained by their positions.

MEDDLING IN UNWELCOME PLACES

As part of her official job in NYCT's Office of Management and Budget, Carol O'Neill is routinely involved in reviewing capital equipment purchases. In early 1994 Carol was attending a meeting on a proposal to purchase a thousand fare-card vending machines to be installed as part of the transit system's overall conversion from tokens to electronic-swipe cards. The discussion raised all sorts of doubts in Carol's mind and looked like an opportunity in disguise. The machines requested were exact fare, no change given, and no dollar bills accepted—hardly customer friendly. And why a thousand machines? It was a nice round number, but a check with other transit systems revealed that far more machines would be needed for a system the size of NYCT.

If Carol were a conventional manager, she might well have sent a long memo questioning the purchase and starting an interdepartmental feud. However, that would likely have resulted in some compromise just as unreasoned as the original request. Instead she decided that she and her people would "insert ourselves into a process where nobody wanted us." She began by raising her questions directly with the requesting department, asking what role it saw for the machines, where they would fit into the overall revenue-collection and customer-service action flows, and how they would affect other functions' operating costs and job designs. The head of the department "was not at all thrilled" by her questions. However, as a result of previously working together, the person to whom the department head reported knew that Carol and her group were trying to serve the overall interests of NYCT and its customers—they weren't meddling auditors causing unnecessary trouble.

So Carol pushed on, leading the formation of a special task force with members from the nine other departments directly affected by the vending-machine purchase decision. She defined the group's purpose very broadly, as: Let's understand where we are really going with automated fare collection and what is going to be our future operating environment. The group looked at the entire set of action flows for customer fare collection, addressed far more issues than how many machines of what kind to buy, and developed a wide range of recommendations for implementation. These included redesigning jobs for greater customer service, doubling supervisory spans for equipment maintenance, and changing station designs and entrance equipment to reduce the total number of station agents needed. The net result was a new fare-collection process that increased customer service, reduced operating costs, and improved capital equipment investments.

Carol played several roles in this process. The first was simply crossing some boundaries in asking questions and forming the group. The second was setting a tone that says, don't take those givens as givens anymore; be willing to expand your horizons a little. The third was creating cautious champions among individuals in the group who would carry the plan back to their departments for implementation. In fact, the group developed even more sweeping work redesign ideas than were included in the official plan. Carol sees this group as a seedbed whose ideas will eventually bloom in other departments.

MODELING NEW WAYS OF WORKING TOGETHER

Most mid-level managers avoid the risk of working outside their formal areas of responsibility. In contrast, Carol looks for windows of opportunity for crossing organizational boundaries when it can be a way to expedite change.

For example, a request by the Metropolitan Transit Authority board (the governing body for NYCT) for a bus depot capital plan to bring the facilities into a "state of good repair" prompted the formation of a cross-functional work group to develop NYCT's first comprehensive strategic plan for bus operations. It addressed everything from route design to the types of replacement buses to purchase, in addition to the depot capital plan. It has proven invaluable in guiding subsequent management decisions, but for Carol the major gain was in "modeling a new way of working together . . . as genuine colleagues working on common problems."

Specifically, three different groups learned the value of crossing borders to work together on common problems and serve each other's needs. The bus operations organization had developed many depot capital plans before, only to have them turned down time and again as facilities deteriorated further. Merely dusting off the old plans wouldn't get the approval needed. Meanwhile, Operations Planning had been trying to get bus operations to work with them on improving current service quality and planning future service design. At the same time, the Office of Management and Budget had been looking for productivity improvements. This cross-functional effort has enabled the three groups to work more closely together on a routine basis.

Obviously, it takes courage and initiative for RCLs to leap over and around the formal structure, even when it clearly stands in the way of change. In many organizations crossing formal boundaries can be close to heresy—and can even lead to career-limiting repercussions. Organizations like Prudential and NYCT have strong structural norms that are seldom violated; so do many smaller companies. Yet, even in those situations, change leaders learn how to safely leapfrog the structural barriers that hamper other mid-level managers. Carol is the first to admit that it does not always work, but when it does, she knows it is because of the credibility and personal relationships she has built up over time. It also works because of her conviction about pursuing the real issues and the right answers, regardless of where they touch the organization.

CLEAN UP THE SCAFFOLDING

Jim Rogers at GE Motors has the right idea: "We have an organization chart. But we don't use it except to send up to corporate (to meet GE corporate human resource information requirements)." When Rogers took over the business, as described in chapter 1, it was dead in the water, with high union wages, old factories, poor quality, and no product innovation in more than twenty years! Profits were nonexistent. The first thing Jim did upon inheriting GE Motors was to look at the structure to see if it was cost effective.

You check the overhead structure and what people are doing, and you say, Is the customer going to pay for this? We went through every single overhead structure we could and said, hey, you have to take out cost. We are going to combine these functions; we are going to take out this layer of management. My attitude was, the house is burning—I may make some mistakes, but we're going to get some big heavy fire hoses out here right now, and if I blow away a few core competencies, I'll put them back.

In this case, the formal structure was blocking change leaders from applying more flexible units and approaches. In other words, the scaffolding was cluttered up with a lot of excess stuff that had accumulated over the years. Jim simply turned a fire hose on it and blew away unnecessary activity and constraints, thereby lightening the structure by 30 percent within his first year.

At the same time, he began creating teams around products sold to discrete customer groups. Rather than displacing the existing structure, these teams provided an alternative or overlay approach for getting people and activity quickly focused on the market. Jim also formed a group at the top to determine strategy, set goals, and allocate resources. Through them he could begin expanding the leadership capacity of the organization.

Through all of this there was never any formal reorganization of the structure at GE Motors. Rogers simply moved much of the old structure out of the way—eliminating its negative influence by streamlining it to facilitate his teams. Yet the formal structure was still there on paper, and occasionally came in handy for routine matters. However, the alignment of the performance activities of the business, and how they were being led, had little to do with the formal structure. By now the old organization structure has completely faded away, replaced by teams. Today, Rogers has trouble even remembering how the place was organized when he arrived.

It is true that within GE Motors, Jim is top management. Within the GE corporate structure, however, he is in a position similar to that of RCLs in that he reports to a higher level authority, does not have complete authority to act as he pleases, and must pursue the kind of change that is consistent with GE corporate aspirations. With regard to structure, he has the authority to change whatever he decides to—so it is interesting and relevant that he concentrates mostly on the flexible units.

2. RELY ON THE FLEXIBLE UNITS

Real change leaders rely heavily on the three most flexible units for getting people organized and focused on performance improvement: teams, single-leader working groups, and energized individuals (champions and mavericks). The secret is not to over-rely on any one of the three, but to consciously and rigorously decide among them based on the performance task or situation. RCLs learn to vary their organizing and leadership approaches to accommodate all three. In the right situations, under the right conditions, and with the right discipline, each can align change activity.

1. Teams are best when the potential for collective performance is high, the solution and approach are unclear, and you have the time and skills to build a real team. In addition to a high level of common commitment, members of real teams shift and share leadership roles and optimize the use of their complementary skills.

2. Single-leader working groups are best when time and efficiency are critical, the task/solution is straightforward, and the potential for high collective or joint performance and skill enhancement is not high. Single-leader groups look like real teams, but their goals and approach are determined by one leader.

3. Champions and mavericks are best when you want individual attention, creativity, and accountability—and when individual expertise is more important than multiperson skills. Though related in their individualism and courage, the maverick descriptor refers to champions who do not fit comfortably into the behavior patterns and norms of their organization.

Teams are particularly essential to broad-based, behavioral change, not only because of their performance advantage, but also because of their learning characteristics (in real teams, each member's skills invariably advance). However, they are being widely misused in most organizations today.* It becomes very important, therefore, for RCLs, as well as top management, to develop a thorough understanding of what a team is and why

---

* Jon R. Katzenbach and Douglas K. Smith, *The Wisdom of Teams: Creating the High Performance Organization.* This book describes how and why teams perform and learn.

it produces extra performance, learning capacity, and change energy. Otherwise, it is difficult to know when and how to use a team to best advantage in bringing about change in any particular change situation.

TEAM "TERMS OF REFERENCE"

The use of teams and other kinds of working groups is a critical part of every real change leader's tool kit. For that reason it is important to understand certain terms that describe the differences as they are used throughout the rest of this book. Most of them come from *The Wisdom of Teams;* more complete explanations are contained in that book. For our purposes, we deal with two broad categories: real teams (alternatively referred to as teams, or high-performance teams) and single-leader working groups (alternatively referred to as single-leader units, working groups, or nonteams).

A "real team" (as defined by *Wisdom,* and as quoted on page 220) achieves higher performance results because of its ability to obtain collective work products from the joint efforts of its members that integrate their different skills. A collective work product is a joint effort that yields a product of high performance value; it could not have been created by any single person. In other words, it requires that team members work together on explicit products, and that the leadership of the group shift among the members depending on the task at hand. Because of the real team's ability to share and shift the leadership role, it has more leadership capacity than single leader working groups, or non-teams. Real teams always have designated or de facto leaders; however, those leaders know when and how to shift the leadership role to other members of the team. This is what the "shared-leadership model" refers to; in fact, a better term might be the multiple- or shifting-leadership model.

Conversely, the single-leader group has advantages of speed and efficiency, largely because it does not require as much development time as the real team. Obviously, it is heavily dependent on the abilities of its leader (whereas the real team can access all of its members for leadership contributions). Within that constraint, however, single-leader groups are highly efficient, and can usually achieve results faster than a real team. The single-leader group's primary disadvantage is in its dependency on one person, and the fact that most of its results are in the form of individual work products rather than collective or joint work products. Its performance results seldom exceed "the sum of the individual bests," whereas the real team obtains "individual bests plus collective (or joint) work products."

Real change leaders have the ability to identify when change and performance situations require real teams, and when single-leader working groups are the better approach. The best RCLs can not only identify the different situational requirements, they can also change and adapt their personal leadership style to fit the performance need. In other words, they can lead real teams, and they can also lead single-leader working groups. This gives them a powerful advantage in volatile change situations that invariably require both kinds of leadership.

USING REAL TEAMS WISELY

Many change leaders learn to communicate and work together. Yet, most small groups that try to become teams fail, because they do not apply each element of the basic discipline required for team performance. For example, one of the department heads at Enron wanted to obtain team performance for his unit. He truly believed that was the way to achieve the performance goals that had emerged from a recent reengineering effort. Despite his noble intentions, however, he was unable to discipline himself to share the leadership role and his direct reports could not commit to a working approach that would enable them to do real work together; they simply could not find the time. As a result, a team never formed, and three of the key members of the potential team left the company.

Many managers do not obtain team performance simply because they assume that teamwork is synonymous with team. The difference is significant relative to performance results. Teamwork implies a set of helpful, supportive interactions that many people can share; a *team* is a small unit that delivers extra performance results. And most managers also continue to believe that the team leader is the answer to team performance. Yet, team performance depends more on a clear, compelling performance target than it does on the unique characteristics of the team leader. Conversely, a single-leader group's performance is heavily dependent on its leader. Yet, the upside potential of that group is also limited by the leader. These distinctions matter a great deal.

A team is a small number of people with complementary skills who are committed to a common purpose, performance goals, and a working approach for which they hold themselves mutually accountable (Katzenbach and Smith, *The Wisdom of Teams*). The primary reason that a team outperforms other like groups is because its members are strongly committed to working together in combining their different individual skills to achieve high performance—by producing one or more important "collective work products." We define a collective work product as a tangible result, such as new services to customers, an improved inventory control system, or a different promotion approach for retail outlets. Collective work products require the skills of several team members working together. They exceed what the members can do working as individuals, and, therefore, the performance result of the team actually exceeds the individual bests of its members. By this definition, there is no such thing as a real team that does not produce extra performance results in the form of collective work products.

Some of the best examples of both teams and single-leader groups can be found at GE Motors, where the performance imperative motivates change leaders to place a high priority on team performance. Surprisingly, CEO Jim Rogers actually sets up leaderless business-unit management groups to run each of the business units at GE Motors; he does not designate a formal general manager of the business unit. Each team is made up of five to six people with different functional skills and business experience (manufacturing, sales, marketing, engineering, product development, and finance). Obviously, they do not work as a team all the time, but they still hold themselves jointly responsible for all operations and results ' of the business unit (in addition to being accountable as individuals for nonteam assignments). The key decisions are made collectively, with strong mutual accountability among the team members. These are powerful leadership units that Jim credits for much of the improvement in GE Motors performance.

When Jim first described this approach, it raised serious concerns. After all, top executives and consultants know that a competitive business unit requires a strong general manager. Teams in the right places, yes, but certainly not running business units without a designated leader. Who could be held accountable for results? The answer is that *the team members hold themselves fully accountable, jointly and individually.*

Jim has had truly remarkable success with his leaderless business units. (Remember, his business performance rose from 0 to over 25 percent return on capital in three years!) But when asked specifically, Does the leaderless business unit approach always work?, he admits that it does not. Aha, so what does he do then? "I pick a leader for them," he replies. That is, he simply creates a single-leader working group (which is what most other business-unit management teams really are anyway). It is clear that Jim's approach may be risky, but it is also potentially very-high-reward. He tries for the real team—if it doesn't work out after a reasonable period, he can always decide to pick a leader for it. All he loses is the few months it took to find out. What he gains, of course, is the potential of the significantly higher level of real team performance.

Real teams, however, require hard work of, and are not without risk to, both members and sponsors up the line. They take more time and patience to form than single-leader working groups, and the definition cited previously must be regarded as an essential discipline if extra performance results are to be obtained; the discipline is simply that you have to be graded A+ in each of the five elements spelled out in the definition of a team (size, skills, purpose, goals, and working approach), or you cannot expect a higher level of team performance. Unless both the sponsor of the team and its members truly believe in the team's purpose and potential, results can be disappointing.

Unfortunately, most executives in upper-management ranks today do not know the difference between a real team (the committed, shared-leadership model) and a nonteam (the single-leader model). As a result, they and their potential RCLs try to "establish teams." But because they are not disciplined about what team performance requires, they get a random mixture of real teams and single-leader groups rather than what they really need. In companies with strong performance environments, this approach will produce some real teams—but they also get too many single-leader groups where they really need teams. Moreover, the leaders of the units are unlikely to consider more than one leadership approach, which is usually their personal favorite. This leaves a lot of performance potential on the table. The choice is too important to leave to chance in today's fast-paced change situations.

USING NONTEAMS WISELY

Real teams go for the upside in terms of performance results. It is true, however, that it takes (perhaps wastes) time and hard work before any group reaches the point at which it can attain higher levels of team performance. It is also true that, because of the discipline required, many groups who could perform as teams fail to attain that potential. The team approach is not without risk and should be viewed as a high risk/high reward option. Real change leaders may not be in a position where they can afford the extra time and risk. If so, the single-leader working group is an efficient, if not the better, choice. Such groups are best under the following five conditions:

1. The sum of the individual bests is adequate; members achieve their best by working on their own at what they know and do best.

2. The different member skills can be applied adequately by simply sharing information; joint work is not required to exploit multi-skills.

3. Past approaches are likely to work well for this kind of task or problem; it is a familiar problem, and the approach is well known.

4. The leader knows best from past experience; he or she can easily determine the best working approach for the group to follow to achieve his or her purpose and goals.

5. Speed and efficiency of time utilization is more important than any extra performance results that a team effort might produce.

Single-leader groups perform faster initially because they are easier to form and more efficient to lead. They also protect against the downside in terms of performance risk, assuming the leader really does know best. Obviously, RCLs play a number of roles with respect to teams and working groups. They can be sponsors, leaders, members, or supporters of one or more team or working group efforts. The critical point for potential change leaders is that teams can be used to great advantage in many kinds of change situations—but they are not always the best answer. *The biggest mistake is over-relying on either teams or work groups; both are essential in a major change situation.* This point is much more critical to RCLs than it is to other managers. Change leaders need the flexibility and capacity to apply both approaches to bring about change. Managers who are simply seeking stability and efficiency can usually get by with either teams or working groups, and, most often, the single-leader approach works best for them.

Real change leaders need to specifically identify those performance-improvement opportunities in their change situations that will be most important to the success of their change efforts. In each case, the RCL should make a conscious decision as to whether the conditions warrant a team effort or a single-leader group approach. Rick Tatman, who is a member of one of Jim Rogers's leaderless business unit teams at GE Motors, uses teams wherever he sees a team-performance opportunity. He recognizes, however, that there are real teams and there are single-leader groups. He also makes a practical and rigorous distinction with respect to how the leadership role needs to shift, depending on the performance situation:

> Everybody here is on one team or another. The real teams, however, are mostly in our business-unit leadership groups and the new-product introduction teams. I would say that close to 75 percent of the rest are more in what you call the single-leader mode, although we are always striving for real team performance whenever the situation permits. You have to remember, though, that some valuable people simply do not want to lead, even in the shifting leadership role mode that characterizes real teams.

Rick goes on to explain that some team situations are more attractive than others, and that the leader's role is often more critical in the "less attractive ones." He believes that "real teams take time, and you cannot always make it happen. We are learning more about how to do it, but it takes time and effort—and we don't always get it right."

For those few situations that really matter in terms of team performance, RCLs must make certain that the discipline of team basics (small size, complementary skills, common commitment to purpose and goals, clear working approach, and mutual accountability) is applied. For those that warrant a single-leader group effort, the RCL can either pick or be a good leader. The chart on the next page is a conceptual summary of these performance look-alikes.

It is important to note that single-leader groups appear very similar to traditional boss-subordinate relationships. The only difference is that the leader and the members think of themselves as a team, and typically assume that the commonality of their objectives plus open communications equates to team performance. Of course it does not, because a single-

PERFORMANCE LOOK-ALIKES

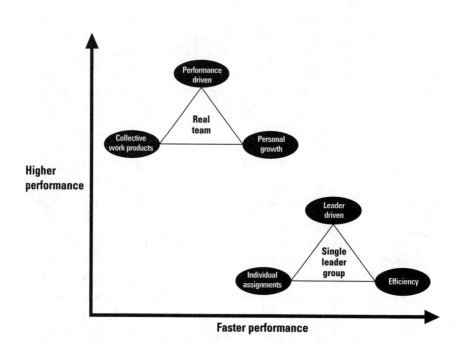

leader group lacks both the discipline that is required for collective work products and the performance potential of a wisely shared leadership approach that characterizes the real team.

EXPLOIT BOTH CHAMPIONS AND MAVERICKS

The individual performer is important in change in those few high-potential situations in which only very talented or motivated individuals can get the job done. RCLs can occasionally save potential champions and mavericks from being lost, since they are often the first to recognize someone who has a unique individual contribution to make to the change effort but is unlikely to fit in well.

True champions are individuals who believe so strongly in an idea that they pursue it against all opposition, and sometimes against all logic as well. Champions sense the need for change ahead of the pack. They are linchpins with an unusual twist—they have a deep understanding of marketplace realities, they passionately believe their organization must begin to adapt, and they are willing to act ahead of top management's support or aspirations. Champions act within the scope that they can reach and often beyond the normal bounds of their authority. They follow the Jesuit belief that it is "easier to ask forgiveness than permission."

These are the people who invent new products, discover new markets, find new resources, land new accounts, and create new approaches. Excellent institutions nourish and encourage them. High-performing companies capitalize on their unique insights. Broad-based change efforts are catalyzed by their creative ideas. Much more so than most managers, RCLs try to find useful roles for potential champions and mavericks, who are often at the heart of innovation.

A number of examples can be found at McKinsey & Company, the management consulting firm where many champions both live and die conspicuously. One is particularly relevant to the subject of this book. McKinsey has long had an enviable reputation in reorganizing large institutions. Several years ago, it became apparent to a few partners that the firm's capabilities in organization were slipping. As in most established institutions, the firm's top leadership was convinced that the problem was largely one of making marginal changes rather than of developing approaches that some leading-edge thinkers were advocating. Steve Dichter was a new partner at that time, and he became a champion for the need to bolster McKinsey's ability to work with companies in major change situations.

Dichter decided to take on this challenge, even though most colleagues and mentors advised him that it would entail considerable career risk. Like most champions, he chose to ignore the advice and the risks, and for nearly ten years has led a variety of significant efforts (both team and individual) to help strengthen the firm's capabilities in organizational change. Some of his actions include:

■ Redefining his job and role to include a disproportionate time allocation to research and development. He let the personnel system know, but did not wait for its approval.

■ Launching a special initiative. Convinced of the need to develop people in new ways, he created a "virtual office," (i.e. a group managed as a unit even though they each officially report elsewhere and are not co-located) drawing together some of the best young people from across North America (and a few from Europe) to work on building their skills and perspectives. The group was motivated by a number of Steve's working visions, including that of "building the McKinsey of tomorrow." Interestingly, all members of the team writing this book are alumni of that initiative.

■   Becoming a role model. His personal commitment and risk taking encouraged others to do more and join the process.

He has succeeded in many ways. But he has also challenged the status quo—and his career path has suffered accordingly. During this period, he has repeatedly been advised and encouraged by senior partners to return to a more normal career path. As with most champions, however, none of that advice diverts him from the pursuit of his personal vision.

"THE CHANGE EFFORT" AT CHAMPION

Mark Childers understands the difference between real teams and single-leader working groups—but he learned it the hard way by working with different combinations over the last nine years of "The Change Effort" at Champion International Paper Company in Stamford, Connecticut. Mark is the senior vice president of Organizational Development and Human Resources for the company. He is not a true human resources professional, however, since he has also held operating jobs in the company's paper plants. A recognized pioneer and leader in self-directed work teams at Champion's fourteen large paper mills, he has been heavily involved in that effort since its inception in 1986. At both plant and corporate levels he is an acknowledged change leader in helping plants convert to self-directed teams.

If you see him in action in top executive discussions, you might not pick him as a change leader. He is quiet, unassuming, and thoughtful. He reminds you of a high school history teacher from some nondescript place like Pierceville, Kansas—warm, friendly, and knowledgeable. When he speaks, people do not always listen because he is informal, if not casual; in fact, they often ignore him at first. They do not, however, ignore him for long because he is always on point, invariably insightful, and never pushes a hidden agenda. To know Mark is to trust him implicitly.

There is no question that Champion International has changed its culture dramatically. Childers believes that the impetus to what Champion calls The Change Effort was a CEO vision and a trial at a greenfield (new) plant in Quinnesec, Michigan, employing a very different set of organizational structures and leadership philosophies. Childer's view of CEO Andrew Sigler's vision at that time (1986) was:

> A company that has nontraditional organizational structures and nontraditional people approaches to operating very good assets [paper machines] and which invests very heavily in training managers and people—changing the whole way the organization worked.

Not surprisingly, CEO vision alone wasn't enough. Fortunately, however, Champion International also had a true champion individual who could translate the top view into something worth working for at the plant level. Steve Goerner was a long-standing operations and engineering manager, who had just returned from constructing and starting up a new plant in Brazil. Working within Sigler's broad guidelines, Steve spent a year studying the latest in pulp-making technology—as well as innovations in people management in a variety of industries. He had the advantage of a greenfield site at Quinnesec, the CEO's support, and his own passion for trying the new approaches he had learned about. As a result, Steve created one of the first truly team-based organizations in the industry. From the start, the entire 620-person operation was organized around 35 or so teams, supported by "shift managers," not foremen, who advised and supported the teams while not abdicating responsibility for shift performance. The teams were made responsible for as many functions within the plant as possible. Many of them worked in what had previously been considered the exclusive domain of management—including the hiring and disciplining of fellow team members, planning, and training. Recently, Champion's Quinnesec plant was rated as one of the best in the world by the Jaakko Pöyry consulting firm, which benchmarks worldwide paper-mill performance across the industry.

A year or two into the effort, Quinnesec certainly was not operating at world-class performance levels, but enough progress had been made for people to recognize it as the prototype for realizing Sigler's vision. In 1986, an aggressive effort was launched to spread the approach across all of Champion's fourteen mills and staff functions—clearly a major risk at the time. Nor was management so naive as to think this would be an easy task. Mark contrasts the company at that time with Andrew's vision:

An old company with mediocre assets, adversarial relationships with unions, top-down management, and top-down information flows and controls.

As might be expected, the company encountered many roadblocks that had not been so imposing at a single greenfield site under the leadership of an extraordinary champion. People lacked the skills, information, and trust to take on the team-based roles expected of them. A whole new set of working relationships had to be forged with the unions. And, most critical, they had to make very fundamental changes in the behavior of existing managers. Looking back, Andrew observes:

> Then the mills were run by old-line managers who had to control the workers and fend off the union; teams were practically unheard of. I guess one or two of the old managers were able to adapt, but mostly we had to find and develop new people to lead the change. The old attitudes and approaches were too intractable. And you could never really tell which ones were going to learn the new game. Often, it was the unlikely characters that you would never have expected to be change leaders. In fact, I still think it is hard to tell beforehand who can lead this kind of change.

Mark agrees, adding that probably not a single mill manager is the same as five years ago and that "a lot of the middle or next level of management in the plant has also been changed." Some self-selected out; others had to be replaced when they could not make the change. As he looks back on the experience, Mark believes it took three to four years of building a new "social system before momentum or critical mass . . . began to take place, and we began to see improvements in productivity, cost improvements, and quality, and all of those things."

This new social system generated—and was energized by—a cadre of individuals who, like Steve Goerner, strongly believed in the new direction. Through a combination of training, experience, and determination, these early change leaders were able to provide others the information, tools, and support needed to make teams work.

In the early years, when the social network was still developing, the change effort resulted in more champions and working groups than real teams. At that time, no one was particularly sure what the difference was, nor had they yet learned all the elements of the discipline required for real team levels of performance. Nonetheless, over time real teams emerged with increasing frequency and impact—pretty much on their own. Certainly the support, training, and systems helped, but the newly formed working groups could not attain team performance levels until each unit learned for itself how to focus clearly on a collective performance challenge, how to share leadership, how to work out its own problems, and how to hold its members mutually accountable. This kind of learning takes time.

Hard-Won Gains

After nine years of extending the original Quinessec approach, Champion today is a very different company with a very different culture. Clearly, it mirrors Sigler's early vision with its modernized paper mills, team-based plant operations, minimal hierarchy, and impressive cadre of change leaders. There is little doubt in the mind of anyone in the company that this change has been achieved largely through the balanced, but opportunistic, use of teams, working groups, and dedicated individual champions. That's the good news.

The bad news is that the company's overall financial performance over the past nine years has lagged its operating performance—due in large part to the difficult, cyclical, commodity nature of the business and some expensive assets acquired in the early 1980s. Put another way, even an industry leader in people productivity has trouble making up for a costly asset base in the short term. Nonetheless, Andy firmly believes that the company's investments in both people and superior equipment will pay off in the long run. He admits that nine years is a long time, but the evidence increasingly supports his claim that the company's culture change has brought it to lead the industry in people productivity and team performance, as well as equipment effectiveness. Analysts are now beginning to admit the financial community's lack of insight into the extraordinary transformation, with one recently noting "the fundamental improvements in Champion's business are still very much under appreciated by a market caught up in history." Another pointed to the tangible payoffs of their change program:

The company has focused on building a strong, efficient work force, recruiting and training to upgrade skills. . . . [It has] also given more responsibility which improved commitment and performance. . . . Productivity [tons per employee] is up 35 percent and costs down 12 percent to 14 percent.

There is little doubt that Champion has positioned itself well for the future through improvement in both workforce and asset productivity. More important to those who lead the effort, however, is their strong belief that The Change Effort has also created an invaluable asset that will never show up on any analyst's spreadsheets. Champion has grown a whole generation of RCLs who now run the machines, mills, staff functions, and even business units. In fact, some from this generation are now among the very top ranks of management. Because of their experiences as RCLs, they can be counted on to continue energizing the company to better and better performance. They know they now have a strong base to build from, and this convinces them that far more can be done. Mark's sentiments echo those of others at Champion:

In all this, I would have to say we have a long way to go. Even after this many years, there's so much potential and so much room for improvement. We're just getting started. But the heart of getting there—breaking up the old stuff—is done, and that is probably the hardest part.

Within the experience, knowledge base, and inventory of change tools and approaches that this group can bring to its ongoing change work at Champion is a very seasoned sense of how to balance the flexible units of the organization for any given situation.

THE WORKING GROUP (NOT TEAM) AT THE TOP

An interesting capstone to Champion's ongoing effort to find the right balance of teams, working groups, and champions is going on today at the top of the company. CEO Andy Sigler and COO Whitey Heist make no secret of their intention to retire from their respective roles within the not too distant future. Two years ago, in anticipation of this transition, they started a process to develop the leadership capacity of Champion's eighteen-person Management Committee.

Not surprisingly, after nine years of change effort, most of this group has had direct experience in leading change initiatives and in making use of the flexible units for organizing people for action outside the formal structure of the company. Mark estimates:

> Half of these people are used to working in teams and have been part of real teams; the other half are used to working in single-leader groups or even groups somewhat beyond that. A lot of our business heads are perfectly comfortable being part of a group and operating as a team member rather than a leader. We've done enough of that to be very comfortable with it, not just at the plant level but the corporate level as well.

Twig MacArthur, the head of a newsprint business that has improved its performance significantly over the last five years, is a good example of such a business head. When The Change Effort began in 1986, however, Twig was in charge of order services, which included inside sales and service as well as production scheduling. He started learning about teams and change along with the rest of the potential change leaders in the middle. Among other things, he led a major task force in 1988 that resulted in significant change and delayering of inside sales, production planning, and production control, the functions widely recognized as the "real guts of the business." When Andy and Whitey reorganized the company into its current business units, they picked Twig to run the newsprint business over a number of other more senior candidates. While Twig has now become more of an executive sponsor of other change leaders throughout his operation, he clearly earned his spurs as an RCL early on.

It might be assumed that a group with such extensive team experience would naturally expect itself to develop as a team. Actually, from Mark's view as a member, their experience has led them to think differently about the Management Committee.

> If it [use of teams] is going on all around you, and you're familiar with how they work, then it makes it easier. If everyone has had four or five years to understand teams . . . then it is even easier to decide [or have the flexibility] *not* to operate as a team. You can use good sense, rather than say the whole company is operating as a team so we will too . . . and then struggle through that and probably fail.

The group did "kick around for six or eight months trying to figure out how we would function," says Mark. But almost from the start, "everybody

recognized we were not going to try to be a team." Their collective experience alerted them to two conditions that precluded them from truly operating as a team: the size of the group and the CEO's personal style.

> We talked with him about it . . . it was a wide-open discussion.
> We just said that wasn't how we wanted to function at this time. It
> wouldn't be a shared leadership mode; he was still clearly the
> CEO and, based on his personality, we didn't think it would work.
> We could work a long time trying to be a team but with the size of
> the group and this other factor we said, naw, let's not do it.

Instead the group has figured out a variety of modes of operating that
actually draw from all the flexible options—including teams. Its primary
mode is as a single-leader working group. Mark sees this approach as having been very valuable to both the group and the company, by providing a
forum for open dialogue on important issues—one of the things a working group does best.

> That's probably a better product than any collective work product
> we might have come up with. When you're all together and have
> dialogue on various subjects it brings people to similar informa-
> tion levels, to similar language around issues so the context
> becomes the same.

Mark believes this kind of dialogue has helped the company a great
deal, simply because it helps produce common views, frameworks, and
even language that results in better alignment of individual actions when
the group is not together. Even this seemingly simple benefit has not come
easily. It took about a year and a half before the group reached the point
where the dialogue moved freely and created the sort of alignment Mark
describes. The group met monthly, and it simply took that much time to
have enough dialogue on subjects such as growth, globalization, and
South American strategy for the members to begin to click in this mode.

To foster these discussions, the group often takes advantage of the
expertise of its membership by assigning what might be considered small
champion roles to individual members.

> We use champions all the time to handle particular issues for the
> group. I do it myself. It might be me going to GE to find out

about what it does around some issue. It might be Ken Nichols, our vice chairman, developing new trend data on some financial area. He would be responsible for bringing that back for the benefit of the whole group.

Interestingly, out of these working group dialogues, team behaviors and collective products do sometimes emerge. Mark points particularly to "brainstorming around strategic direction and priorities, where Sigler will drop back into not being the main spokesman and be a participant in that activity." Out of those sessions comes "pretty good in-depth work" for which the group has taken collective responsibility.

Subteams have also emerged from the larger group. A good example is the issues team, composed of a subset of the Management Committee. The issues team is responsible for identifying and prioritizing issues to bring to the larger group. Because it is a smaller group and has a clear work product in evaluating company issues, Mark sees it operating "pretty much as a team." When the full Management Committee takes up one or more of the issues prepared by the issues team, one thing they consider is whether it warrants chartering a special-initiative team. Drawing on their collective experience in knowing where and when forming a real team matters, they look for issues that are of high-potential priority to Champion, have collective work requirements, and require a complementary set of skills and insights to work effectively.

When the full working group (Management Committee) determines that an issue warrants a subteam effort, it charters one or two of its own members to put together a cross-functional team. It is these specially chartered, issue-based groups that Mark sees as really functioning as teams most of the time. For example, they have set up a purchasing subteam and a best-practices subteam that work as real teams, both in areas of high-performance potential.

As we observed a special initiative teams on which Mark serves in action, it was interesting to note that he often functioned as the de facto leader, even though he was clearly the junior member of the group—in age, position, and stature. In fact, he is perhaps the only one who is not a likely candidate to run the company at this point in time. Why is he usually the informal leader? He knows how to get difficult tasks like this done; he is a completely nonpolitical executive; and he is trusted by those above and below him. Actually, there was no official decision that he should lead, it just happened.

Champion's nine-year "change effort" has clearly changed the plant operating culture, workforce productivity, and performance. A recent internal analysis shows that running the mills better is adding $1.35 to earnings per share and saving $650 to $700 million in capital spending. More important, however, it has also produced a new breed of leaders who have now evolved into top leadership positions. The RCLs who once worked at lower levels to develop teams and working groups across the plant are now running most of the company. And their time is now coming at the top, since one of these change leaders will most probably become the next chief executive. And as a result, The Change Effort is likely to continue its impressive course.

3. RESTRUCTURE AS NEEDS BECOME CLEAR

Real change leaders can help top management better understand if and when a structure change can make a difference in performance results. To illustrate how RCLs deal with these different restructurings, we will describe one example of changing the formal structure early in the change process and one that involved waiting as long as possible.

A CASE OF MOVING EARLY: MEPUS 1990

In 1990, Mobil's Exploration and Production Division in the United States (MEPUS) changed its formal organization structure from a functional, and hierarchical one to a team-based one. These changes were part of the MEPUS story in chapter 1. Basically, the old functional organization was reconfigured into several asset teams that were given overall, cross-functional responsibility for a geographically grouped set of production fields. The teams were headed by asset team leaders who served as general managers and change leaders with profit-and-loss responsibilities for that piece of the business. This move to asset teams was a total reorganization that came out of many months of study of MEPUS's business processes and the new-culture, empowerment, and high-performing-organization training and experimentation that had been under way since 1988. MEPUS leaders became convinced that their rigid bureaucratic organization simply could not function in their current business environment.

In one sense, this reorganization occurred well into MEPUS's major change efforts, since a number of cultural and cost-reduction change efforts had already taken place. Most of these, however, had modest impact on people compared with the fundamental changes that took place as a result of the two special team, problem-solving efforts that had helped MEPUS face the realities of the marketplace, as described in chapter 1. During the two years between the reorganization in 1990 and these efforts in 1992, performance did not improve. Since the reorganization itself did not produce immediate changes in performance, one might well conclude that the reorganization was unnecessary. However, three RCLs at MEPUS now look back on that structure change as a necessary early action, though each draws different lessons from the experience.

Greg Cox, who led the later change effort that achieved $300 million in expense savings, recognizes the common fallacy of thinking "that the first (and maybe the only) answer to any organizational problem is to change the formal structure." Yet he also believes the MEPUS situation in 1990 was one of those where structure change was essential first.

> Having many interdependent teams working together [requires] a structure to support that. You can't say we're going to do that and still have a functional structure. There were so many barriers . . . structure change was necessary.

Charlie Spruell, to whom Greg reported, looks back on the reorganization similarly, as a step that had to be taken to keep moving forward. It was a necessary experiment (and risk) from which they learned a great deal about teaming and working together.

> We started from a very strong functional organization in which exploration, production, engineering, and finance were the structural underpinnings that mattered. We went to eighteen asset teams without really being sure it would work. We were just groping for a way to get more efficient.

It was more than two years before MEPUS would develop the market insight and performance results to lead the industry. But MEPUS's change efforts might have stalled altogether without the initial reorganization in 1990. It laid the groundwork for their later success.

Tom Timmins also lived through the reorganization, as the producing manager. He agrees with the decision to reorganize, noting that having the wrong structure can really impede implementation. He also points out that "[a new] structure alone does not really help much in a change effort." While it can sometimes be necessary, it is seldom sufficient. Moreover, the hidden costs of the reorganization are significant. In this case, the restructuring not only had to address the formal structure, it had to establish new work flows. In the process, it broke some very critical informal people-networks.

> It is the informal people-networks that you cannot draw on charts or design into processes that matter most. If you do not worry about those when you are changing structures and formal

processes, you can have a real mess on your hands until those networks get reestablished.

The collective lessons of Greg, Charlie, and Tom are well taken by RCLs. Sometimes changing organization structure is necessary early in major change. Yet that jolt does not happen without a price and, in itself, will not lead to performance improvement. A change leader's work is only just beginning after a reorganization. It is one step along the way, and it must be followed by the rebuilding of lost networks and the refocusing of people's attention back on the performance challenges of the marketplace.

WAIT AS LONG AS POSSIBLE

Changing the formal structure late, as a catch-up effort to realign the formal structure after you have already worked to improve performance results, offers significant advantages. Once the people across the organization are actually working on new ways to improve performance, RCLs can learn exactly where and why the formal structure is not working. They can also better determine and learn, by using the more flexible units, the specific realignments in the formal structure that are most needed, and where structure realignments can have the most positive impact on change and performance going forward.

For example, chapter 1 drew on Michael Keith's work in getting AT&T's new middle-market sales organization working on the few things that mattered to its midsize business telecommunications customers. In this case, the formal structure change that created Michael's middle-market organization actually came after nearly two years of bottom-up team and process efforts had improved sales performance (the effort by Mary Livingston and her Change Management Organization). During this period, the flaws in the formal structure became clear. For example, under the old structure, a sales account executive typically had ten to twenty midsize customers in his or her account module, along with two or three very large customers. As you might expect, the few big accounts received 80 percent of the attention of the account executive and senior sales management. Besides deserving more attention, the midsize customers also had service needs and buying processes that were distinct from those of very large customers. The creation of the formal middle-market organization involved a massive redesign of account modules around only midsize customers, plus the hiring of new account executives, the creation of new middle-market branches, and the transfer of large accounts and some account executives to another sales organization focused only on large customers.

These structural changes might have been made much earlier. In fact, reorganizing was the usual means of addressing sales-performance issues at AT&T. The Business Communications Services sales force at AT&T had been reorganized so many times in the ten years since the break-up of AT&T in 1984 that veterans lost track as they started counting the reorganizations on both hands. The good news is that these structural changes were an easy way to launch a new attack on performance problems. The bad news is that they seldom resulted in commensurate performance improvements.

This time, however, Mary and her Change Management Organization did not take the easy way out. Instead they focused their energies on developing and spreading the sort of front-line, performance-improvement processes described in chapter 4 (and further detailed in chapter 7). No doubt, the existing structural problems created some complications, but those problems were manageable compared to the disruption, loss of focus, and false sense of having solved the problem that reorganizing first creates.

Even more important in Mary's mind, however, was that by focusing first on performance improvement, her approach enabled account executives and sales management to spend their time really working their market and customers in new and different ways. As a result, the problems with the formal structure became much clearer throughout the organization. In fact, some sales branches began to informally realign their account modules in advance of the formal middle-market reorganization. By the time it became official, many people in the organization already knew from experience why the change was needed and what improvement it should bring. They understood both the purpose of the reorganization and how the new structure would work.

AT&T's middle-market experience highlights three basic reasons RCLs often choose to change structure later, after first working with other elements of change.

1. RCLs have a far better idea of what really needs to change. Changes are based on what is needed to support continued performance improvement rather than personal preference, or opinion, or predictions of how people will respond.

2. The usual disruption and loss of productivity from structure change is minimized because people understand better both what must change and why, and have already begun to build new capabilities.

3. Any delusion of being able to fix a performance problem simply through structure (especially on the part of senior management) is avoided; RCLs know from other experiences that there are other more important determinants of performance improvement.

THE KINDS OF CHANGES THAT HELP

Of the many possible changes to the formal structure, real change leaders can make the most use of three fairly straightforward options. These are neither grandiose nor complex—which is probably why change leaders use them the most often. Three brief examples of each illustrate how.

1. Flattening and eliminating layers—to get everyone closer to the front line and to speed communications and decision making.

Don Tate of Sealed Air recalls that as World Class Manufacturing began to take hold in the plants, and machine operators became directly involved in problem solving and decision making, middle management found its position threatened. "Middle managers were walking the floors and, all of a sudden they were not part of the workforce, they were struggling for control of the business." Consequently, he reduced their ranks and reoriented those that remained, "changing the middle management role from managing as a control freak to coaching and motivating."

This is similar to what happened in many General Electric plants that underwent CEO Jack Welch's now-famous "workplace redesign" changes. A visit to GE's electrical products plant in Fort Edwards, New York, for example, when it was two years into its workplace redesign, was revealing. The company had essentially eliminated two layers of middle management in a 400-person plant, and installed a handful of special coordinators whose job was to serve as an extension of the plant manager in enabling twenty-seven self-directed work teams to achieve their team-performance potential. The coordinators, several of whom were once traditional mid-level managers, are now working in support of teams.

2. Moving staff functions into the line—to build skills, save costs, and gain better perspectives.

As part of the overall change program of AT&T's Business Communications Services sales force, headed by Mary Livingston, the major reengineering effort described in chapter 7 was launched to cut overhead by half ($150 million) and to increase the effectiveness of four management processes in supporting the front-line sales force (compensation, business planning and management, human assets and learning, and product marketing interface). One of the main ways the objectives were met was by taking out most of three layers of staff and giving the sales branches direct responsibility for most of the processes.

For example, compensation had been administered through national plans which were complex and inflexible, heavily reliant on expensive information systems, and very staff intensive. Worse still, they weakened any sense of field ownership. By turning sales performance evaluation back to the branches, the administrative costs were greatly reduced and sales managers assumed far more accountability for defining and rewarding actual sales force performance.

The same sort of change occurred with training. The central "sales university" which local branches had relied on for training was disbanded. Core elements of training design remained centralized to assure consistency and take advantage of national resources, but training delivery became entirely a branch responsibility. The cumulative redesign of training, compensation, and other human resource processes gave the branches the responsibility for the overall development and performance direction of their people. Such processes had been seen as "individual islands that did not connect" when managed by remote staffs. Now they came together at the branch where they could effectively and flexibly be used to support performance objectives.

3. Regrouping into small units—to change points of focus and coordination.

Teams are the classic way to regroup rapidly and target new issues or opportunities in almost any organization. Both real teams and single-leader groups can be helpful. When Enron decided to reengineer the back-office support units in the Enron Capital and Trade Services business, the company did it with a series of teams and single-leader groups. Some of these became critical parts of the formal structure going forward. The structure that came out of MEPUS's second reorganization was based on the small-unit asset teams that were re-formed around core and noncore assets.

When Texas Commerce Bank (TCB) decided to go after everything that frustrates the customers and the employees, it went from 6 task forces to 176 action teams and working groups and back again to a different configuration of teams, task forces, and working groups for implementation. TCB's formal organization now includes many of these small-unit approaches. The focused, small unit—be it a real team or a single-leader group—remains the most flexible organizational unit for either performance or change.

ORGANIZING WRAP-UP

Achieving some ethereal "organization-of-the-future" is not seen by RCLs as the primary target or end point of change. They move toward new organizational designs only insofar as the designs provide the best way of aligning and motivating their people to improve performance. There was a time when the strategy of an organization truly was replicated in its formal structure. A former CEO of Prudential once claimed, "Our strategy is our organization." Today, RCLs don't start out with an objective of creating a new type of organization per se. Their organization incorporates both formal and informal elements, and it evolves as they find and further incorporate different combinations that work. Ed Whitaker, CEO of Southwestern Bell, recently told a group of top executives of the Southwestern Council that "nothing is permanent or forever; we are prepared to change any aspect of the organization to meet the market need."

It is as foolish to argue for a totally team-based approach as it is to ignore the power of teams in key places. It is equally foolish to argue for a completely horizontal organization or a nonhierarchical organization. It is naive to expect one type of organizational approach to save all companies, and it is equally naive to expect the same change process to work in all situations. One of the main reasons that command-and-control has fallen out of favor is that it was too heavily relied upon in situations where other options used in conjunction with it could have helped. Yet, upon reflection, it becomes clear that there will always be situations where good old command-and-control is the best way. In short, beware the self-proclaimed change masters who push you toward their one preferred solution.

Nor is the consideration of organizing options solely the province of top management in a change effort. All RCLs need to think about the multiple options they have for aligning the behaviors of their people. They may not be able to use all the options they are aware of, but they certainly will have more than one at their disposal. Teams, single-leader groups, and champions add up to a pretty good set of options for attacking change—even when they must work within an unfriendly formal structure. RCLs need not fear trying a variety of combinations from this arsenal, nor can they afford to be discouraged if the first few tries do not work. Moreover, no combination will work forever; changing conditions demand new combinations.

In the end, what works for RCLs in organizing for change often finds its way into the ongoing organization as well. Recall the change effort at TCB, examined in chapter 4, where literally thousands of people and recommendations are in need of supporting changes in the formal organization. Some of these happened in real time during the "Process Improvement" effort, but others are yet to come. While still in the midst of the implementation phase, Anita Ward could already see the effects the experience is having on the organization and anticipate the implications.

> [The] process is going to force us into a different formal organizational structure—both for successful implementation and because our customer and employees are going to drive us there. . . . You'll end up seeing more team-based structures, more self-managed teams. Before, if I had given anybody here a paper on self-managed teams, they'd have said I was nuts. But that's what we have now. Essentially what we've done is changed our structure.

To Anita, the informal structure has really become the formal structure, heavily biased towards teams and working groups, since that is what worked for the TCB change leaders in their high-involvement change effort. In other situations, a different balance of flexible and less flexible elements will make sense.

PART III

LEADERSHIP CAPACITY AND GROWTH

MOMENTUM

How do I build "momentum" and keep people pulling in the same direction?

■ *We got off to a good start, but now a lot of people are starting to work at cross-purposes.*

How do I hold people's motivation and energy at high levels over time?

■ *Most people are beginning to get tired of all this change stuff. Can you really expect them to keep working harder and harder for very long?*

What can I do to increase the pace?

■ *We have a solid start, but the game may be over if we do not really get moving.*

How many different sets of change tools and approaches do I need?

■ *Yesterday it was Quality. Today it's Reengineering. How can I avoid leading the "program of the month"? Should I stick with one program or change to another?*

How do I increase both the pace and performance impact over time?

MAJOR CHANGE EFFORTS ARE SELDOM SELF-SUSTAINING, EVEN WHEN THEY GET off to a good start. In fact, the primary problem that most major-change efforts encounter is stalling or becoming hopelessly diffused after the first several months. The reasons are perhaps obvious, but nonetheless important. Major change efforts take much longer than normal improvement projects or programs (most of which are less than one year). Broad-based change invariably lasts longer than expected—it takes years rather than months to complete. As a result, people develop a natural and increasing desire to get back to normal or business as usual. They tire of the extra effort and workloads that accumulate.

People also develop a need for closure, or completion, along the way. As Anita Ward pointed out in chapter 4, ". . . They need some time to rest, reflect on their accomplishments, and regroup for the next push." It is easy to mistake these interim stopping points as the time to declare victory and return to normal, or less intensive, effort.

There is a need for rejuvenation that requires more than traditional management can provide. Top management often overlooks signs of eroding momentum. Even when they do recognize it, more pronouncements and special programs from on high seldom provide the answer. Nor is yet another task force likely to make much of a dent in the growing confusion. Most middle managers want to regain control of their units. They want to get back to meeting budgets and sales quotas. The last thing they need is another set of extra change tasks added on to their normal work requirements.

Change leaders use a wider variety of approaches to get people into action—and to build momentum over time. They seldom rely on only a few tools or sources of ideas. One of the ways they generate momentum over time is by integrating different ideas and tools to create new approaches. They get the best contributions from a wide range of people by taking risks on different people and new approaches that traditional managers avoid. When Sally Beck of Enron was seeking new leadership capacity for the next wave of improvement goals in her group, she faced such a conflict. Some of her people were urging a shift to a team-based organization, which Sally favored herself. Others argued that there was no way most people were ready for real teams, and that she should simply get stronger supervisors in place. Rather than simply deciding between teams and stronger supervisors—or compromising by calling her supervisors team leaders—she worked hard with her people to develop a single-leader approach that would evolve into real teams in key places over a specified time period (two years). This is a riskier approach, but one that offers much higher performance potential. Traditional managers seldom take this approach, because they have neither the mind-set nor the tools to do so. More than fifty years ago, Mary Parker Follett argued convincingly that performance suffers when leaders decide to override, or compromise among, conflicting interests. Instead, they need to work hard to incorporate the best of each. According to Follett, "Compromise does not create, it deals with what already exists; integration creates something new."*

Building momentum in a broad-based change effort is a tough job that gets tougher as the effort continues. To address this challenge real change leaders:

1. **Build a diverse tool kit and develop a variety of approaches—** to increase their options for addressing different performance challenges.

2. **Rebalance the mix as they go**—to exploit different combinations, as well as new ideas and approaches to both deliver results and rejuvenate the effort.

3. **Increase the mass and velocity over time**—to obtain better and better performance results.

---

* Elliot M. Fox and L. Urwick, *Dynamic Administration: The Collected Papers of Mary Parker Follett* (London: Pitman, 1973).

1. BUILD A DIVERSE TOOL KIT

Real change leaders know what is required for better results and merely try to get the targets, tools, and approaches together that work best to achieve those ends. It is virtually inevitable that they find or develop a combination that works—simply because they keep trying different ones until they like the rate of performance gain.

The main mission of RCLs is to get better results and keep the momentum building. The results get better because each successive round builds off of the previous round of results and learning. In fact, a great deal of the momentum that you see among their people comes from the enthusiasm and satisfaction of getting better and better relative to the competition—and the expectations of their leaders. This is why most RCLs prefer to work in a mode where they are not pushing programs from on high that do not appear relevant to the day-to-day business problems of front-line managers and people.

To that end, RCLs tend to follow two simple guidelines, which differ from what other managers typically do, and which tend to build more lasting momentum for change:

1. They get a few basics in place that others can apply more broadly and encourage that application without overcontrolling it.

2. They expand the use of tools and approaches that work into other situations.

GETTING A FEW BASICS IN PLACE

Sometimes top management provides good air cover—actively supports the RCLs' change efforts—and sometimes not. In either case, RCLs must have at least a rough idea of what matters for performance in top management's view, plus a solid grounding in what the marketplace requires. Without a point of view that integrates both of these elements, it is extremely difficult to get started in the right direction.

When Dermot Dunphy, the CEO at Sealed Air, created his controlled crisis by raising corporate debt, he provided the impetus for the World Class Manufacturing effort. This provided a very clear picture for

RCLs early on. It was also a good example of getting a few basics in place that enabled dozens of plant managers to apply their own initiatives to get a broad base of both momentum and performance improvement. Clearly, a broad-based effort was necessary to service $302 million in long-term debt and rebuild the company's net worth. The pivotal organizing event was a meeting of several plant managers in Florida. In just four days, these managers combined their collective understanding of market requirements and top management priorities to craft a set of measures for each of the six WCM principles and to set a first-year improvement goal for each.

Don Tate, a regional manufacturing manager who was later named vice president of manufacturing and given overall responsibility for WCM, remembers what it took to make that meeting work. It started a few months earlier, when a small group held a one-day meeting with Richard Schonberger, the author of *World Class Manufacturing,* to "talk about the philosophy of WCM and try to get a feeling of ownership with some key managers in the company to get things going."

Informed by a survey of major customers and some basic cash-flow analysis, a small group worked with Schonberger's principles, "Sealed Airizing" them into the six WCM disciplines detailed on p. 44. They also started preparing for the Florida meeting. Copies of Schonberger's book were widely distributed and assignments made to make presentations on different sections of the book. People were also charged with developing starter lists for what measures and goals to set for each discipline. These starter lists served the dual purpose of getting the managers to think in advance about measures and giving the Florida participants some starting blocks to build on.

Don estimates the plant managers applied "60 percent art and judgment and 40 percent facts" to come up with proposals for measures and goals. Through all of this, Don pushed for simplicity. He specified that the working groups put forth no more than three measures for each of the six WCM disciplines, "so we didn't get lost." At the meeting, the individual book reports and starter lists of measures and goals that each manager had developed prior to the meeting were discussed and debated in small groups to get people working on the problem collectively. Don believes the four-day meeting was really key in developing ownership:

> The meeting was a lot of discussion, and it was dynamic. There was . . . freedom to increase the goals . . . but they were pretty

well set since a lot of work went into it before . . . so the meeting was really selling and fine-tuning. At the end . . . everyone went home with a charter.

Once managers were back in the plants, they immediately started tracking and posting the new measures (often requiring new equipment, training, and processes on the plant floor) and identifying the problems that had to be fixed to reach the annual goals spelled out for each discipline. Cross-plant comparisons were published by discipline so each plant workforce could see its own results alongside those of other plants, which helped develop a sense of mutual, as well as individual, accountability. Consolidated summaries from all plants were also tracked and charted in the corporate office "war room." This helped standardize some of the goals. Clearly, the success of Sealed Air's WCM effort was not the result of anything special or magic. Don remembers running into just the sort of resistance you might expect:

There were challenges in the plants, that is, people said, this is just another program that will come and go. Getting ownership into the workforce was not real easy. It took constant reinforcement. . . . Our tracking system let people know that we were serious about it. It didn't go away.

Obviously, getting a few basics in place can help people get started quickly on generating results. As more and more people work against the same basics, there is another powerful benefit with regard to building and sustaining momentum over time—people reinforce one another's determination to overcome change resistance and to keep performance moving up. When the plant managers first convened in Florida, each was committed to his or her own particular managing and organizing approach. They were all good managers with limited change experience. As the discussions developed, and the managers began to share many ideas, as well as improvement suggestions and best practices (such as how to reduce inventories or how to simplify quality control), they also reinforced one another's commitment to higher performance.

This reinforcement continued long after the Florida sessions, because the managers continued to exchange information and ideas. Thus, they were building momentum that would extend into each of their plants—and later across plants—to produce better and better results over time. As Fred Smagorinsky observes in retrospect, "I don't think any of them realized how much they could accomplish in the way of change until they started translating and working the WCM principles together." By so doing, they became increasingly excited about the possibilities, reinforced one another's commitment to get better results, and took the few basics back to their individual plants to use as a basis for getting more and more people into action.

LEARN WHAT WORKS AND EXPAND

The traditional manager is content to work his own territory efficiently and effectively. He does not search for ways to apply what is working in one kind of situation to a completely different setting. The change leader is constantly looking for ways to expand things that work, both within his own formal area of responsibility and in other areas. His concern is overall company performance, not simply getting his own act on center stage.

When Fred Smagorinsky was interviewing for a job with Sealed Air in 1992, his main question was, Do they really need me? They're doing a pretty good job here. He saw the job as "a kind of stewardship of the overall WCM program." Fred surmises that the vice president of manufacturing, Don Tate, "felt like he had taken it as far as he could as part of his regular job . . . they had reached a plateau and weren't necessarily sure how they wanted to proceed next."

So Fred found himself in a common RCL situation: coming into a change program in midstream that wanted a fresh boost, some additional momentum, and a bit broader scope: a phase two, so to speak. From the start, Fred felt he had inherited "a nice little package" in WCM. "The thing that I was most thankful for coming in was they didn't start with process measurements. They didn't say, How many teams are we going to form? How many people are we going to train? or anything like that. They said, How are we going to define success?" The basic principles were sound, the performance focus was clear, the measures were tight. How hard could this be?

Fred could have approached this job opportunity as a traditional manager rather than as an RCL. Many would have started by designing a set of process measurements to be installed across the plants and making a push for more training, team building, and cross-plant comparison reports.

Most of their emphasis would have been on telling and prescribing, while staff change leaders like Fred are in the game of encouraging ideas and solutions from the people who must make them work. It is perhaps a subtle difference, but a very significant one nonetheless. Fred found ways to expand what was working in one area into other areas where he could identify similar performance situations and skill-set needs.

In many ways this is analogous to the "edging out" approach that Clifford and Cavanagh discovered when they looked at what the best performing midsize companies did, in their book, *The Winning Performance,* a chronicle of what the hundred best-performing midsize companies do.* These companies expanded by taking what was successful in their initial business concept into other business opportunities that had similar characteristics—edging out, rather than leaping into completely different and unfamiliar territory, or simply staying comfortable and content in their initial boxes. Real change leaders like Fred use the same kind of approach to build momentum, by taking what they have made work in one area, then adjusting and applying it in areas where similar conditions and skill sets are required. Fred did it in Sealed Air by edging out, plant by plant, then working across functions, and finally working jointly with customers. This is an obvious extension, but one that traditional managers seldom pursue.

EXPANDING PLANT BY PLANT

One of Fred's first moves was to expand on what was working with WCM by adding a critical, but very simple, new element—a bottom-up problem-solving process. The initial just-do-it approach to WCM had not included the sort of structured processes or tools described in chapter 4. Initial gains had been made without their benefit, but the need for the increased efficiency and effectiveness of a more disciplined approach was apparent.

Fred did two things to make a more structured problem-solving process work at Sealed Air. First, he kept it very simple. To this day, the WCM effort is nothing fancy—no monogrammed binders or special courses, just a few minutes of explanation and some simple forms. Second, he did not roll it out everywhere as an involvement process or a training program, as traditional managers of quality programs do. Instead, he expanded it into

---

* Donald K. Clifford, Jr., and Richard E. Cavanagh, *The Winning Performance: How America's High-Growth Midsize Companies Succeed* (New York: Bantam Books, 1985).

the more obvious and natural areas of clear performance opportunity. He simply showed up at a plant with a few problem-solving tools in hand and worked directly with plant teams on real problems. This may sound too modest an effort to many managers, particularly some of the recent wave of participative managers, or, as identified in the next chapter, misguided change leaders, who seem to believe in involvement for the sake of involvement, and to think that more is better, and sooner is faster. Misguided change leaders try to obtain more impact by getting a lot of people involved in a hurry—instant teams everywhere. While this may well create momentum, it is diversionary, rather than performance focused. As more than one such leader has said, "If we just get lots of people involved, it is bound to add up to higher performance." This idea is all right, but the sequence is all wrong.

Instead, RCLs like Fred start with a clear picture of the performance results needed—and then decide who needs to get involved in what to deliver better results. They seldom go for all-out involvement in the early stages of change, though they appreciate the importance of getting the best from all their people over time.

Fred certainly heard the admonitions of some around him urging getting lots of people involved early. But Fred is stubborn; his instincts said go slow, get a few basics in place, find what works, and build credibility first. Then edge out, or expand, when specific, related opportunities present themselves. This approach accomplished three important things:

1. It got immediate, tangible results by solving real problems.

2. It built momentum among a larger group of plant managers by introducing them to the idea of using a new, structured, participative approach to problem solving.

3. It established Fred's credibility for being able to help plants in ways that mattered, an especially important consideration for enabling him to later edge out in bigger ways.

Simple as this sounds, however, it did not always work. In the early days of trial and error, Fred made a number of changes in how he set up the meetings, introduced the tools, and worked with people. With each session, however, he was able to learn from what worked and did not work in the previous efforts, as well as to adopt the ideas and approaches that worked in similar situations. Not only did these changes increase the validity of his approach, but they also built momentum that both lasted and increased over time—because other people experienced the satisfaction of achievements they had not anticipated. As the changes were applied across the plants, structured problem solving became a permanent part of the Sealed Air vocabulary:

> Now problem solving is something people talk about all the time. I will be in a management meeting, and an operating problem will come up, and someone will say, Why don't we do some kind of problem solving on that? They never would have said that three years ago.

By getting people to experience the satisfaction of contributing more than they thought they could, Fred delivered improved results, learned what worked, and set in place a set of action flows whose results provided much of their own momentum over time.

EXPANDING ACROSS PLANTS

The next obvious opportunity to edge out with this approach was in cross-plant issues. Initially, all the WCM efforts were plant-by-plant, rather than systemwide. Previously, company-wide gains were just a roll-up total of individual plant improvements. Fred realized, of course, that there could be significant gains by attacking cross-plant issues in a similar way, that is, by edging out. As a result, he was more than ready to act when such an opportunity walked into his office in the form of the division controller, exclaiming, "Freight [costs] are blowing out [of control]. . . . What do we do with all of this?" It turned out to be an interplant issue, so Fred said:

> Well, why don't we talk to the plants involved. Let's ask them to form an ad hoc team . . . to reduce their freight. We checked with Ted Bell, division vice president of manufacturing, sent the right guy at each plant a letter, set up a conference call and said, "Here are the four steps, you all know them, so let's solve the problem."

Fred continued to check in with the interplant team by conference call to be sure they were staying tight on their objectives and time line. Sure enough, the team cracked the shipping-cost problem, and several plants benefited instead of just one. While the nature of the opportunity in this instance was cross-plant, the principle at work remained the same: Fred took an approach that had worked in one area and looked for the right opportunity to apply it in a similar area. In doing so, he delivered better results, while building momentum by enabling others to then apply the approach on their own.

Moreover, he continued to build momentum by working next across functions, attacking a freight issue that required problem solving across manufacturing, sales, and customer service. And finally, he even found the ultimate "edge-out" opportunity through joint efforts with customers. In 1994 Sealed Air launched its Team 2000 Growth Alliance Program with over sixty of its distributors. Sealed Air's own cross-functional problem-solving groups now join with distributors' counterparts in a cross-company team. Together they are eliminating redundant costs, reducing inventories and shortening time intervals in the entire chain of supply. Team 2000 illustrates how developing and expanding a structured process for performance improvement can eventually become a keystone of a company's strategy.

Perhaps the essence of how RCLs expand and build lasting momentum, however, is best described in football terms—looking for the opening and running through it—sometimes aggressively, and sometimes unobtrusively. Invariably, however, the momentum comes from enabling increasing numbers of other people to apply a few simple basics on their own—and encouraging them to help others do the same.

2. REBALANCE THE MIX

The change program for the AT&T–Business Communications Service (BCS) sales force grew out of a long-standing concern over the central sales force's performance. Chapter 2 describes how Mary Livingston developed her own personal vision, along with a set of working visions, to bring about change in that environment. She headed the Change Management Organization (CMO) that was established by Lou Golm, the president of one of the world's largest sales forces, to lead an effort that Lou envisioned would significantly improve the performance capabilities of BCS. In leading this effort, Mary worked with several other change leaders at BCS. It is a good example of how RCLs learn to use and balance different tools across an extended change effort consisting of three parts: 1) diagnosing performance needs; 2) building a set of change tools and approaches; and 3) achieving critical mass.

DIAGNOSING PERFORMANCE NEEDS

Mary formed CMO by recruiting about thirty top salespeople and sales managers from across the country, with two things in mind. First, to be accepted by the sales force, the CMO effort had to be seen as being of the sales force, by the sales force, and for the sales force. So, she screened for people with good sales records and strong networks into the organization—thus, whatever came out of CMO would be seen as guided by people from the heart of the sales force. Second, she wanted to model ways of working that did not follow the usual hierarchy:

> I was really trying to guard against leaders who told people what to do and didn't do things themselves—I wanted everybody to do real work—I wanted to make sure that other people felt like they could make equal contributions.

That meant finding people who were more committed to improving the sales force than to climbing another rung on their career ladders. In fact, those who signed up not only gave up their current positions (including commission income), but they received no guarantee of a position afterward. Their future in the organization depended on the success of CMO. Not everyone who joined worked out, but by laying out the expectations early, Mary greatly improved her odds of getting change leaders.

The effort began with a series of analyses to assess "true" sales performance. Unfortunately, CMO could not rely on the existing sales-results tracking systems or measures, because they did not provide an accurate, market-based view. They only reported sales made, not sales missed. They also did not distinguish whether sales were lost because of sales problems or product and price deficiencies. To get a more realistic view of what was happening in the market, several tools were used:

- Telephone surveys of thousands of businesses (customers and non-customers);

- Hundreds of in-person interviews with buyers on their decision processes;

- Dozens of interviews and focus groups with salespeople to debrief them regarding both wins and losses; and

- Fact-based analyses of competitors' sales force size and practices.

These efforts resulted in a segmentation of customers by size (e.g., total spending on telecommunications) and type of usage (e.g., international calling). The analyses revealed what percent of total buying decisions were being covered by the sales force and, for those covered, why decisions were lost. Based on this data, Mary's team determined that sales could increase by over a billion dollars if both coverage and sales effectiveness were increased by roughly 50 percent over existing levels.

More important, the firsthand experience of participating in the new work opened the eyes of many in the organization to their performance gap. Scores of other potential change leaders were recruited from the sales organization to help with the analyses, particularly the customer interviews. Many became convinced of the need to change only after hearing directly from customers about the shortcomings of the sales force. The data produced by those diagnostics proved to be of lasting value, says Mary:

> I don't know how many times that data has allowed me to go back when people started to get distracted and say, That is not what the data told us. It has allowed a lot of us to have discus-

sions based on more than just opinion. It took a long time for people to accept it, but now I see it showing up regularly in presentations . . . it cracks me up.

BUILDING A CHANGE TOOL KIT

Mary knew a change challenge of this magnitude would require more than any one approach (e.g., quality, reengineering) could provide. Reducing high staff costs, for example, requires a different approach from raising low customer coverage. As they progressed, Mary and the change leaders kept adding to their tool kit of different approaches to meet the various challenges. "Now they seem like fairly simple tools, but frankly, they were new to me then. We come back and use them over and over, depending on what the initiative is." Basically, her team's tools and approaches fall into four broad categories:

1. Making the change clear and tangible. The rigorous marketplace diagnosis described in the last section made the change situation very clear to Mary and her extended team—but not to the rest of the organization! To correct that problem, they developed not only the working visions described in chapter 2, but also a number of other valuable approaches.

To begin with, Mary and Lou Golm convinced sales-organization leaders to spend a significant portion of their time leading the change (Lou himself set the example by spending 25 percent of his time leading the initiative), as well as shaping and delivering consistent messages to the organization:

> I saw their role as making sure that this was hooked in reality. I wanted insiders that would help advance these ideas among their peer groups and the field, and would take real leadership of it so that it wasn't staff-think. I wanted them to make the product their own, to give real content input, not just cosmetic touches, to make it a real live thing in the end.

Next, Mary and her team developed new performance measures, both to give a better sense of market performance and to track the impact of the new sales efforts. Finally, they took advantage of every opportunity—formal and informal—to talk to the sales organization about the challenges. They made sure that every change effort was clearly related to the performance imperatives, rather than an activity for its own sake.

2. Structured, bottom-up performance-improvement processes. These were designed to ensure that superior value was delivered to "very large" and "large" existing customers. Within this existing base, much of the problem was understanding the customer's business and the full range of possible sales opportunities that existed. Mary's group designed two well-structured change processes to develop an understanding of needs, identify specific sales opportunities, and turn those opportunities into sales. (Two separate approaches were required, because the two customer groups followed very different buying practices.)

These two efforts were rolled out nationwide, with teams from CMO helping the sales branches with the implementation, which encompassed hundreds of salespeople and thousands of customers. In the course of the implementation, the RCLs set specific targets for new opportunities and new sales. Guided by these targets, AT&T's share decline in these markets was being reversed. And, rather than being one-time events, these performance-improvement processes were incorporated into the ongoing sales approach. Again, the momentum was sustained over time by different combinations of tools and approaches, and by the improved results that were in and of themselves invigorating to the people involved.

3. Focused skill-building programs. These were developed to upgrade the capabilities and performance of sales managers responsible for sales to small businesses. With hundreds of thousands of customers and relatively high turnover of salespeople in this segment, performance-improvement processes like those for large customers were not appropriate. Instead, the hundreds of sales managers in the Commercial (small market) sales organization were identified as the pivotal people for improving the sales effectiveness of thousands of salespeople. A program titled World Class Sales Leadership was inaugurated. It focused on developing the sales managers as coaches (rather than administrators or super-salespeople), and gave them a new, ongoing management process for assessing and developing core sales skills with their teams of salespeople.

4. Reengineering teams to fix the infrastructure. The initial diagnostic work that Mary and her team carried out had also established that the company had about twice the sales overhead per person as its major competitor. This issue was left on the back burner while initial efforts concentrated on sales-performance improvement. As budget pressures mounted, and management worked to hold earnings amid declining prices, overhead became the logical target. The only alternative was to cut feet-on-the-street (salespeople calling on accounts), which meant lost revenues.

Simultaneously, the performance-improvement initiatives were generating concerns about sustainability: would the new business processes become just one-time events if they weren't built into ongoing management processes? For example, the emphasis to better understand customer needs that was an integral part of the performance-improvement processes was bumping up against incentive systems the product marketing organization had built to push certain products.

After reexamining and updating the original overhead analysis, upper management set an objective of cutting overhead by half ($150 million) and improving the effectiveness of management processes. "That was an incredibly significant decision, a very big risk," Mary recalls thinking. "I don't think they had a clue as to how we were going to achieve that objective." Upper management's answer was to put Mary in charge again. She was initially overwhelmed by the new task. "It was one of those times when I had to reach deep inside and remind myself that I have been overwhelmed before and that somehow it can be done. We'd always found a way before, so you suck it in and move forward." So Mary embarked on yet another approach, this time getting the Infrastructure Reengineering initiative under way by configuring all the activities not directly related to selling into four basic management processes and forming a redesign for each: compensation, business planning and management, human assets and learning, and product marketing interface.

Overall, the reengineering effort was clearly successful on the cost side (45 percent reduction). As for effectiveness, results were mixed. Some processes were more thoroughly redesigned for effectiveness than others. Other processes were very well redesigned but called for skills and perspectives beyond the immediate capability of the organization. A case in point was the business planning and management process. It was redesigned to turn a top-down, sales-quota-allocation exercise into a bottom-up market analysis, forecasting, and goal-setting process. One of the centerpieces of the design was the chalk talk, in which branch managers would present their local market analyses to a group of fellow branch managers and product house staff members, for a joint review and problem-solving session. It was a big leap for an organization with hundreds of thousands of accounts, little experience in local market analysis, and a tradition of being told what to do and how to do it. The organization's management initially never really bought off on the design, but Mary remained philosophical and realistic about the outcome, and noted a year later that significant progress has actually been made. Originally, a major objection to the redesigned process had been that the organization lacked the necessary skills. Now, just by going through the "chalk-talk" process, the skills are being created: "you do it, you slop around, make mistakes, and learn from each other." Rather than wait for skills to be developed, Mary has learned that "sooner or later you have to take the training wheels off and just let it go."

The need for multiple tools and approaches—as well as the difficulty in integrating them—is a common theme among most change leaders. Too many change efforts start with one or two very strong thrusts, but falter unless different kinds of tools are applied over time. Mary's story highlights both the power and the frustrations that change leaders experience in trying to balance and rebalance multiple tools and approaches. There are bound to be setbacks, failures, and shortfalls—and it is easy to lose sight of the gains. Overall, however, the impact of this kind of balancing act is orders of magnitude greater than what could be expected with a less chaotic, well-organized, traditional management approach. Keeping the momentum going demands this kind of rebalancing—and when it works, the flow of new results almost always generates increasing momentum across larger numbers of people, as they actually experience the exhilaration of better performance results themselves.

From a top management point of view, an overall change effort can be viewed as an integrated process that involves a balanced set of initiatives of three basic kinds: top-down direction setting, cross-functional system and process redesigns, and bottom-up performance-improvement programs. While few change leaders think in these terms, it is clear from observation that they apply a similar mix. Their working visions and clear performance measures and accountabilities are top-down; their redesign of business and management processes are cross-functional; and their use of structured problem-solving approaches, teams, and working groups are often bottom-up efforts.

3. INCREASE MASS AND VELOCITY OVER TIME

Real change leaders do not measure their success by reaching some given end state. They believe, as Jim Rogers of GE Motors says, "Our best is always ahead of us!" Thus, they instinctively work on increasing the momentum over time. As in physics, momentum is a function of *mass* (the number of committed people, at all levels, working to improve results) and *velocity* (the speed at which results accrue and/or new initiatives ramp up).

EXPANDING THE CAPACITY FOR CHANGE

Compared to RCLs, most managers have a narrow view of the leadership and change capacity in their organization. They tend to think of the leadership as residing in a few people who occupy the designated manager positions in the formal organization structure. The managers are the ones who make the decisions and assignments that others carry out. People below managerial levels are not supposed to lead and do not expect or know how to lead. In contrast, change leaders honestly believe that all but the laggards and malcontents have the capacity to lead in their work assignments—at every level. They recognize that some people simply do not wish to exercise that capacity, but they are constantly encouraging everyone to try, even if it is only in small ways.

Steve Uthoff describes it well. As described in chapter 3, Steve is the change leader who helped to convince the two top executives of Browning-Ferris Industries (BFI) that major change was the issue. He sees any organization as a simple distribution of people. A small percentage of the organization (5–10 percent) already "gets it"; they are the first wave of potential RCLs, when given reasonable direction and opportunity. To Steve, such people "contribute throughout their lives, whatever the cause, wherever they are . . . they are pushers and givers who are willing to make this place better." Another similar proportion of people will never "get it" and must eventually be culled out. Steve concedes, "They just don't respond to the idea of a company culture that says we'll somehow be 10 percent better each year than last. Instead, they just want a job that lets them collect money and go home."

Then there is a large group in the middle that can be swayed either way. Steve describes these as the people who exclaim, "Why, I had no idea!" They are individuals who need a bit of a push to step up to the challenge, in a sort of spontaneous self-identification. Usually, this occurs as a result of new information, new awareness of a pathway to improvement, new tools and guidelines, or simply encouragement and support. These people can be influenced to try new approaches, learn new skills, take initiatives, and speak out with new ideas. They can lead others around them, even when their official jobs do not imply leadership. But without some kind of positive new impetus, they remain neutral forces at best; at worst, they join the forces of resistance, because of the influence of the naysayers.

Most real change leaders share Steve's view. When RCLs think of expanding their change capacity, they mean enabling the minority who naturally get it to help capture the latent leadership capacity and change initiative from others. Steve describes this as "working the geometry" (looking to start and further a progression of 2, 4, 8, 16, etc.):

> The geometry comes into play when you show somebody a better way and they become so enthralled with the solution that they tell all their peers, This works!

Randy Howard of UNOCAL had a similar view in mind when he thought about how to increase the leadership and change capacity of his efforts:

> These are the people who will encourage that involvement of the broader group. It's those twenty or thirty who are truly empowered, and they will give you the biggest benefit.

This is a completely different mind-set from that of most mid-level managers, who typically believe the power should reside in the top 10 percent—who must think, decide, and determine how the mass should behave. This attitude is usually attributed to top management, but it is clearly not restricted to that level. Traditional managers at all levels instinctively believe that working with the few key people is the best way to ensure business performance and is the most efficient way to spend their time. There is little question that this practice is time efficient; it is not, however, very change effective.

CREATE PERSONAL GROWTH OPPORTUNITIES

To RCLs, capitalizing on latent leadership and change capacity implies getting the most from each and every person. This requires providing personal-growth opportunities. The best change leaders become masters of this craft and are seemingly immune to any fear of taking risks on their people. The three main organizing elements covered in chapter 6 (real teams, single-leader groups, and individual champions) can all be used to create opportunities to get people involved in ways beyond their normal positions and responsibilities. Real change leaders are intent on getting people to perform outside their boxes, while traditional managers want to keep people within their boxes.

The "discipline directors" in Sealed Air's WCM effort are a good example. Nationally, and at every Sealed Air plant, there are individuals designated to track and champion efforts to meet the goal for each of the six WCM disciplines. The person chosen may or may not work in an area closely related to the discipline; he or she may or may not be in management. Though no official position or promotion is involved, these roles are highly regarded as personal-development opportunities ("precious things" in Don Tate's words). The people in these roles are periodically changed to open the opportunity to others, keep perspectives fresh, and avoid burnout. While continuity is a consideration, Don believes that "people get burned out on things and are looking for something different . . . changing their jobs keeps the motivation level and their enthusiasm going."

In selecting people for these positions—whether it is senior management picking a plant manager to play the role nationally or a plant manager picking an hourly worker to play the role at an individual plant—Don says you "screen carefully and make your best possible decision" on who will perform the role well and grow from the experience. For example, in picking a safety director, "you usually find your best people, who have the strongest commitments to safety, and they become your leaders." Sometimes, however, an exception to this logic proves the better choice. For example:

> Our safety director for the company today got the job because his plant had *poor* safety performance! He has been an outstanding safety director because he began focusing on being an example with his own plant's safety and made a dramatic turnaround. He knows firsthand what it really takes to improve plant safety.

The secret to providing personal-growth opportunity, obviously, is the willingness to take a risk on those who might not be the easy choice.

Keep Trading Up

Real change leaders also look for every opportunity to trade up. They work hard to upgrade and capture the potential of the people they have, but they also move quickly to replace those who just do not have it. For example, in picking people for the discipline director roles, Don and others at Sealed Air do not hesitate to "change out" individuals (return them to their regular jobs) when "they aren't buying into it." These roles are too critical to squander. World class performance allows no room for mediocrity.

Greg Cox of MEPUS believes in the idea of trading up for traditional leadership positions like manager and supervisor as well as for nontraditional team-member and leader roles. Mobil now selects people for leadership positions based on a set of criteria that puts more emphasis on characteristics required for real change leadership than on those found in traditional manager-performance appraisals. Greg says:

> Every time a change opportunity comes up, we want whoever we put in the spot to be a better change leader than whoever left, based on the new leadership criteria.

Randy Howard of UNOCAL reminds us that RCLs often have to start with the cards they are dealt. Trading for a better hand has to wait for later rounds of play. He realized early on that he had some difficult people-issues, but he also realized that there was a great deal that he could accomplish without immediately confronting those issues and causing the potential disruption and gridlock of fear that might well result:

> So I went after the biggest chunk of savings first, got a mass of people moving in the right direction, and then I could go back and solve the individual people-problems.

Don Tate has found that the idea of trading up works all the way back to hiring. As a result, he has become very disciplined in hiring people over the last several years and has given a very high priority to making sure that Sealed Air gets the best people for their change situation:

We look for a person who is both skilled and very oriented toward multitask jobs. [We believe] that person will be motivated by this environment because of the flexibility, freedom . . . and a lot of responsibility.

This emphasis has led to changing hiring practices in all Sealed Air plants. One new "capacity" criterion that Sealed Air has adopted is to hire only those believed to be promotable into at least two different positions within twenty-four months.

REALIGN TO ELIMINATE BARRIERS

When parts of their organization are not aligned with what RCLs are trying to accomplish, it creates drag on the momentum. Often the causes are not immediately apparent, and the solutions can be very difficult to implement. Consequently, RCLs tend to work on this alignment only after they really understand through experience where the real rubs are. They are usually well advised to work around them as long as they can. Using energy to deliver results early invariably makes more sense than fighting internal wars.

Once the organizational drag becomes a serious barrier, however, and the change required is clear, the change leader has to deal with it. This often means a redesign of business or management processes. As discussed in the preceding chapter, if RCLs can make do for a while, they will be able to use what they learn from earlier performance efforts to help design the changes (e.g., use of cross-functional teams, four-step problem solving). For example, MEPUS is now in the midst of a major overhaul of its human resource functions. Why now? As Greg Cox explained, by the time the initial, intensive performance-improvement effort ended, the need for this was much more clearly evident. The new human resource strategy MEPUS is now developing has over a dozen components, covering everything from employee development to workforce planning. In classic RCL fashion, Greg's answer to why this was not done sooner is very pragmatic:

Those [human resource management processes] are the hardest things to change. They are very ingrained; they have been around a long time. . . . [Moreover] we couldn't have made the changes before, because I don't think we knew what we needed. Only through our team-based, bottom-up results process were the needs identified.

Instead of changing the human resource functions, Greg and other RCLs have simply been working around them. He admits to pushing the old system pretty far, but you get to a point where additional progress means you have to change it. Because they worked around the system initially, however, they are now in a much stronger position to make changes. Greg says:

> You really have to show that you have pushed it. You've got to have some credibility that you've worked with it the best you can. You've got to demonstrate that this is what you've tried and that this is what works and what doesn't.

KEEP PEOPLE FOCUSED ON WHAT MATTERS

Momentum is lost any time people start pulling or pushing in a wrong direction, and any time they forget or lose conviction about why they are working so hard. Hence, RCLs must constantly recommunicate, retranslate, and reemphasize the core messages about what matters and why. With time, any change program will go through many initiatives and cycles. Confusion and the flavor-of-the-month syndrome can become real issues. RCLs avoid confusion by delivering a consistent message and by using simple pictures.

A Consistent Message

After seven years of WCM at Sealed Air, Don Tate knows the importance of a persistent, consistent message. He wants the person listening to him to realize, "He [Don] is not going away, and he is not going to change his mind; he is going to keep talking about the same things." Don even speaks of the message of WCM as one of spiritual conversion: "It is almost like a religion. It's a commitment that people believe in and wake up tomorrow morning believing in no less than they do today. Everyone strives to be better each day than the day before."

In the same vein, it is important to avoid confusion as new initiatives and buzzwords come along, by showing their link to your original themes or principles. It is a matter of protecting the integrity of your own brand of performance improvement. As Don says:

> You do not make it the program of the year. It is a program that you believe in for the distance. It is fine if you want to give away [coffee] cups, but do not make it the "program of the year."

Over the years, many things have changed at Sealed Air, but WCM has been a constant. It is Sealed Air's own brand for problem solving and performance improvement. Using it as a brand, change leaders are careful to maintain its name identity and integrity, accepting no substitutes or knockoffs. Even Fred Smagorinsky has to be careful not to confuse terms:

> Our last newsletter was on reengineering, and I showed it to [CEO] Dermot Dunphy in draft form. In it, I called reengineering an evolution of WCM. He looked at it and said, "No, no, no—not an evolution of WCM—it's not what WCM becomes—it's an outgrowth of WCM . . . we're still going to have WCM."

It is very important that RCLs use themes and principles consistently as ways of guiding people in identifying their own self-starting actions for performance improvement. One way that Steve Uthoff of BFI reinforces the most important aspects of the change effort at Browning-Ferris is something he calls "the right-hand side." He actually means the right-hand side of a single chart from a presentation developed for launching the BLUEprint initiative. It's a simple from-to chart, with the left-hand column describing BFI today ("Best in the industry—maybe," Steve says) and the right-hand column describing where BFI must be in three to five years ("A superior company," as Bill Ruckelshaus staunchly maintains):

> That chart is a vision of how we are going to manage . . . not a vision of what business we'll be in. It's a chart describing what kind of place this will be.

Steve uses the chart as the heart of a speech he "has learned to give in my sleep." Like the working visions described in chapter 2, the words on the chart may not seem very insightful to people outside the company,

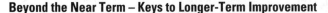

BLUEprint for Improvement

Beyond the Near Term – Keys to Longer-Term Improvement

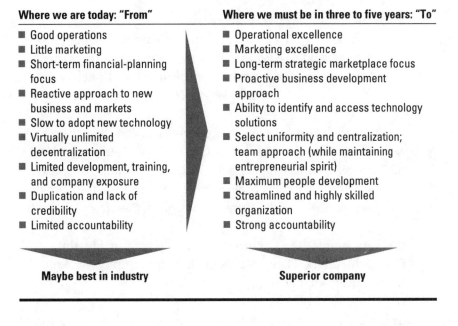

Where we are today: "From"	Where we must be in three to five years: "To"
■ Good operations	■ Operational excellence
■ Little marketing	■ Marketing excellence
■ Short-term financial-planning focus	■ Long-term strategic marketplace focus
■ Reactive approach to new business and markets	■ Proactive business development approach
■ Slow to adopt new technology	■ Ability to identify and access technology solutions
■ Virtually unlimited decentralization	■ Select uniformity and centralization; team approach (while maintaining entrepreneurial spirit)
■ Limited development, training, and company exposure	■ Maximum people development
■ Duplication and lack of credibility	■ Streamlined and highly skilled organization
■ Limited accountability	■ Strong accountability

Maybe best in industry   **Superior company**

but they are making the change real at BFI. They enable Steve and other change leaders to describe a set of future work and marketplace conditions that do seem different and better than those of today. The words work largely through repetition; Steve gives the speech an average of once a week. BFI's chairman, Bill Ruckelshaus and CEO, Bruce Ranck, also use the chart, making it hard for someone to ignore it or believe it will go away. For those seeking further reassurance, Steve points out that the chart itself also conveys longevity:

> The chart clearly says three to five years. That gives it longevity. People understand this program will be around and what these changes mean, and that this is a big investment in skills and attitudes. We tell them that the only competitive advantage comes from skills and investment in training people. Trucks don't matter and computers don't matter for very long; it's really up to people. People understand that.

While the official BLUEprint effort is primarily focused on three areas of performance improvement, placing that effort in the context of a wider change picture has allowed Steve to prompt action across the organization:

> Bill, Bruce, and I met with each department head and went over this chart, asking, What are you doing in your department now and over the next five years to take us to the right side of this chart? If you don't see your role very clearly, we will help you with what it is. We have been very encouraged by the reactions.

For example, Dave Hopkins, the controller at BFI, told them, "My group's role is to reengineer these back-office processes." Steve says that he, Bill, and Bruce were virtually blown away by how thoughtful Dave was and the enthusiasm that he and his people showed. When Steve told him how impressed they were with all the energy he described, Dave responded with:

> It is very simple. The controllers are really enthused by this BLUEprint effort. They see it as the first opportunity in a long time to really change things.

In fact, Steve has had to turn away some who came to him wanting to "license" the BLUEprint name to put on their pet project. "You have to watch that there are no pretenders out there using this as cover," he says with a smile. While he does some brand protection to maintain the integrity of the change program, in most cases people come with really good ideas. It is not a problem he minds having.

SIMPLE PICTURES

RCLs often find it extremely useful to have simple ways of showing how all the pieces fit together. These aids are not magic, but they serve as memorable symbols and reminders of many aspects of the overall effort which people can quickly call to mind and respond to. They are much more than gimmicks to the people who use them.

SEALED AIR'S NUMBER ONE CARD

Talk to anyone at Sealed Air very long and he or she is likely to pull out a "Number One" card. Dermot Dunphy is known for pulling it out whenever speaking with employees and reminding them, "Don't leave home without it." This simple card knits together all the performance priorities and values of Sealed Air. It's been around for almost as long as WCM. Don Tate recalls, "The endorsement of the strategy for World Class Manufacturing sort of drove the Number One card. Within six months of the start of WCM, we had publication of this card." It is not just another clever wallet card for the change leaders at Sealed Air. For example, Don (who has it as a plastic page divider for his time-manager notebook), pulls it out and tells how he used it just that day with a customer. In fact, he goes through each element on the card in telling his version of the Sealed Air story, as depicted in the chart on p. 273.

The MEPUS Mountain

There's a chart at MEPUS that everyone involved in the division's performance journey since 1987 seems to remember and pull out in conversation. At first it was a very crude hand-drawn picture of a mountain (p. 274). At the top is "HPO," for High Performing Organization. Along the ascent of the mountain are the names of all the initiatives they been through, starting at the base of the mountain with the formation of MEPUS in 1987.

Greg Cox recalls that MEPUS did not have this big picture in 1987. It was actually developed in 1992 as part of the change effort, at a time when the division was really trying to sort out what was important and where it was headed. MEPUS used the HPO vision as the top of the mountain it was climbing, and it became a symbol to which various change initiatives could be related. The picture helped to show that different initiative names did not mean random flavors-of-the-month. Having the HPO flag at the top reminded people of what they were really trying to achieve. The mountain in the distance was later added to make it clear that this was not a one-peak, one-time assault (although they'll take it one peak at a time).

Ken Miller refers to the chart to make a slightly different, but reinforcing, point. At the time the picture was developed, people had just been through another downsizing, and though beginning to get focused on real performance improvement, were wondering whether all the reorganization, culture building, and process design work of the previous years had been worth it:

The issue is why do I have to continually change? People tend to think of change as a one-time event. What we have learned is that we have to build a message to people that we expect the changes to be continual and that you have to try a lot of different things to find the ones that work. You have to look at past efforts and say, If I had not done those things, I would not be able to do what I am doing now. We used the mountain to say that.

For Ken, the idea of continual change—trying things, building on experience—is "an important thing to get people's minds around." It's also an idea he sees taking hold at MEPUS. "One big difference that I see in the organization now is that people are much more accepting of change. It's a way of life."

MOMENTUM WRAP-UP

The momentum-building efforts of change leaders at Sealed Air, AT&T, MEPUS, and BFI follow a pattern that is increasingly evident in successful major change situations as the efforts proceed. Early on, RCLs simply use a variety of different tools to get people into action—tackling performance-improvement opportunities. As the effort continues, however, it becomes necessary to use different combinations of tools and approaches, always looking for opportunities to get more people experiencing the personal satisfactions of achieving better and better results. Over time, RCLs adjust the mix of tools they use, blending top-down, bottom-up, and cross-functional approaches to rejuvenate and excite people and deliver superior results. Finally, RCLs think explicitly about expanding momentum over time by getting more and better people working to improve performance.

DON TATE'S EXPLANATION OF SEALED AIR'S NO. 1 CARD

Customers

Prior to the implementation of the strategy, we had a survey done of our customers. It came back that we were a bit arrogant. That was an awakening. The company was really proud of its success, but our pride had become arrogance. Having customers come first on the card reminds us that we can be great at all of these programs to improve manufacturing but, without customers, it doesn't matter.

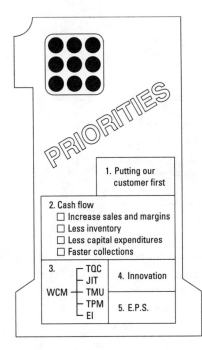

Cash flow

With the recapitalization, cash flow obviously became the second priority. Cash flow was broken into these four headings for improved focus.

WCM

That's how we get there; our strategy for success.

TQC:	*total quality control*
JIT:	*just-in-time*
TMU:	*total materials usage*
TPM:	*total preventive maintenance*
EI:	*employee involvement*

Innovation

We had been very innovative in the early days, spending money to develop new processes and machines. But the company was getting somewhat complacent. With the recapitalization suddenly money was not readily available; much more justification was required for project appropriations. So we said, "Okay, wait a minute, let's go back and get sharper in our mental skills, let's be more innovative, let's utilize existing equipment expenditures better before we ask for more."

Earnings per share

Some people ask when you show them the card, why isn't this first? The answer is take care of other things first and E.P.S. happens. Plant managers had a heavy focus on their cost of production (or margin). We said forget about that part. Make all the programs work, and then look at the profitability. If they work, then profitability occurs. You can be so focused on the bottom line that you never make it happen.

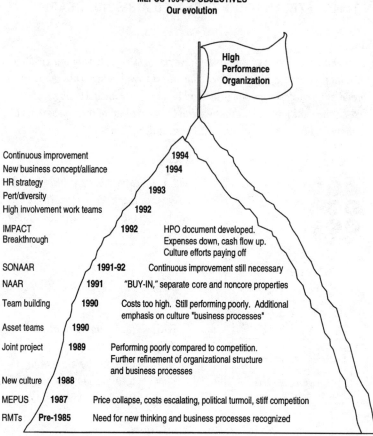

MEPUS 1994-96 OBJECTIVES
Our evolution

High
Performance
Organization

Continuous improvement — **1994**
New business concept/alliance — **1994**
HR strategy
Pert/diversity — **1993**
High involvement work teams — **1992**

IMPACT — **1992** — HPO document developed.
Breakthrough — Expenses down, cash flow up.
Culture efforts paying off

SONAAR — **1991-92** — Continuous improvement still necessary

NAAR — **1991** — "BUY-IN," separate core and noncore properties

Team building — **1990** — Costs too high. Still performing poorly. Additional
emphasis on culture "business processes"

Asset teams — **1990**

Joint project — **1989** — Performing poorly compared to competition.
Further refinement of organizational structure
and business processes

New culture — **1988**

MEPUS — **1987** — Price collapse, costs escalating, political turmoil, stiff competition

RMTs — **Pre-1985** — Need for new thinking and business processes recognized

SKILL BECOMING MORE THAN A GOOD MANAGER

Why aren't there more RCLs? Do I need or want "the skills" to be one?

- *Most people around here don't look or act much like RCLs, nor does our formal management development program focus on them.*

I think I'm a good manager. Why is that no longer enough?

- *RCL sounds different from good manager, but I like being a manager. Why not simply find RCLs to work for me? Do I really need to develop new skills myself?*

Exactly what new skills will I need to manage change going forward?

- *I've never seen a list of RCL skills, nor have I seen change leader skills on any resume or job description. Are they all that different?*

How do I acquire these new change skills?

- *Sounds like you have to learn them on the job. How do I get the right kind of assignments to build these skills myself and for potential RCLs that work for me?*

What good will RCL skills do when this change stuff is over?

"BECAUSE IT IS A BASIC SKILL THAT YOU CAN ALWAYS USE, THAT'S WHY!" responded the mother of one of us many years ago. She had just been accosted by her fourteen-year-old son for an explanation of why he had to be the only freshman boy in a high school typing class with more than twenty girls. Obviously, he was too young to appreciate some of the side benefits of this situation. The year was 1946, and the scene was a small farming town in the sugar beet country of Colorado, where most girls as well as boys might well have questioned the practical value of typing skills. Mom in this case was clearly in-command-and-control—so, typing it was.

Years later this same male typist became one of the first senior partners at McKinsey to master the personal computer and has since blessed his mother's foresight a thousand times over. Today, of course, PC skills are typical even among senior executives, but there was a time when the entire notion was ridiculed, just like typing, as a clerical skill unworthy of anyone with executive potential. Most of us can recall clearly the excuses that ricocheted around the corporate hallways: it's the latest technology fad; it takes more time than it is worth; my secretary can always do it; I can always learn it if I really need to; it is not the best way to leverage my time; I have more important things to learn. In short, no self-respecting general manager, let alone an executive leader, would waste valuable time on this kind of "techie" clerical work.

Times change. Today, if you were to eliminate PCs, E-Mail, electronic document transfer, and computerized spreadsheets from our skill sets, most of us could scarcely function. Our leadership capacity is now highly dependent on these skills. Those of us whose mothers had the foresight to provide us with basic typing skills might have found it easier to work with PCs initially, but we still had to spend many months, if not years, mastering additional skill sets before we could operate at the levels of executive computer proficiency that are now commonplace.

We believe the same to be even more likely with the emerging change leadership skills required of RCLs. None of those described earlier in this book graduated into their managerial roles with change leader skills and attitudes well in hand. Yet, many executives today still minimize change skills as being nothing more than good hard work against a set of clear priorities. They behave as though change leadership is simply a modern version of the fundamentals of leadership or good general management skills in action. And clearly, at some level of abstraction, this is true. However, when it comes to getting hundreds of people to learn and apply new behaviors and skills that are outside their comfort zones, managers had better be equipped with more than a standard set of good-manager skills and fundamental leadership characteristics. There are critical, demanding, and different skill sets and leadership approaches to be mastered and applied. Nor can good managers get away with simply hiring others with those skills, if they aspire to play a leadership role in their institutions' broad-based change efforts and future success.

This chapter is devoted to three critical aspects of becoming a superior RCL:

1. **What skills and mind-sets are required?**

2. **What leadership roles come into play?**

3. **How and why to become a superior RCL?**

1. SKILLS AND MIND-SETS REQUIRED

To argue that good leadership will instinctively bring about change is equivalent to arguing that Michael Jordan could easily play right field for the New York Yankees—or that any natural athlete can perform at Olympic levels in any event. The specific skill sets matter every bit as much as the proverbial "natural people skills" that most managers claim—just like athletic skills do in the Olympics. And those skill sets require careful identification as well as training, practice, and dedication to master. Moreover, these new change skills are as important to potential change leaders as are their industry experiences or business-management skill sets.

But is it really fair to compare the "good manager" in a major change situation to the "natural athlete" in the wrong event? After all, good mid-level managers are the product of a great deal of both formal and on-the-job skill development; they are not playing in a game that they were untrained for, are they? Unfortunately, we believe they are. The corporate change game, as it is played across the mid-levels today, is not the same game as ten years ago. Nor is it the strategically logical, clearly organized, and carefully planned playing field that most business schools and corporate executive training efforts prepared us for. Instead, it is a game of rapid, recurring, and unpredictable fluctuations, in which success or failure is largely determined by the adaptability of managers in the middle—who must learn difficult new skills on the job.

Throughout the preceding chapters, many examples of the work of RCLs in leading their people to change and achieving better results have been cited. Many of the activities described are the same as those that any manager might be involved in these days (setting performance priorities, managing a reengineering project, forming teams, measuring customer and worker reactions). For that reason, it is worthwhile to be explicit about how RCLs think and act differently—and more effectively—than the typical manager in the same situation.

CORE SKILL SUMMARY

This section summarizes briefly, by chapter topic, what the primary RCL insights and skill differences are relative to those of most other managers.

BALANCING THE SCORECARD

The essential difference between skills required of traditional managers and those of the change leader in achieving performance results has two dimensions: balance and rate of climb. Managers typically view performance as meeting the earnings targets that will satisfy shareholders. They manage by objective, with the dominant focus being on annual cost and revenue targets set by high-level executives. Good managers are distinguished by their ability to set and meet tough earnings goals and plans. They increase these goals each year based on top management guidelines. Customers and employees are a means to those ends.

The RCL goes beyond the financial dimension of performance—without sacrificing it. RCLs view customers and employees as equally important constituents for whom the company must perform. They learn to convert top-management financial performance imperatives into meaningful terms and add equally binding targets for satisfying their customers and developing their people. They also learn to influence high-level executives to include more than economic goals in their performance aspirations, and, in fact, often set higher goals than top management expects of them. By staying on top of what goes on in their marketplaces, they gauge their performance against external benchmarks, not internal precedents. They go on to develop the tightly linked and well-rounded set of measures that let everyone know "what's important around here." Few RCLs yet have the benefit of Jim Rogers's "weather-map" scorecard on workplace satisfaction (described in chapter 1), but most of them search for ways to accomplish the same thing.

FINDING WORKING VISIONS

Good managers rely on formal statements of corporate mission, which they may modify slightly to reflect the implications for their units. Increasingly, managers at all levels are enamored with vision-shaping exercises in which statements from the top are the subject of down-the-line discussion groups for purposes of creating buy-in. Sometimes these exercises also result in modifications in the original statements, yet the changes remain modest. The good manager believes that visions must come from the top and behaves accordingly.

RCLs believe that good visions are theirs to form at any level, and they develop a skill for seeking and nourishing informal and formal interactions to that end. Seldom do they launch formal vision exercises, but they are keenly aware of informal situations that can lead to the set of words and images that will energize and align their people for change. They seize those opportunities because they know that the value of vision comes largely through intense and informed dialogues among many different people about "why we're doing this." This leads them to the words and images (seldom their own) that constitute a working vision. The very best RCLs also develop the skill to recognize when the words and images need to be changed. "No graffiti" plays out in the transit system in New York, but change leaders continue their dialogues toward a new working vision.

INSTILLING CONVICTION IN OTHERS

A major difference between traditional managers and RCLs lies in the change leaders' recognition of their need for, and skill in, instilling courage for change across a broad base of people. Managers see it as an issue of motivation rather than courage. Hence, they follow one of two traditional approaches to increase the motivation for change. The first is positive encouragement and incentive. They try to paint positive pictures that too often deny the realities in their marketplaces, sponsor lots of involvement and participative management initiatives, and encourage teamwork among people for elusive nonmonetary rewards. The second is to apply pressure and increase anxiety levels by emphasizing headcount reductions and tight cost control. They usually have little tolerance for those who buck the system.

In contrast, RCLs are pragmatic realists. They are extremely skilled at bringing marketplace realities into clear focus for their people. They have learned how to help people face and deal with difficult facts without allowing them to become either discouraged or overly anxious. They do not believe that denial or fear is the best way to get people to change. They are able to maintain a sense of urgency without creating undue anxiety. Finally, they have learned to reduce the fear of failure that prevents people from taking risks. As Rick Tatman of GE Motors, whose team fell short of its goals, reminds us, "you just have to go back to the customers and learn what went wrong." It also helps that Tatman has the full support of CEO Jim Rogers, who believes:

> I prefer that we miss high stretch goals now and then rather than discourage the stretch by punishing all shortfalls. I try to celebrate the hell out of achievement and progress here, even when

some of it falls short of what the team goals may have been to begin with. I do not believe you gain anything by public floggings of people who have given their best, but were largely beaten by the circumstances.

GETTING THE MOST OUT OF MANY

This is perhaps the most significant difference between good managers and RCLs. The good manager believes that people perform best when job assignments, work plans, and time lines are clear. They preserve a clear hierarchy of control, and the organization is run by "a few good men." Good managers follow a fairly elitist philosophy in the development of their people, believing that a few high-potential winners in the work force will determine change success. A good organization structure for these managers is one in which management time is deployed to the key decisions and interactions. There is also a fairly clear separation between the thinkers and the doers in the structure.

In contrast, RCLs believe strongly in getting the maximum out of most of their people. They are as concerned with leadership and initiatives from the middle 65 percent as from the top 10 percent. They develop both skills and working approaches that place them in more direct contact with people down the line, and a much higher proportion of their time is spent doing real work as opposed to reviewing and approving the work of others. They rely more on structuring pathways in which large numbers of people can exert initiative. By being disciplined in these approaches, RCLs realize performance gains never imagined possible. Steve Uthoff of BFI recalls many a manager telling him, after sitting in on their first breakthrough team session, that "I had no idea there was this kind of potential!"

SHAPING AND USING ACTION FLOWS

Another difference between most mid-level managers and change leaders is the RCLs' relative emphasis on horizontal action flows versus vertical information flows. Most managers, because of their reliance on functional controls, operate in an environment of up-and-down (vertical) information, approvals, and decision making. They like the comfort of having deep functional expertise to rely on and are uneasy without that kind of quality and behavioral control. This does not imply that they are still wedded to the extreme command-and-control approach, but they do rely heavily on individual accountability and functional expertise for both key decisions and operational efficiency.

RCLs operate from a more horizontal mind-set, concentrating on designing and using action flows that will deliver value to the customer rapidly. Their customer and competitor knowledge and start-to-finish understanding of critical action flows are superior to those of most other managers, and they work constantly to improve them. They have learned to apply a number of tools and approaches (such as cross-functional teams, new measurement systems, and reengineering) to reorient the mind-sets in their functional organizations and pull together all the pieces for the customer. Kevin Desmond (chapter 5) pinpointed and connected the missing elements along the line to make the A train a true "showcase" for public transit in New York.

RELYING ON THE FLEXIBLE UNITS

Most managers still see the organization structure as the primary alignment mechanism for channeling behaviors and skills. When change is necessary, good managers tend to start by changing the organization structure and end by putting different people in the boxes. If that does not work, they change the names and faces until it does. Good managers may try teams these days, but invariably the single-leader type, which limits both performance potential and capacity for change.

RCLs use whatever works, but they seldom start with structure. They recognize that changing structure alone seldom leads to performance improvement. Doing so also carries a high price in terms of internal disruption. Instead, they use informal, ad hoc networks and find ways to cross functional boundaries and hierarchical levels by focusing on action flows and objectives, not on functions and positions. Rather than relying on rigid structures, they first use real teams, single-leader working groups, and champions to ferret out the problems and opportunities and get some tangible results. Rick Tatman describes how—even in a team-driven environment like GE Motors—most of the teams start out in the single-leader mode. He also points out, however, that the intention is for as many of these groups as possible to achieve real-team performance levels.

The ability to differentiate between real teams and single-leader working groups—and use each as needed—is an increasingly critical skill for RCLs. The best change leaders learn to function in both roles and know when each makes the most sense. They consider structure only after they have worked the potential of these flexible units; then structure can be used to help lock in performance gains, often by eliminating layers, moving staff functions into the line, and regrouping around smaller, customer-focused, team-based units. Even after such formal moves, RCLs continue using the flexible units as needed, keeping in mind the attitude expressed by Jim Rogers: "We have an organization chart. But we don't use it much as it changes so frequently."

Building Momentum

The most difficult part of a change effort comes after "phase one." Unfortunately, most managers—and even developing change leaders—concentrate on getting the extra burst of energy in the first phase. They believe that if you carefully plan and execute a few top-down programs and initiatives, and follow up with the prescribed performance-improvement processes (off-the-shelf quality or reengineering programs), the change will happen: the rest is implementation. Of course, they create and maintain formal tracking and reporting systems, coordinate activities, and allocate resources across special projects. They consistently work a priority list, item by item, in order of importance—always trying to "get back to normal" as soon as possible.

Change leaders instinctively recognize that the toughest part comes after phase one. They understand the physics of managing change—the need to increase both mass and velocity to build momentum over time. They also suspect that another change effort is very likely to follow closely on the heels of the current one; there probably is no getting back to normal. Once a few basics are in place, RCLs start improvising, experimenting and revising approaches on the run. Whatever success they achieve with a new approach in one area becomes a candidate for application in other areas. They constantly work a changing mix of initiatives to keep the momentum going—and to generate increasing momentum. They build a diverse set of tools and approaches that they can draw on as circumstances require.

The best RCLs display highly developed skills for integrating across conflicts and strongly adverse positions. They have experienced the difference an integrated solution represents and will work hard and take risks to obtain it. In the process, they are also continually looking for and creating opportunities for people throughout their organizations to take on new challenges. They also have the mind-set of expanding the pie rather than trying to get a bigger piece for themselves. They simply do not have time to get involved in political turf battles. George Devlin would never have cracked the code on Compaq's manufacturing process if he had been worried about his own advancement prospects.

MIND-SETS THAT GUIDE RCL ACTIONS

There is more to real change leaders than the insights and skills reflected in the preceding summary. They also hold certain mind-sets that make them more effective than other managers in change situations. These mental attitudes strongly influence RCLs' interpretation of, and response to, change situations.

TRY IT, FIX IT MENTALITY

Sometimes change leaders look like they might be trying to fail. They don't always get it right the first time. Sometimes their cut-to-the-heart-approach is too quick or simply misdirected. At other times they take calculated risks, especially on people, in the hope of having greater impact or accelerating a person's development. Steve Uthoff of Browning-Ferris Industries has made more than one such bet in the BLUEprint initiative. For example, a district manager he knew to be among the hardest to convert was picked to lead the first pilot breakthrough team. "In the back of my mind, I thought that if we could succeed with him, he could become a powerful spokesman for the effort with the other managers. I wasn't absolutely counting on it . . . but it did come through." That time it worked: the district manager gave an effusive testimonial at the next worldwide managers conference. But Steve has also had such attempts go the other way, and when that occurs, he has had to dig his way out and quickly figure out another approach. Still, he believes it is critical to keep taking these kinds of risks to keep the momentum building.

One reason change leaders are so willing to try a new approach is that they have so sharpened their skills of observation and comparison that they can recoup quicker, as well as learn more from trials and errors, than most other managers. An important reason is simply the proportion of real work that they do. While most mid-level managers are intent on designing solutions in advance, staying out of the fray, and leveraging their individual time, RCLs are intent on getting into the murk and mire to learn whatever more they can that will better inform their next moves. The emphasis on experimentation here could create the impression that they operate without deliberate thought and intent—that they shoot from the hip. Instead, their mode is deliberate and reasoned, but quick to react and adjust as soon as new/better information is available. Hence, they are taking a page from most proven problem-solving processes. It is the old plan-do-check-adjust approach that good problem solvers always employ.

They are also rigorous about reprioritizing opportunities and cutting losses. When most managers make a decision, they tend to ride it out and do everything possible to prove the decision was right, rather than admit to a poor choice. Because RCLs are so intent on reading what the marketplace is telling them, and because they are determined to get results, they seldom hesitate to admit to mistakes or question their previous decisions. Harriet Wasserstrum of Texas Commerce Bank (TCB) describes how she made a mistake but quickly got on with more important priorities:

> We have one team that I am not expecting any recommendations out of. Maybe if we had a more politic outsider [leading it] it would have worked better, but it is my biggest failure. At some point I could have dropped everything to run it myself, but I had more important things to do.

Too many general managers in this set of circumstances would have focused on justifying the decision, covering up the failure, or blaming someone else. Wasserstrum simply wrote it off and kept her focus on those of her two dozen teams that really mattered.

COMFORT IN UNFAMILIAR TERRITORY

Change leaders do not follow tightly defined job descriptions or clear lines of authority. In fact, they seldom have any official authority for much of what they do. At NYCT, Carol O'Neill's formal authority is limited to certain administrative budget procedures (not even budget approval); Kevin Desmond is only supposed to gather service data and set schedules. Yet each of them skips across, around, and through the organization's structure and formal lines of authority to get things done. They are careful to avoid serious violations of protocol, but they rarely think first and foremost about what they can and cannot do, who they can and cannot call, or how they can or cannot propose an idea. If they did, they would accomplish far less. Instead, they think first of what is the right thing to do and who they need to involve to get it done.

Experienced RCLs develop a comfort with the ambiguity of their real authority. Much of this comfort comes from realizing that formal authority is not needed to get people working hard and delivering tangible results. The comfort also comes from learning over time just how far the boundaries of authority can be pushed without anyone pushing back. It is usually far more than expected, as Mary Livingston of AT&T's Change Management Organization learned with time:

> I didn't have absolute authority on anything, but I can't ever remember somebody saying stop. I didn't push the boundaries anywhere near what I could have done. If I had it to do over I might take more risks . . . part of the growth experience for me is getting out of this checking first with everyone mode and just pushing it.

The other area of ambiguity or uncertainty with which RCLs learn to contend is working outside their past experiences and normal work settings. In fact, they are often tapped for difficult change assignments precisely because they are not familiar with a particular area or function of the organization. One important criterion in picking several of the action team leaders at TCB was that of wanting an outsider who could bring a fresh perspective, raise tough questions, and keep the team from falling prey to old thinking and assumptions. Even in familiar territory, any change assignment is almost sure to require change leaders to work with and through a number of people with whom they do not normally come in contact.

Real change leaders find comfort with such situations, because their mind-set admits to missing critical knowledge and instinctively seeks to enlist the people who can provide the missing pieces. Change leaders know they cannot bluff their way through without the relevant business know-how. Change is hard enough when a change leader is familiar with the territory and the sources of knowledge; when the territory and sources are unfamiliar, the task is much more difficult—and the gap-filling mind-set more critical. As RCLs broaden their knowledge, they also gain increasing confidence to take on whatever challenge comes their way. This confidence, in turn, reinforces the mind-set that helps them work in unfamiliar territory.

CREDIBILITY AND TRUSTWORTHINESS

RCLs operate with a basic mind-set that their ability to effect change is almost entirely dependent on the credibility and trustworthiness they have established with others. They understand that, by the very nature of the process, changing people's skills and attitudes cannot be accomplished simply through the exercise of power. Other managers assume that they must rely on their authority within the hierarchy, believing they can both direct the changes to happen and delegate much of the actual work to others. Their credibility and trustworthiness, while no doubt important to them personally, is not considered all that important in getting others to change. Instead, they believe they can manage change at arm's length, through the system—not through their personal credibility. Consequently, people may respect and listen to them, but seldom commit to, confide in, or trust them.

By contrast, RCLs believe their personal credibility is more important than their formal position of power. Credibility is what they think enables them to inspire confidence among the people they must influence to take initiative and personal risk. If people believe that RCLs know what they are talking about, RCLs can quickly move them toward change, because less explanation and interaction are needed to obtain commitment. If RCLs have credibility based on past experience and demonstrated contributions, people accept their higher standards more readily. The best change leaders show their personal credibility both in what they have accomplished and in what they know about the change task at hand (almost always demonstrating this know-how through real work). They also show credibility through their straightforwardness in dealing with people's concerns and suggestions. For Dennis Stoker of AT&T, this base of personal experience, good and bad, was essential to his ability to introduce new sales-performance-improvement processes to branches across the country.

> You need a personal resume that is credible. I had a predominance of experience in selling—in direct selling. That credibility was essential for me in communicating and making [this effort] happen.

Trustworthiness is different from credibility, but the two are certainly related. Personal trust is less a function of what change leaders know and demonstrate than it is of how they treat other people, particularly under conditions of stress, and how much they show that they really do care about what is important to others. For example, Carol O'Neill reflects that it took considerable time for her and Kevin Desmond of NYCT to establish enough of a trust base to begin to make the critical changes in which they believed so strongly. As Carol says:

> The thing that comes out of these kinds of efforts [e.g., the task force effort on bus strategy] is the basic respect and trust for us that we are not auditors and that we really care about the operation.

Charles Bennett of Mobil's MEPUS emphasizes that the effectiveness of the performance message is based on building personal trust, and that trust cannot be established in one conversation or by only talking business:

> You can't always be throwing the business side at them either. You've got to get the personal side in. I very rarely lead off a conversation by talking business. It's more like, hey, how was your week off? You have to help them see that you care about them.

But change leaders cannot expect to get that personal trust up front. They have to live it every day, and recognize that people are looking for RCLs to fail and be inconsistent.

KEEPING THE PEOPLE AND PERFORMANCE BALANCE

RCLs are ever mindful that change is about both performance and people, and that managing change requires constantly balancing the two. After having been through multiple initiatives over many years, Greg Cox of MEPUS sees this as his most basic challenge:

> Some people are really good at analyzing what is important in the business. But they're not worth a darn at working with people. You've got to create a sense of urgency about the target, and you've gotta let people feel like they're participating in this whole process as a human being at the same time.

RCLs realize that if they lose consciousness of this balance, they can easily end up erring in either of two directions. Overemphasis on the hard, demanding elements of performance can lead them to forget about *how* that performance is being gained. The resulting gains cannot be sustained, because too little attention was given to changing the skills and attitudes of people. Conversely, focusing only on the process of change and the involvement of people can easily lead to a period of temporary good feelings, followed by a time of acrimony when no performance improvement results.

Fred Smagorinsky of Sealed Air has seen the failings of both "process managers who don't have credibility because they're not achieving results" and "results managers who really don't care how they get there." Consequently, he sees himself in a continuous "balancing act between results and process—problem solving and people development." For him:

> Having that balance of seeing what you're going through, but also making sure that you're going to get the results you want is really, to me, what makes the difference. . . . The hard thing is to know when you need to shift modes . . . not that I always know, but I know it's important to know.

2. LEADERSHIP ROLES THAT COME INTO PLAY

The landscape of any major change effort will reveal dozens of different types of change leaders. Examples of some of them were given in earlier chapters. Looking across these different profiles, it is not difficult to identify patterns that might be helpful for RCLs to recognize as they work to position and further shape their own roles and careers. Beyond the broad categories of traditional manager and real change leader, a spectrum of different change positions can be identified, including front-line supervisors, senior change sponsors, change experts, staff support leaders, potential or developing change leaders, and misguided change leaders. We will describe how the more important of these impact on RCLs under three generic headings: traditional managers, executive sponsors, and change leaders.

TRADITIONAL MANAGERS

Traditional managers, sometimes referred to as "good general managers," have always been considered the bedrock of business leadership. The only problem with them was a shortage of supply. In fact, most top executives still lament the shortage of good managers at virtually every level. The term *good general manager* has become synonymous with what leadership in the past was all about—decentralizing into business units and operations or staff departments to pursue sound strategies with flawless executional consistency. The best managers have always had the ability to integrate across functions (marketing, operations, finance, etc.) to optimize profit results. Unfortunately, there now appears to be a growing abundance of not-good-enough managers in the middle ranks, who are being rapidly put out to pasture by all the restructuring, downsizing, delayering, and reengineering efforts. Large numbers of these managers in the middle are now treated as the bad guys—whether in companies with good or poor performance.

They are finding themselves vulnerable and in excess supply for two reasons: fewer are needed, and their skills and mind-sets do not fit the patterns of change. First, fewer are needed, because recent changes in management practices (like total quality and reengineering) have shifted significant responsibilities to the front line; there is simply less to be commanded and controlled. Those managers once viewed as critical controllers of people and activity are now considered unnecessary overhead. The delayering at GE Motors and increasing spans of control at Sealed Air are good illustrations of the reduction of positions once filled by traditional middle managers.

Second, their leadership approach is not well adapted to an era of rapidly changing markets in which flexibility and tapping the hidden reserve of the workforce is increasingly mandatory. Consequently, when they try to manage change efforts by using new-style approaches (like reengineering and teams), they tend to get old-style results—lower costs and fewer heads, but no net-productivity gains or changes in people's skills and attitudes. Many have not yet been able to retool for this new environment—intractable attitudes and mismatched skill sets hold them back.

Nonetheless, it is unfair and incorrect to vilify them or to assume they will disappear altogether. Much as some may wish it to be otherwise, there are still times when command-and-control management works effectively. We would all like to believe, as Mary Parker Follett and other early management theorists pointedly articulated, that people do not respond to taking orders nearly as well as they do to other motivators, that, "power over" someone offers far less potential than "power with" someone.*

On the other hand, the pragmatist in all of us knows that, despite the noble aspirations of many top leaders, command-and-control approaches are unlikely to magically disappear, simply because there are times and situations where command-and-control works. Marvin Bower, founding partner of McKinsey & Company, Inc., puts it succinctly, "The insidious thing about command-and-control is that it works!" And as more than one of our RCLs point out, ". . . and when you need it, you really need it!"

Moreover, few traditional managers today are the "command-and-control freaks" they are sometimes painted to be. They are typically intelligent, effective leaders who establish directions clearly, pick and develop the best people carefully, and make tough decisions quickly. They are organized, analytic, logical, and dispassionate; they know how to leverage their time and utilize their resources, including people. This is in marked contrast to the best RCLs, who leverage the leadership potential of their people—and thus obtain far greater amounts of personal initiative and innovation, as well as productivity.

---

* E. M. Fox and L. F. Urwick, eds., *Dynamic Administration: The Collected Papers of Mary Parker Follett* (New York: Pitman, 1973).

In almost any organization, real change leaders will have to deal with many traditional managers in the course of their change work. Traditional managers present both a challenge and an opportunity for the RCL. When they hold key positions in organizational areas in which the RCL is pursuing change, they are likely to be points of resistance. After all, the change leader questions traditional priorities, practices and measures. Change leaders also violate functional boundaries and involve people in the workforce who have traditionally been mostly "controlled." RCLs need to anticipate these points of resistance and at least try to win the grudging acceptance (if not conversion) of traditional managers.

When traditional managers are assigned to change initiatives, RCLs must consider ways to involve them constructively to avoid having them disrupt the effort. The key is to find roles that fit their existing skill sets and mind-sets. For example, traditional managers can actually be very useful in implementation phases, where effective execution of clear-cut requirements is needed. They can also manage project pieces of an overall effort with clear deliverables, like determining changes in customer buying practices. And whenever headcount reduction is the name of the game, a few old-school, command-and-control managers will always get it done. It is important to remember that they know how to run things well—they just do not know how to change things well! It is premature to bury them.

EXECUTIVE SPONSORS

Senior executive sponsors are an extremely important source of support for the RCL. They are the more senior, experienced executives who recognize the value of the RCL role, but may be unable to fill that role themselves because they are too far along in their own career, constrained by their position, or lacking in will or capability. They are, however, very good executives who have come to recognize that the organization really does need the initiative and innovation of more than "a few good men."

These leaders were sometimes the early and essential mold-breakers in strongly established cultures like those at Mobil. Paul Hoenmans and Walt Piontek filled that role in the early stages of Mobil's North American change effort. Without the willingness of these courageous executive leaders to step back, take risks on unproven people around them, and break down old communications barriers, the next generation of change leaders would have had much tougher going. RCLs can gain valuable support and sponsorship from such executives—and it is important to recognize this and to cultivate their support. The following are examples of different kinds of sponsorship and support by four strong executive leaders.

CONSISTENT SUPPORT OVER TIME

In the Champion change effort described in chapter 6, each member of the top line of business leaders became an executive sponsor supporting the development of many change leaders. Perhaps the best example is Ken Nichols, the company's vice chairman and chief financial officer. Nichols is a tall, slender, soft-spoken leader who has earned the respect of virtually every manager and change leader in the company. Despite his lack of plant operating experience in an environment in which the operators become the leaders, Nichols is renowned for his intelligence, integrity, and wisdom. He has been CFO for more than ten years, and may well have been an early change leader prior to that. In his current position, however, he has created literally dozens of real teams and working groups across the finance and accounting services departments throughout the company. These teams have earned the respect of the operating teams as a result of their consistently high service-and-cost-performance results. He understands clearly the importance of team performance, and is a model executive team player within CEO Andrew Sigler's Management Committee working-group effort.

VISIBLE SUPPORT AT CRITICAL JUNCTURES

Bruce Ranck, president and CEO of Browning-Ferris Industries (BFI), is an example of top-level executive sponsor leadership behavior at its best. Bruce came up the hard way at BFI and, as a result, has earned the respect and admiration of the executives and managers below him. As described in chapter 3, BFI is a classic decentralized company with more than 600 local business units worldwide. Many of the local district managers, as well as the division managers above them, are good managers in the best sense of that term. In large measure, the company's success has been a result of Ranck's outstanding ability to lead a highly decentralized organization by capitalizing on its growth opportunities. You will recall that the Black & Blue team's conclusions about the need for change differed from Ranck's initial expectations and argued for changes that went well beyond the decentralized philosophy that he ably personifies. In fact, the Black & Blue team was at first anxious about presenting its findings in many areas for this very reason.

They need not have worried. Bruce not only listened carefully, he pushed them further in their thinking, and encouraged and supported the new initiatives they recommended in operations as well as marketing. Most significant, according to Steve Uthoff, Ranck put the power of his position squarely behind the effort. He also removed significant obstacles that had both symbolic and change value. The most notable was the elimination of an outmoded budgeting-control system that most people considered an immovable object. He exemplifies the kind of executive change leadership at the top that enables RCLs and potential RCLs to survive and grow.

DYNAMIC SUPPORT UNDER PRESSURE

Greg Petsch at Compaq has moved so rapidly from manager to executive sponsor in his company's whirlwind change effort that he may have leapfrogged the RCL role himself. In 1991, Greg was one of three or four key general managers in the company's manufacturing operations. On October 8 of that year, he got a call to come to the CEO's conference room to talk about a layoff, which occurred a short three weeks later. Greg frankly admits to his surprise: "Never thought we would get to that point at Compaq." Almost overnight, it was a new ball game. On October 23, Rod Canion was replaced by Eckhard Pfeiffer as CEO, Petsch became his head of manufacturing, and Compaq's dramatic and continuing change was under way. Petsch describes the dimensions of that change, which are truly remarkable in a three-year time frame:

> On October 31, the manufacturing organization had 3,600 indirect employees and 3,300 direct employees—a ratio of 1.1 to 1. We built 910,000 computers at three sites. We began a process in April or May of 1992 that we called workforce rebalancing. This past year we produced roughly five million computers; we are at five sites; we work seven days a week, twenty-four-hours-a-day in all factories—and we had only 2500 indirects.

> We virtually took out three layers. A line supervisor, for example, in 1991 managed twenty people, tops. Today you see some line leaders managing a hundred people. An average is eighty.

Greg can look out of his eighth-floor window in Houston and point out the several manufacturing buildings that were built as this expansion occurred. Compaq used to operate each building as though it were in a separate city; now manufacturing is a single, integrated system. The organization laid it out over four phases, changing not only the physical facilities, and the workplace layout, but also reshaping the roles of managers into those of change leaders. The role of a front-line supervisor, for example, evolved into what Greg calls coach, as Compaq implemented what it calls high-performance work teams. Middle managers, now clearly developing into change leaders, must learn to use the disciplines of problem solving. The results have been incredible.

> Now it is all integrated. So now you start building the unit and you burn it [test it] in two hours versus ninety-six hours. It used to be that you had people trained in work technology in one building and then in another building you had people trained in assembly and tests. Now you are actually expanding your breadth to cover the whole business [in a compressed area].

It was a big adjustment for both managers and the workforce to make, but they lost very few in the process. As Greg says, "there was a strong pride in working at Compaq." He admits that the weak job market in Houston at the time probably helped keep the better workers from leaving. For whatever reasons, however, Compaq did not hire anyone until early 1994—*despite the fivefold increase in output.*

Greg's role as an executive sponsor of mid-level change leaders is clearly evident in this story. Literally dozens of managers and supervisors were redirected to lead teams and integrate processes. The workforce was reconfigured into teams, single-leader units, and integrated action flows. In fact, these units are not only highly productive, they are motivated to continue to reduce the number of people required to deliver the results. As Greg points out, because of their very attractive profit sharing:

> They all receive bonuses not graduated by grade or salary; their work groups realize that the common denominator is headcount. They start to think about how they can do things differently on the floor versus adding more headcount. They realize that fewer is more in their pocket. This kind of change is clearly to their advantage.

Petsch has the mind-set of an executive sponsor and leader of change. He questions everything and everybody. He always wants to know why—and why again. He keeps relentless track of productivity results, and is expanding his organization's ability to track customer reaction. He believes in his people, and knows that he must have RCLs in all parts of his expanding organization who can extract extra initiative and performance from people in any way they can—be it through teams, work groups, or fundamental process redesign. Real change leaders flourish under his sponsorship.

THE KINDLY HIGH SCHOOL PRINCIPAL

Lou Golm at AT&T has been described in a recent business magazine as having the demeanor of "a kindly high school principal," but he made things happen in his executive sponsor role for the Change Management Organization described in chapter 2. Mary Livingston provides a useful illustration of the specific things Lou did that made the difference for the CMO:

- Created a full-time change team (the CMO) by pulling top-performing people out of the line sales organization;

- Protected the change program from recurring rounds of budget cuts;

- Protected individual team members from mandated workforce reductions;

- Protected the change initiatives in times of pressure for the sales force to deliver short-term results; and

- Kept the change initiatives from getting tangled up in "quick-fix" programs which were also under way at the time.

It's these kinds of specifics that make executive sponsors critical for RCL efforts over time. We see four distinguishing characteristics of these executives that set them apart from their peers and counterparts:

1. A stronger and earlier sensing of the need for a broad base of real change leaders and workforce initiative-taking down the line;

2. The willingness to really listen, question the established way, and motivate less experienced, lower-level people to step up;

3. The courage to shield their people from the system; and

4. The power to clear the way by removing obstacles and barriers for potential RCLs below them.

Real change leaders can both encourage and capitalize on the transitional change managers with whom and for whom they have the opportunity to work. These managers are invaluable allies to RCLs in the quest for change.

In the foregoing examples, the change efforts that executive change leaders like Nichols, Ranck, Petsch and Golm led and enabled were greatly advantaged by their personal leadership. Even more important, perhaps, it is because of their efforts and initiative that so many RCLs are now emerging in their respective change efforts. As BFI's Todd Strong testifies, "I had the weight of Bill [Ruckelshaus] and Bruce [Ranck] fully behind me from the start of the Black & Blue team's work," without which Todd believes he could not have successfully influenced the local district managers to launch the new breakthrough process that drives the operational change effort at BFI.

POTENTIAL CHANGE LEADERS AND RCLS

Not all potential change leaders make it to RCL levels, but they have a better chance than most traditional managers. The difference between good managers and potential change leaders lies mainly in their intent and trajectory. Not all of them will become RCLs, unfortunately, either because they fail to develop the range of skills required or because they are not given enough opportunity. Many potential RCLs have cut their old general-management umbilical cords and are embarked on a life of their own in acquiring the change skills described earlier. However, they have yet to develop either the discipline or the advanced skill sets required to function as RCLs.

Todd Strong of BFI is one good example, because he is a battlefield convert who went from good manager to change leader under fire, somewhere between the Black & Blue team and BLUEprint change efforts.

Todd is an excellent general manager in his own right, who has gained new change skills and perspectives. He was one of the select crew initially picked by Ranck for the Black & Blue team effort. Like most top executives, Bruce is an excellent judge of people. As an executive change sponsor, he also knew that the Black & Blue team would need buy-in and support down the line. Obviously, change leaders like Todd could make a big difference in the credibility of the entire effort.

While Todd remembers a little skepticism from a lot of district managers during the Black & Blue team's diagnostic work, he remembers more skepticism in getting some of the recommendations implemented. It took courage, trial and error, the strength of past relations, and lots of frank back-and-forth communication to convince hardened managers to do their day-to-day job differently. Getting people to change when they do not report to you requires more than a new skill set—it also requires a different mind-set, plus a great deal of sensitivity and patience. Most RCLs on special assignment have to master that capability, while it is less necessary for line executives and managers.

Terry Atwater of GE Motors illustrates a different kind of potential RCL; he was almost born one. When first introduced to us, Terry said, "My career goal is to master change in a global context." In fact, on his formal employment record he lists his career objective as "to lead and implement change in a global and dynamic environment." Terry is not an Ivy League MBA. He graduated from Western Michigan University, went on to GE's manufacturing management program, and started work at GE's Astro Space Satellite Division as a sourcing specialist. He lists his accomplishments there in terms of concrete changes in cycle time, scrap reduction, and increased use of small, disadvantaged businesses by the division. From there, he served a tour with GE's Electrical Distribution and Control Division in Puerto Rico, before joining the GE Motors effort in Fort Wayne, Indiana.

In each of his job assignments to date, Terry firmly believes he was adding critical building blocks to his leadership skills that would help make him a change master in a global environment. Terry looks and sounds like what we suspect many emerging RCLs will be like in the future—dedicated to building superior change leadership skills. He sees each assignment as an essential building block toward the ultimate skill set and leadership approach that will qualify him as a superior RCL.

Terry's outlook on change and change management was instilled by his parents as he grew up in Waukegan, Illinois. His father is an entrepreneur who owns both a machining and a distribution company.

Through his father's work, Terry got a firsthand view of the ups, downs, and changes of business as he grew up. His mother is a registered nurse, who often "put in the long hours that kept the family going." From them he learned that "if you're going to continue to grow you're going to have to change . . . times change and you have to change with them." Terry sums up his philosophy of life with an acronym—AAA:

- Attitude—to achieve you have to have the right attitude and apply yourself to the situation.

- Aptitude—you have to have knowledge on the subject; if you don't have it, beat the learning curve and get it.

- Action—execution is the only thing that makes all this stuff work.

The words are his own, but the thoughts come directly from his parents.

Terry also believes that his attitude about change is very typical across the new breed of change leaders that he knows. "It used to be that maybe 45 percent of the people with leadership potential in situations similar to mine were in a change mind-set; now it is closer to 95 percent. Those who like what they do around here are invariably change-oriented and are developing significant change skills." Terry also comments on the importance of this mind-set in new recruits. "When I joined the company, the focus was mostly on leadership potential, broadly defined. Now we place a very high emphasis on people's ability to adapt to and initiate change; team orientation is also a major factor." Since Terry is on the GE Motors recruiting team, he speaks from firsthand knowledge.

Terry's chosen role on a special team exploring outsourcing opportunities, was consistent with the fact that he was its most junior member. "I put myself in a grunt position," he says, explaining that he felt this was the best way to both enable the effort to succeed and to expand his own skills and credibility across the organization. He is now functioning as the leader of a single-leader group, and he anticipates that his next assignment will give him a chance to function in a shared-team-leader role in a real-team situation. He already recognizes that he needs to acquire both sets of leadership skills if he is to attain his full potential within GE Motors specifically, and within General Electric more broadly.

Terry is not atypical, nor is he simply using the latest buzzwords on change. He firmly believes that the world of change—be it continuous or episodic—is here to stay. He also recognizes that the skills required are not simply the natural by-products of good management practices. He therefore intends to pursue a set of career assignments that will enable him to learn the basic and advanced skill sets, how to apply them in different combinations depending on the change situation at hand, and how to upgrade his skills in these areas over time. He realizes he has to learn these skills on the job.

Whether they are good-manager battlefield converts, or people who emerge from the workforce ranks, potential RCLs evidence these same five characteristics:

1. Strong experience and know-how regarding action flows and customers;

2. Close, peer-like relations with front-line supervisors and workers;

3. Instincts to do more than step back and let it happen;

4. Determination to find a combination that works;

5. Undisciplined use of a limited and not yet fully developed set of tools and approaches (RCLs access a wide range of options and apply them rigorously, e.g., using multiple leadership approaches—teams and single-leader groups—as appropriate).

They have nonetheless mentally cut the cord that binds them to any past constraints and are determined to move up the RCL capability ladder. It is important for potential RCLs to be honest in assessing their skills and experience gaps. Unless they recognize their shortfalls as well as their strengths, they cannot expect to achieve full RCL potential.

EXPERT CHANGE AGENTS AND SPECIALISTS

It is very important for RCLs to know about change experts and other specialists, simply because they are ever present in change today. Virtually every change effort of significance draws upon high-powered change experts or specialists of some kind, either internal or external. These include a wide range of people, from top management change gurus like Rom Charam and Noel Tichy, top management firms like Bain, Booz-Allen, The Boston Consulting Group, and McKinsey, all major accounting firms, and specialized process consultants of all kinds. This group can also include top individual functional experts or turnaround specialists—hired guns, so to speak. We recognize, since we are consultants, that our comments on this topic are suspect—but external change specialists, such as consultants, are nonetheless an important part of the RCL story because internal change leaders inevitably have to work with them. For the most part, however, the best RCLs are discriminating users of change specialists, be they internal or external, firms or individuals.

Change leaders need to develop the ability to evaluate, select, and integrate specialized expertise into their efforts. Unfortunately, extreme positions or policies on the use of outside expertise by top management can subvert the RCL's discrimination. Many stalled change efforts have been the result of overuse and over-reliance on consulting that actually prevented or diverted potential RCLs from building critical change momentum. In other cases, a top management philosophy of "no consultants" has handicapped change leaders from getting catalytic support in key areas. While the Texas Commerce Bank is justifiably proud of its own accomplishments, it had the benefit of ex-consultant and reengineering expert Anita Ward, and her staff of experienced internal consultants, to help fill the gap.

The secret that RCLs have discovered, however, is that there are ways in which change expertise can catalyze their own efforts, and there are ways in which it becomes a crutch or an inhibitor. When top management involves RCLs in a way that permits them to discriminate, the likelihood of a good combination is higher. In deciding when and where outside change expertise is appropriate, the following characteristics of change specialists are important to keep in mind:

1. Unique ability to apply strong, special expertise and know-how in high-leverage areas; they are professional trouble-shooters. Superior expertise leads to better judgment calls with minimal analyses.

2. Superior experience on the special issues that permits them to provide high value quickly in appropriate situations in different company settings.

3. Fees and *costs* can be excessive unless they are used where the trade-off benefits are clearly favorable to the company.

4. Different specialists offer widely varying "tailored approaches" which may or may not include taking time for teams, skills, etc. It is critical to make sure their approach fits the need.

5. Provide an objective point of view and raise the tough questions that more closely involved people may avoid or overlook. However, they can also be subject to their own prejudices and set approaches or become aligned with factions within the organization that erode their credibility.

In short, they offer advantages and disadvantages. Discriminating use of change specialists can often make the difference between getting the unique skills that RCLs need and getting mired down in unnecessary process complications or getting undermined in terms of internal ownership and development. RCLs must stay alert to make the right choices. Mary Livingston's (AT&T) experienced observation is on point:

> Working with consultants was a new experience for all of my teams. We had a rocky start, probably because we looked at consultants just as a supplier and didn't own our work. After a few "woodshed" meetings and "shared expectations" sessions, we ultimately leveraged what both groups brought to the table in a formidable team effort. . . . So the lesson is, know your consultants if you are going to be part of a team; be clear on what you are working toward; and start figuring out how you are going to work together.

Misguided Change Leaders

Al Bandino of Finser, a financial services company in North America,* thinks of himself as a change leader. He believes strongly in worker empowerment. Change to him is all about getting people at lower levels involved so they can express their feelings, communicate with one another, generate ideas, and become committed to the company's change vision. He also believes that reengineering is the road to empowerment. He led a reengineering effort to rethink a set of core processes at Finser, and, while the effort was going on, sales dropped 30 percent—in large part because of the redesign diversion. Throughout this catastrophe, Al continued to argue for having faith that the redesign would pay off. He increased levels of investment in staff and technology, virtually lost the ability to speak in plain English rather than empowerment and reengi-

---

* Fictitious name and company.

neering-ese, and put a heavy stress on training and brown-paper-on-the-wall, process-mapping approaches. Before he was through the effort produced more than five hundred pages of useless documentation. Al is no longer at Finser.

He blames his fate mostly on top management, who he says do not really understand how important people are, and are not really committed to the principles of reengineering. Al says, "The relentless hierarchy at Finser kills initiative, and causes people to become complacent, nine-to-five workers." Al is a badly misguided change leader.

Dick Washburn is a misguided change leader at Brookington Transportation in California.* As one of the leaders of the company's quality effort, Dick became known as a process staff guy who was primarily concerned with whether the company went with the quality philosophy and programs as prescribed by his favorite quality expert. He insisted on training all 15,000 employees before any performance-improvement efforts were launched, and the first quality teams were focused on noncritical tasks like the redesign of the employee-break rooms. As the effort began to flounder, he insisted on management testimonials to quality—and then berated management for handling real business problems without using true quality tools. And, of course, he was a master of tracking activities like meeting times, attendance, and numbers of participants.

Misguided change leaders like Al and Dick are all too common in mired-down change efforts. They do not really bring it all on themselves, however. Their mind-sets and managerial approaches can almost always be traced to a set of reasonably valid ideas and theories that they have learned from others, and that they somehow misunderstand and misapply. Misguided change leaders are characterized by four common and easily identifiable attributes and characteristics:

1. An unrealistic view that change—in and of itself—constitutes high performance. "Change is all around us, and we must all change to survive."

2. High involvement activities that detract from real work and performance results. Feelings and interactions displace facts and results; accountabilities are obscured.

---

* Fictitious name and company.

3. Adherence to a personal-favorite leadership approach, and use of off-the-shelf approaches that emphasize technique over real understanding and involvement.

4. Excessive dependence on guidance from the top, by both expecting more from, and blaming more on, top management.

It is not easy to correct or even neutralize the behavior of misguided change leaders. When confronted directly they will react negatively, often becoming naysayers if the RCL efforts do not support their version of what is required. If left unchecked, they can consume critical time and resources in activities that have little or no performance impact. Over any extended time period, their approach creates disillusionment, because it sets unrealistic expectations that can discolor the entire change effort. Real change leaders attempt to correct this problem before too much damage is done. Of several possible antidotes, three deserve special mention:

■ **Get misguided change leaders involved in real work** with people who have a more pragmatic perspective on what the change requires. It is much easier to create working situations where they can discover the difference themselves than it is trying to influence them with rhetoric and logic.

■ **Find ways to steep them in marketplace realities** by direct exposure to what competitors are doing and how customers are reacting. Experiencing these realities firsthand is always better than hearing about them secondhand. Unstructured customer visits are usually easy to arrange, and they can be very effective eye-openers for people who have lost touch with how the customer really feels about products, services and competitors. Make sure they also understand the fundamental economics of your business; this may open their eyes to why some things matter more than others.

■ **Expose them to real change leaders in other settings.** Seeing how others do it differently can be very convincing. They will see how RCLs define and measure real performance improvement, use a variety of tools and approaches depending on the situation at hand, and work effectively with top management in providing the necessary direction and leadership for real change.

3. HOW AND WHY TO BECOME A SUPERIOR RCL

The road to becoming a real change leader is much easier to describe than it is to travel. Not only are there many forks in the road, but everyone's idea of the destination is somewhat different. Most of the people we interviewed already think of themselves as the RCLs that we describe. Nonetheless, all are intent on adding and honing skills that will make them better. Certainly, this is the right mind-set.

Becoming a superior change leader implies a discipline and level of commitment that is unrelenting. In almost every company we visited, the stories of RCLs are accompanied by stories of difficult personal sacrifices. Not everyone is prepared to make those trade-offs. As a matter of fact, most people do not actually decide to become change leaders, as Terry Atwater at GE Motors has; the decision usually just happens as a result of personal predispositions and pivotal career events beyond the person's control. A few examples of such decisions are given in this section. For those good managers and potential RCLs who would like to improve their odds of acquiring real-change-leader skills, this section also suggests some traditional management assumptions to discard. Finally, because the world of large, complex institutions needs more change leaders, it is worthwhile to recap the rewards of being an RCL.

PREDISPOSITIONS AND PIVOTAL EVENTS

In talking with RCLs, their natural predispositions and preference for the work they do comes through. For example, Greg Cox of the Mobil MEPUS $300 million effort to become "the one others copy" is well known for his long-standing dissatisfaction with the status quo. He is never unconstructive or belligerent about his concerns, but he is certainly not bashful either. As he explains:

> I'm never satisfied with things the way they are. I always want to change them. I know there's a better way; I just enjoy the battle, I suppose. I guess I tend to always kinda fall into, or get picked for, or end up doing this kind of stuff.

Charles Bennett, from the same change effort at Mobil, probably metamorphosed into a change leader as a result of his unabashed love of working with people. Charles says, plain and simple, "This is what I love to do. I was doing it anyway."

Yet, even when individuals are naturally inclined toward change leadership, fate plays an important role in the making of an RCL. Often without realizing it, they find themselves facing an obstacle or opportunity that constitutes a pivotal event in their career. These events shape their basic convictions and develop the skills and perspectives required of RCLs.

Mike Vaccaro (chapter 3) worked at all aspects of process design for twenty years at Prudential. Yet, not until he was tapped to head a major reengineering project did he begin to see his work as more than a paper exercise. It was when he found himself on center stage arguing for radical changes before his unit's president that he made the transition to RCL. For George Devlin (Introduction), head of Compaq's manufacturing operations in Scotland, there were two such events. The first came early in his career when he had to close a Digital Equipment plant and swore to himself that he would never get into that kind of situation again. The second came when Compaq woke up to the threat of low-price competitors and he discarded conventional practices to reduce his plant's manufacturing costs by 66 percent, this time without a layoff.

Such events can be near religious experiences that shape entire careers. Many years ago Dick Krause, now Manager of Fort Wayne Operations for GE Motors, arrived at a plant in Maine where the workforce was known for drinking on the job to stay warm through the bitter cold winters and where the manager in charge would fire people in staff meetings for giving the wrong answer. He soon realized a previous scheduling foul-up had left his unit with only half the time needed to build a million-dollar piece of nuclear power plant equipment. So he turned directly to the unionized workforce and admitted he didn't know how to make the equipment, let alone make it in half the time. After their initial disbelief at being asked rather than told what to do, they started working with him. Dick had them sit in on production planning meetings and show all the ways they could save time by changing the usual fabrication sequence. Almost miraculously the job was finished on schedule. To this day Krause remembers the morning the train pulled the finished piece out of the shop.

> We had sixty guys screaming their heads off because they had done something nobody thought they could do. That was an

emotional experience for me I can never forget. It was like a born-again Christian experience. It just completely changes the way you think.

Not every RCL has this dramatic an event to convince them that everybody has more to contribute than most managers typically give them credit for. And few RCLs go all the way back to 1970 to recall such events. They do, however, attest to the value of similar baptisms of fire in reshaping their leadership approach. The transforming effect of such trials is similar to that experienced by high performing teams. The research behind *The Wisdom of Teams* suggests that these remarkable units (which outperform like units by several times) are very rare and do not occur on purpose. Instead, fate favors them in a counter-intuitive way—by putting an insurmountable obstacle in their path that would destroy most other teams. The commitment required to surmount the obstacle is what produces the high performance capability. All high performance teams sight such pivotal events in relating their formation. Dig into the background of almost any RCL and you will find stories of similar formative experiences.

ASSUMPTIONS TO DISCARD

Our work uncovered a number of wrong assumptions about what mid-level change leaders do and do not do. The more limiting ones, unfortunately, stem from traditional patterns of good management practice that have become firmly established and are, therefore, hard to abandon. Nonetheless, the following five assumptions will seriously hinder any prospective change leader's ability to become a superior RCL in almost any kind of major change situation.

1. **"A few good men" can determine what is best for all.** Instead, while RCLs recognize the value of a close group of strong colleagues and teammates, they also see the purpose of that team as developing the leadership potential of a larger number of people at all levels and in all functions. The only group excluded from this purpose are those who underperform through lack of effort and commitment.

2. **Climb up in the hierarchy for reward and security.** RCLs are focused on making a difference, and developing their leadership

skills. They do not measure these aspirations in terms of hierarchical levels, faster promotions, or even higher compensation. They are building resumes that will be respected and valued by any organization that faces major, recurring change—and they have the confidence and courage to move when their current organization does not recognize the value of their skills.

3. Leverage your time by delegating and directing other people to increase your achievements. RCLs see efficiency of time utilization very differently. They invest their time, whatever it takes, in groups or one-on-one encounters, to develop the performance levels and leadership capacities of others. Meeting with six different people in the course of an hour to tell them what to do is not their idea of efficiency or effectiveness.

4. Make all the critical decisions yourself if you want things done right. The best RCLs make relatively few decisions themselves. They are not reluctant to trust others with important decisions. In fact, they have cultivated a strong base of decision makers around them, and they decide themselves only when no one else is in a position to do so. They do not, however, avoid the tough decisions.

5. Avoid mistakes and failures if at all possible, if you want career success. RCLs expect to make mistakes and to fail along the way to their ultimate performance aspirations. They learn more from mistakes than their counterparts do, and they are not discouraged by interim or temporary failures. They even survive and grow through major failures. They do not define career success as the absence of failure! They know that failure can be just as rewarding as success—it only takes a bit longer for the benefits to materialize.

WHY DO IT?

The reasons for working hard to acquire the skills and experience required to become an RCL seem obvious to those who are well into the journey. Not surprisingly, a primary reason is simply the satisfaction of helping other people grow. Fred Smagorinsky of Sealed Air sums it up this way:

> The most successful [change leaders] in this kind of an environment have a combination of being very driven, very results-

oriented. But they also get a huge personal charge out of seeing people develop and achieve.

To conclude this chapter, we simply share four other reasons that RCLs have given as to why they believe the road to becoming a real change leader is well worth the journey. Some are self-serving, some noble, and some very pragmatic. All in all, they add up to a compelling argument.

1. **Unique opportunity to learn and grow.**

   I saw it as a great opportunity for me to learn. I'm very uncomfortable if I'm doing the same thing. I've never done one job in the same place for more than a year and a half to two years. I need that. I get charged up with more learning. If I'm not learning, you won't see me smiling. (Charles Bennett/MEPUS)

2. **Importance and meaningfulness of the work.**

   From a standpoint of personal reward, it has made my life and job a lot more vital, interesting, and important . . . this stuff has a certain appeal and intrinsic value. Doing this has elevated what I do to a different plane. It makes this position a little more noble than peddling long distance. (Ray Butkus/AT&T–Middle Markets)

3. **Fun of working with good, dedicated people.**

   You can work just as hard in other kinds of jobs and not feel like you had the same impact. It is very tiring and very frustrating, and beating your head against the wall isn't all that much fun. On the other hand, the fact that there are people out there to work with that are trying to do the same thing— they keep you going and make it fun. (Mary Livingston/ AT&T–CMO)

4. **A chance to reenlist.**

   The change effort of AT&T–Business Communications Services sales force had two major phases. At the end of the first phase, Mary Livingston gave everyone in her organization the chance to either quit or reenlist, with no hard feelings or repercussions either way. She asked everyone to send her a letter or E-Mail saying how they felt, what they wanted to do, and why. In their candid responses, people weighed the positives and negatives and shared their personal feelings about the work they were doing. Mary says most of them enthusiastically reenlisted. Their reasons for reenlisting speak to both their personal values and their convictions.

WHY CHANGE LEADERS DO IT

■ *I have a missionary's need to see some of our work really take hold—that's the ultimate pay dirt for me.*

■ *Although our work is often extremely challenging, I truly love being here, and believe that together we can do great things for the company.*

■ *The time I have spent with CMO has been the toughest, most challenging, and most rewarding time of my career.*

■ *I am fully committed and very excited about having the opportunity to work on a team of energized individuals who are focused on making a difference.*

■ *My personal commitment to the team has increased with time: the more I know them, the more I commit. They give me reasons to trust.*

■ *The prospect that our collective effort could have a profound effect on the future of AT&T is both challenging and exciting, and I look forward to being a part of it.*

■ *I want a job to look forward to in the morning and not want to leave in the evening.*

■ *I believe in what we are doing, knowing in my gut and heart that the future of our business will, in a very real sense, be fashioned by the fruits of our labor.*

CHAPTER 9

NEW BREED

THE NO-EXCUSES MIND-SET

NOT THAT LONG AGO IN THE WEST, THERE WERE TWO WIDELY PRACTICED WAYS to break a wild horse for riding and ranch work: rodeo style and ranch style. In rodeo style, one cowboy would bite down on the ear of the animal while a second cowboy would saddle and mount it. When the ear was released, the horse bucked until either it was subdued, or it threw its rider unceremoniously into the dirt. The entire process took less than fifteen minutes and resulted in a snorting, stubborn animal. In marked contrast, ranch style required several days, because a serious effort was made to gentle the horse before riding it. The animal was first corralled and broken to post-tie, halter lead, and saddle-blanket lead before any attempt to ride. Both styles worked, but the ranch style usually resulted in a more responsive, trainable, and useful animal. Many who grew up in and around the Big Horn Mountains in the mid-1900s developed the skills for either style and became professional horse wranglers and rodeo riders.

In recent years, a hybrid style has emerged in which an experienced trainer quiets and breaks a horse to ride in a day or two—usually without ear biting, wild resistance, or bucking. It is a clearly superior approach for large ranches, but one which most traditional horse wranglers do not apply. Consequently, a new breed of horse wrangler is taking over, and, as a result, a great many traditional wranglers are out of work these days. While some could probably master the new approach, their basic habits and mind-sets preclude them from making the effort. Instead, they sit

311

around the feed stores and pool halls lamenting the good old days of real cowboys.

This is analogous to what seems to be occurring in many middle management situations. While there have certainly been more than just two styles of management in the past, most mid-level managers seem to fall into one of two management camps, which can be roughly categorized as *budget beaters* and *participative managers.* Budget beaters are command-and-control managers who set and make tight annual budgets no matter what. Over time, the problems the budget beaters encounter include not getting the better people to work for them, not extracting initiative and innovative ideas from their people, and not delivering more than cost-reduction results.

Participative managers are at the other extreme. Their problem is not being tough enough. Their people like them, and feel good about being involved, but they take a long time to generate improved results. Sometimes, in fact, business performance erodes because of their lack of discipline in making the numbers. Participative managers also seem unable to make difficult people-decisions and have a tendency to focus on the feelings and interests of their people at the expense of what is in the best interests of the customers and shareholders of the company.

Despite these problems and failings, some middle managers in both categories have been able to rise to senior management positions, usually developing some elements of the other management style along the way. However, far too many of these middle managers are now finding themselves plateaued and in excess, often because they still rely too much on one style, or become confused trying to find a compromise solution between the two extremes.

As in horse wrangling, a new breed in management is emerging. These are the change leaders who not only have developed the skills discussed in the previous chapter, but who have also developed a balance and flexibility in terms of how they apply these skills to particular performance situations. They are learning, usually through change experiences, how to recognize different performance needs, and how to vary and customize their styles and skill sets to fit different needs. If tight control and consistency over time are required, they function in traditional management modes; if change and innovation are required, they function as real change leaders. In short, they are becoming very adept at matching their leadership styles and skill balances to the situation at hand. Few of these managers will be referred to as "a great cost-cutter" or "a good people-guy."

Instead they are identified as *the people to handle the really tough and impor-tant change assignments, whatever they are.*

The best RCLs develop a unique combination of skills, values, attributes, and attitudes for a wide variety of change and performance sit-uations. They are able to meet increasingly demanding standards for bet-ter and better performance results. But they do it by capitalizing on the hidden potential of their people, and without sacrificing the longer-term quality and service requirements in their markets. They also demonstrate an unusual ability to apply different leadership approaches—single-leader and team—when and as the circumstances require it. They have learned how to obtain better people-results as well as better performance-results. Last but not least, they seem to be motivated more by making a difference than by climbing up through the hierarchy.

When these new-breed change leaders rise to meet more demanding change challenges, they face a never ending task of maintaining the opti-mum balance between faster and better results, and more mass and momentum of people. As this flexible new breed emerges, the old-style, unidimensional middle managers will increasingly end up like the bitter cowboys of the past. Paradoxically, except for their attitudes and mind-sets, many could master the skills and develop the flexibility and agility of the change leaders who are beginning to replace them. To some extent, this may be because they are not given the right guidance and opportunity to develop by those above them. Unfortunately, however, this places a big-ger burden on their own initiative to learn new skills and adapt.

Our final chapter is intended to be a positive wake-up call for mid-dle managers and potential change leaders alike. The time is right for them to strengthen their balance of skills relative to the situations they face, and to develop attitudes that will enable them to exploit the new-breed poten-tial. This aspiration can lead potential change leaders to higher levels of personal impact and satisfaction, no matter how their future career paths unfold. It is not surprising that RCLs demonstrate the same pragmatism with respect to their own careers as they do with the business situations they face—they are more concerned about making a difference than climbing the ladder. The remainder of this chapter summarizes what lies ahead for RCLs in two sections:

1. **Adapting to the situation: "vary the balance."**

2. **Looking to the future: "make a difference."**

1. ADAPT BY "VARYING THE BALANCE"

Different change and performance circumstances call for different combinations of managers and change leaders; both are essential for successful change. Each individual change assignment also calls for a different mix of skills and leadership approaches, even within the same institution. One size will not fit all, and an individual who tries to roll out what worked in previous situations will soon end up like the forgotten cowboys. The right balance is particularly significant to RCLs, not only because of the need to adapt their own approaches, but also because they need to work with different combinations of managers to get the job done. Even something as fundamental as the relative importance of the RCL role, versus the support and counterbalancing roles of other managers, is determined by the specifics of the situation. Understanding situational differences, therefore, can help RCLs determine both the extent of their opportunities and where and how best to integrate their roles with those of others. It also helps in determining the relative importance of particular change skills, as well as the leadership style most likely to be effective.

Four broad categories of change situations, while by no means all-encompassing or comprehensive, illustrate how the specifics of the change situation affect the relative importance and mix of RCL skills, roles, and styles. The key is to become oriented quickly, and then find the right balance. The four categories are:

1. Mature, established institutions trying to augment or accelerate growth—most major oil companies (Mobil and Shell), large financial-service companies (State Farm), and mature manufacturing companies (Ford).

2. Strongly positioned businesses seeking transformational change—Texas Commerce Bank, Kodak, and Burlington Northern Santa Fe Corporation.

3. High-growth businesses facing rapid change—Compaq, Enron, and Microsoft.

4. High-performance organizations seeking continuous growth and improvement—General Electric, Levi Strauss, and Hewlett-Packard.

MATURE INSTITUTIONS AUGMENTING GROWTH

Despite the prevalence of change, there are many large and successful institutions that are not attempting major change. Some, like The State Farm Insurance Company or Southwestern Bell Corporation, are performing well and can rely on their fundamental values and traditional management philosophy to sustain that performance; they do not appear to require or warrant the risk of disruption implicit in more fundamental change aspirations. Others, unfortunately, appear to have waited too long, and to have essentially over-relied on their traditional good general managers to maintain forward progress (well-publicized past shortfalls include those of General Motors, Westinghouse, and IBM). A critical oversight in these situations would seem to have been not realizing the value of obtaining a critical mass of RCLs early enough to stay apace in their changing markets.

In such situations, what are often touted as major change programs in fact are not. Instead, the programs are mainly dependent on accelerating the efforts of traditional managers. The few mid-level change leaders in such situations, therefore, find themselves constantly struggling to create a higher sense of urgency for change. The inertia of business-as-usual creates difficult barriers. The answer is for senior management to visibly commit to building a stronger sense of urgency for change. In this case, one of the top RCL priorities must be that of trying, directly and indirectly, to influence top management to provide this catalyst. A brief reprise from previous chapters summarizes how RCLs can best exercise this kind of influence:

1. **Bring the marketplace realities more clearly into focus.** RCLs find ways to convey to top management a more direct picture of how customers and competitors are reacting. They try to clarify senior management's view of the world by providing better internal feedback as well as more accurate and compelling external perspectives. As change leaders at GE Motors in chapter 1 emphasized, you cannot deny the reality of the marketplace, no matter how wrong you think the customer or your competition may turn out to be.

2. **Experiment with ways of getting front-line views more clearly recognized at the top.** RCLs have a unique perspective for translating what front-line people really feel—it is a perspective that top management both values and needs, but may not always appreciate.

RCLs must find ways to hear, filter, synthesize, and present the essentials to senior management. The focus groups with employees at Texas Commerce Bank (chapter 4) is an example of this kind of feedback at work.

3. Access the experience and perspective of outside experts whose credibility is respected at the top. Many companies are currently redesigning the role and composition of their boards to help provide this perspective. In addition, academics, peers in other companies, and even consultants should be considered. Internal change leaders can sometimes be helpful in enabling credible outside sources to interact with senior management on crucial topics. The reengineering of back-office systems at Enron was a case of change leaders and outside parties working jointly to reinforce the urgency of change.

4. Collaborate with other change leaders in demonstrating the need for change. RCLs combine the results, ideas, and findings from multiple smaller efforts to provide a more complete picture of the situation. Several RCLs working together in integrating their ideas and approaches usually will be more powerful than any individual efforts to swing senior management away from the comfort of conservatism. The initial work on redesigning the policy change process at Prudential by Mike Vaccaro and Mike Pleskow (chapter 5) is a good example of combining forces—an effort that led senior manager Don Southwell to expand Vaccaro's initial action-flow effort across a much broader base.

Sometimes the only practical course for an RCL in these situations is that of waiting and watching for signs that top management's perspective is beginning to shift. Striking out in quixotic fashion without the required urgency seldom leads to favorable results—either for the company or for the change leader. The harsh reality is that no matter how hard or what RCLs try, they may not always experience results similar to those of Steve Uthoff at Browning-Ferris Industries or Carol O'Neill at NYCT in influencing the view at the top. In such cases, it is easy for change leaders to lose faith and either leave or drop back into a more traditional manager mode. This is potentially counterproductive, for change leaders will not be ready when the time becomes right, and an important opportunity might be lost. The process of bringing senior management along can be time consuming, and it is important for prospective change leaders to maintain a high degree of patience as they wait for the right moment to push forward as RCLs.

TRANSFORMATIONAL CHANGE SITUATIONS

An increasing number of public and private institutions today claim to be facing transformational change—aimed at changing the behaviors and skills of large numbers of people. These situations are often distinguished by a feeling of instability, especially with respect to change leadership. Consultants and task forces often fill the roles of change specialists, and the key is for internal change leaders to develop RCL capabilities that enable them to gradually take over the key change-agent responsibilities. Sooner or later, successful major change becomes an internally driven effort in which the primary change-agent roles of front-line communications and motivation are filled by internal change leaders as opposed to outsiders or temporary task forces. To that end, change leaders need to learn how to utilize such outside experts and special task forces as catalysts and special resources, without becoming dependent on them. The secret is for RCLs to work concurrently with special resources, while also beginning to fit into and fill pivotal leadership roles within the permanent organization.

While there remains a continuing overall need across these kinds of companies for good general managers, there is also a growing need for change leader skills and styles to augment the efforts of traditional managers. These situations usually offer RCLs their best opportunities to make a real difference in institutional performance and change. It is here that development and recognition of the need for RCL leadership takes place most rapidly. Not surprisingly, this is also where opportunities for personal growth and impact are highest.

HIGH-GROWTH, RAPID-CHANGE SITUATIONS

High-growth, rapid-change situations mean attractive job opportunities. That is why companies in these situations can often attract the better people at all levels. Companies like Compaq, Enron, and Microsoft are front-page news as they scurry to stay on top of exploding demand opportunities, while aggressively countering rapidly changing competitive environments. Successful companies in these situations have to undergo almost constant change to maintain their competitive positions. As a result, companies such as Wang Computer and IBM have paid huge prices for maintaining the status quo for too long. While companies in rapid-change situations can provide an exciting environment, they do not afford much time for potential change leaders to develop and broaden their skills or to experiment with different leadership styles.

At the top of these companies are some of the strongest general-manager leaders. A few RCLs are beginning to appear, but for the most part, leadership remains a top-down game played by uniquely talented individuals operating in the strong, single-leader mold. Because of the pace and urgency of their situations, these leaders often rely on internal and external change specialists, whose experience and judgment can quickly leverage change in the right directions.

The pace and intensity of these situations force a de-emphasis on mobilizing and energizing lots of people. Time does not permit it. This is in stark contrast to other situations in which long-term, continuous improvement, rather than near-term agility and flexibility, can be key to survival. Those who have the strategic acuity and vision to deliver against very high expectations will advance; those who do not will be quickly replaced. Here, it is the excitement of the growth, rather than the evolution to high performance, that motivates. A few RCLs somehow emerge— as they always seem to do—but for the most part, change is dependent on senior management and highly motivated individuals, operating mostly in single-leader groups to produce the right moves in the right time frame.

Obviously, high-growth situations attract some of the most talented top leaders. They attract mid-level change leaders as well. As a result, it is highly likely that companies in these situations will not only anticipate changing leadership requirements—but will readily discover the potential value of real change leaders. In the heat of their current battles, they may have little time to help potential change leaders build new skills, or to shape developmental roles for them. They simply hire them as they need them. But as their battles subside, they are likely to start developing more of their own. In the short term, they may have the luxury of filling change leader voids with outside change experts and specialists. Over time, they will want their own cadre of RCLs.

By definition, high-growth situations are relatively short lived. As a result, the imbalance in a company's current leadership approach becomes more of a problem over time. At some point as the business matures, organizational and institutional infrastructure can become as important to sustained success as natural marketplace momentum. The better institutions will recognize this and begin to develop the skills to manage in a less growth-fueled, chaotic environment. It stands to reason that these companies will begin to need a more balanced cadre of change leaders, even before the growth/rapid-change era is finished. It also stands to reason that RCLs who are already operating in rapid-growth situations will find ways to quicken bottom-up-involvement processes, thereby obtaining more of the benefits of an energized workforce faster. Their natural focus on the marketplace will help them respond to the inevitable move to a less dynamic environment, and they will continuously push back on senior management to understand and find the right balance between short-term, market-based initiatives and longer term, institution-building initiatives. It is their hunger for marketplace reality, and their willingness to do whatever it takes to get results, that make them increasingly invaluable in high-growth, rapid-change situations. Certainly, this has proven to be the case at both Compaq and Enron.

HIGH-PERFORMANCE ORGANIZATIONS

Sustaining high performance over time is the ultimate objective and challenge for most companies, although it is both hard to achieve and harder to sustain. It is a bit futile to attempt to list high-performing institutions, as these things can change quickly. Nonetheless, since this book is not about such institutions, in either descriptive or normative terms, a few examples are worthwhile reference points. They include companies like Frito-Lay, General Electric, UPS, Hewlett-Packard, J.P. Morgan, Levi Strauss, and Emerson Electric. Those on the threshold of sustained achievement over time would include Microsoft, Compaq, and Enron.

Such institutions instinctively strive for a balanced distribution of potential leaders, be they good traditional managers, executive change sponsors, or real change leaders. Because of their performance ethics and strong management capabilities, many of the best managers in these companies are able to handle the change situations that arise—suggesting that the need for RCLs might be lessened. In fact, in these situations it can be difficult to distinguish between the best general managers and the best RCLs. Perhaps it is not that the need for RCLs is less, but that the change leader skills and roles are being provided and filled by more traditional management sources. Typically, these companies also make less use of outside change expertise. This may also be related to the capabilities of their strong management groups. It seems likely, however, that over time these companies will realize the value of additional RCL capabilities and will begin to develop it from within their own ranks. Given that most of these companies have highly advanced organization-development functions, one catalyst for this may be a realization that RCL experiences can be incredible learning and growth opportunities for talented junior management—a relevant point as more and more traditional management jobs are eliminated.

Another compelling reason for high-performance companies to develop change leaders is that these institutions are not immune to the need for major change, in which the focus of the change activities must shift from incremental to fundamental. The efforts by Hewlett-Packard to revitalize its personal computing business is a well-known example of how, even companies with the strongest performance records and reputations can encounter marketplace discontinuities that require an aggressive, ramp-up change. Similar examples (General Electric, Texas Commerce Bank, and Enron) are described in the earlier chapters.

Until recently, high-performance companies have not been particularly known for empowered or democratic management approaches. This is probably because they were able to meet their performance objectives through a strong, top-down leadership approach combined with highly developed management processes. More recently, however, companies are following the lead of GE, Motorola, Hewlett-Packard, Procter & Gamble, and Levi Strauss, and are beginning to recognize that continuing to attain higher levels of performance will likely require a more engaged and empowered workforce. In fact, Jack Welch, chief executive of GE, now recognizes one of his toughest challenges as that of releasing "type three" managers from the organization. Apparently, these are managers who usually meet or exceed their financial targets, but do so at the expense of, rather than because of, the people working in their organizations. A well-known phrase at GE is that "the numbers no longer prolong or protect you" if you don't energize and motivate your people.

High-performance companies, like RCLs, are pragmatic and expedient in their approach. They tend not to be wedded to business-as-usual, no matter how successful they have been. Thus, their focus on sustained high performance will drive them to doing whatever it takes, which will in all likelihood be the development of more RCL roles and a greater RCL presence in the future.

2. MAKING A DIFFERENCE IN THE FUTURE

The roles that real change leaders play in many different change situations are increasingly crucial. Being effective in these roles requires a unique set of skills, mind-sets, and personal traits. Moreover, the roles and challenges that change leaders face will differ by the specific change and company situation. Thus, it is inarguable that the benefits for a company of having enough RCLs in appropriate positions are great. But what about the benefits for the RCLs themselves?

What's in it for them, not just from a career standpoint but from a personal-growth standpoint as well? Where do the personal gains come from, and how should potential change leaders think about their careers when faced with an opportunity to become an RCL? While there is certainly no single or definitive answer to any of these questions, a set of consistent themes emerges when RCLs themselves are asked these questions. The primary reasons why RCLs have valued the experience were highlighted at the end of the last chapter. In addition, there is a similar set of themes that come out when RCLs reflect upon the road that lies ahead of them.

WHAT LIES AHEAD FOR RCLS

Above all else, RCLs are determined to have an impact and make a difference in whatever they are doing. In that context, it is important to understand that whatever they are doing is not necessarily limited to playing change agent roles in major performance improvement or change efforts. Many RCLs move back and forth between traditional management jobs and change assignments—but what they retain from their change experiences are invariably useful in more normal jobs. The unique perspectives and different lenses through which they have been able to view the organization in general, and the front line in particular, are extremely valuable. They understand better how things really work, and how to communicate better with people in different settings.

These new perspectives will continue to shape and guide them, whether they return to management ranks, or stay in change agent roles. Their enhanced sense of purpose and drive for accomplishment will show through no matter what position they end up in. When Randy Howard was recently promoted to a senior management position in charge of all of UNOCAL's supply and transportation functions, he did not leave his RCL skills and mind-set at the refinery. A higher position was not going to prevent him from doing the same types of things that he had done as an RCL managing a plant.

> When I got into this job I didn't start with a series of meetings or briefings. I wanted to really understand how the business worked, what were the drivers, what were the real opportunities. So I just started getting out to the facilities and terminals, getting into workboots and a hardhat and talking to the front-line managers and workers.

> Just like in our program at the refinery . . . this was not only the best way to really understand how the business worked, but it enabled me to demonstrate my commitment to a balanced approach, and my desire to understand the perspectives of the people actually doing the work. The business and personal rewards are too great to think about going back to another management approach: this is the way that I work.

Like most RCLs, Randy will continue to be a real change leader even if he is never truly in another change agent role. The skills he honed at the Los Angeles refinery will be equally important to his personal impact in whatever job or challenge he might face in the future. Wherever they are, RCLs become addicted to the benefits of getting results faster and better than those around them, and they are not about to break the habit. They also believe that their unique skills and experiences will afford them plenty of options, "here or elsewhere." It is a good bet that they will pursue other options, if necessary to find situations where they can have the greatest impact, from a bottom-line standpoint as well as a personal standpoint. This knowledge, as shown in chapter 3, instills a sense of confidence in many RCLs, and thus lessens their concerns about either their level in the organizational hierarchy, or their long-term prospects with a particular institution. Their view of the future is to end up in situations where they can energize people of all kinds in making things happen, as is expressed by one RCL:

> I do not know where my next job will come from, since I seem to be working my way out of this one—but wherever it is, I intend

to be making a difference and building up the capability of the people I work with. If it isn't with this company, it will be with another one.

Similarly, when Harriet Wasserstrum of Texas Commerce Bank (TCB) was asked what would happen to her when the process-improvement effort moved into its implementation phase, her reply reflects the same attitude of optimism about an uncertain future:

> I was so busy that I really didn't think about it until my team leader started saying I should be worried about what I was going to do next. So I asked Marc [CEO Marc Shapiro], who said that I will wind up implementing some of the recommendations, doing one of the big operations projects, or running a business. Which covers anything. He said my biggest problem will be choosing from among the options he will offer me.

As Randy Howard explained, change leader experiences often raise RCLs' expectations about both the challenges they might tackle and the work environment they prefer. The satisfaction of leading and energizing people to higher accomplishments makes their return to lower-energy, lower-performance settings very unlikely. To avoid this, they will recreate jobs, redefine roles, break the rules in terms of traditional expectations, or simply leave a situation. Luckily, however, this works both ways. Ray Butkus of AT&T, for example, modified his expectations with respect to leaving to join another potential employer, making his commitment to AT&T even stronger. He refused a lucrative offer from a Fortune 100 company in another industry because:

> It was in a very slow-growing industry and a very old, bureaucratic company. I thought about it—did I want to go to a slow, bureaucratic company from a large, kind of bureaucratic company where interesting things are happening? No way!

John Wood, who led the AT&T–Profiles effort (a critical piece of the AT&T–CMO effort described in chapter 3), clearly raised his sights in looking for the next, bigger challenge, particularly with respect to energizing and tapping the full potential of people:

There's lots to do out there. I could easily go do something else on a broader scale requiring even more change with even more challenge. Particularly now that I've got a heck of a lot more confidence in the ability of people to do more than just intellectualize different ways of getting work done and becoming a high-performing team. People actually want it, if you put the right vision out in front of them. Whatever I end up doing, I know one thing for sure: I can never go back to the old way!

Whatever the industry, and whatever the change circumstances, RCLs stand out as those people who are determined to make a difference in the performance of the enterprise. It seems almost self-evident that many will become senior-level executives and even CEOs.

MORE RCLS AT TOP LEVELS

In fact, there is already an emerging group of top executives—emerging CEOs—who definitely display the characteristics of RCLs. It is impossible to prove either empirically or intuitively that RCLs will increasingly find their way to the top. It is also hard to imagine that this is not inevitable. No one seriously argues that major, transformational change is not increasingly upon us. Nor does anyone dispute the difficulty of accomplishing such change, particularly in complex organizational situations in virtually every sector of the economy. Thus, the only question is whether or not change leaders in the middle make the difference and are, in fact, themselves different. That they are is the thesis of this book, and the logical extension of that thesis certainly would place more and more RCLs at top levels in organizations of the future. Consider these examples.

JIM ROGERS AT GE MOTORS

Rogers's results have already been cited; they are hard to argue with. And in many respects, he is a product of the Jack Welch school of CEO leadership. In other important ways, however, he is more like his RCLs. He is personally connected to the marketplace realities his businesses face; he works competently in both team and nonteam modes; he nourishes champions and mavericks; he relentlessly searches for new ideas and ways to keep performance results climbing; and he is a legend in his own time among his people. Taking nothing away from Mr. Welch, Rogers is more like the RCLs of today—and perhaps more indicative of the CEOs of tomorrow. If you trace his background, it is RCL all the way.

"It's just the way I learned to manage," says Rogers. Now, it is certainly clear that Rogers is really a CEO, and, therefore, should not be considered a legitimate RCL. The problem is his behavior. He simply refuses to behave like anything but a real change leader. He won't dress like a CEO, he won't act like a CEO, and he won't even spend his time like a CEO.

He grew up in Melrose, Massachusetts, in a family with four brothers. His dad was a fireman and his mom ran the household. He "never had much but never wanted for anything." Jim and his brothers all played sports, and he ended up going to Rutgers, where he played basketball for a while. He is clearly not tall enough for basketball, but nobody ever told him that, so he was an all-star player. He got his first job at GE by walking into the Lynn, Massachusetts plant and asking if it had a management training program. It had one all right, and took him on—but the program was not exactly what he had hoped for. In fact, most of the time he was bored, hated the bureaucracy, and really couldn't wait for the end of the day so he could play basketball. After six months, he says:

> I finally came to the conclusion that the boredom was my problem, not the company's problem. So I got off my ass and said, I can do my job in an hour and a half; why don't I find out what's going on in the business?

He started walking the factory floors, getting engaged on his own initiative, and saw he could get some things done. One thing led to another until higher authority invited him to move onward and upward, and he did. Jim went from a staff analyst job to eventually running an $80 million business, and has been climbing ever since. He spent some time in the performance-oriented GE Capital business, and then moved to North Carolina, where he proceeded to turn around the manufactured-housing business—by walking the floors, energizing the people, and driving for performance results through teams, single-leader units, and individual champions. In each case, he continued the basic approach that worked for him at Lynn—becoming engaged on his own initiative, listening to and energizing people, and getting things done better and faster. Pretty soon he found himself being asked to take on the $1 billion GE Motors business and transform it into what it is today.

Somehow, this sounds like a story of how you might get to be a real change leader, not a CEO. On the other hand, is it possible that Rogers is some kind of advanced alien form of CEO that we might expect to see more of going forward? Let's hope so.

MARC SHAPIRO AT TEXAS COMMERCE BANK

Shapiro succeeded one of the most notable CEOs and institution builders in Texas history, Ben Love. Ben is an impressive, charismatic leader who, for more than twenty years, built a performance record that had no equal among the regional banks of this country. He also developed a very high-quality group of general managers and leaders. Like all banks, TCB went through difficult years in the late 1980s, and Shapiro intends to restore the bank's performance to that of the Love years. However, he is in the midst of a massive change effort that has yielded $50 million in profit improvement and has involved nearly 4,000 of the bank's 9,000 employees. The effort is changing the entire leadership philosophy of the bank— and Shapiro gives much of the credit to his emerging group of RCLs (a term he actually uses). His behavior mirrors theirs to an increasing and surprising degree. Love and Shapiro are both admirable leaders. Each molded his leadership to fit the circumstances of the performance situation. In fact, Shapiro is a product of Love's leadership approach, but his own is much more like that of an RCL.

ANDREW "I" VERSUS ANDREW "II" AT CHAMPION

Finally, consider this brief vignette on "Andrew Sigler I" versus "Andrew Sigler II." His leadership behavior has changed significantly during the cultural transformation at Champion. During the very tough turnaround years for Champion in the 1980s, Andrew I was as tough and demanding a CEO as you could find. His personal and physical stature dominated most key decisions, and he was respected, if not feared, by many. He shouted at and intimidated his executives often, although most came to realize he was not really mad at them. More important, he led his executives with clear personal vision, control, and inspiration. And he succeeded in changing the culture across a dozen old-style paper mills that now operate with self-directed teams at operating efficiencies that are among the best in the industry. This was a major change accomplishment of significant dimension. It is no accident that he also sits on General Electric's board of directors.

Andrew II looks exactly like Andrew I, but he behaves very differently. In the process of developing the structures, systems, and processes which have enabled RCLs to develop at Champion over the last eight years, he has significantly changed the way he runs the company in ways that parallel the behaviors of the best RCLs. Andrew II began to appear on the scene a few years ago. He still appears outspoken and intimidating to the casual observer, but his behavior in top executive circles is almost a complete reversal of his previous patterns. He has seen what RCLs, whom he affectionately and colorfully describes as "unlikely characters," can do in the plants—and he wants that kind of team behavior and performance reflected at the top. His "unlikely character" reference actually conveys the great affection and respect he has for his plant-level RCLs, and he uses it to emphasize that they are not in any way like the "MBAs with dark suits and pastel shirts" who, in his view, personify entitlement rather than performance ethics, and deliver little value. The sort of change Champion is undergoing requires everyone—from the mills to the executive suites—to change. He knows that if his own leadership pattern and that of the next round of executive leaders does not keep step with the changes in the workforce's behavior, they will fall short of the organization's needs.

Call it what you like—new paradigm, old leadership resurgence, or forerunners of a new breed emerging—it is still hard to lightly dismiss this emerging RCL leadership pattern. We suspect that the Jack Welches and Ben Loves of the world can always lead large organizations successfully. We also suspect, however, that the Jim Rogerses and Marc Shapiros of the world increasingly will be better able to change broad-based behaviors and skills—and do it while delivering better and better performance results. The need for a critical mass of such RCLs across the middle is already hard to deny; the need for RCLs at the top is an intriguing, speculative prediction.

CEO positions will not be the only path or ultimate destination for RCLs. In fact, it would be very un-RCL-like for real change leaders to waste a lot of time really worrying about climbing the hierarchy, versus continuing to have an impact and making a difference. The pragmatism of real change leaders also forces a realization that the minuscule number of CEO jobs makes the attainment of that position unlikely, even for the best performers with the most powerful skill sets. This is in marked contrast to the thousands of places and positions in virtually every company and organization in which RCLs can have an impact and find personal satisfaction. Thus, the future, while clearly lacking guarantees, tends to look bright for those who have become RCLs and experienced a high-performance situation. It would also be a good bet that, no matter where they are, they will be spending more time thinking about how to handle their current challenges than wondering what specifically will be next for them. They will be looking to the future with a sense of excitement rather than one of uncertainty.

FINAL THOUGHTS ON THE FUTURE

The skeptics can always argue that RCLs are doing nothing more than what good managers have always done. They are smart, honest, hard workers, who figure out how to get difficult jobs done on time. So what's the big deal? *The big deal is simply that such people are in very short supply!* Moreover, everything has sped up exponentially, stimulating the greater demand for RCL capabilities. Maybe the formula is no more complicated than doing what has to be done, but if so, why don't more people do it? We think the answer has two parts: they know it is not that simple, and they do not know what will work. That is why we wrote this book.

We also do not believe that it is that easy. The basic principles of people management have been well articulated for decades, but only recently are they receiving the emphasis they deserve. The new change thinking is available in every bookstore, but it has yet to permeate very far into the best practices of the corporate establishment. Most large organizations have not recognized the critical roles that RCLs must play down the line in their organizations. What they have recognized is that their middle management layers have become less effective, and they have responded by dumping middle managers overboard to lighten the boat! Getting rid of ineffective middle management is easy. Developing RCLs to fill the crucial change-skill gaps is much more difficult—and much more important.

If nothing else, we hope this book will provide encouragement to those RCLs who are squarely in the middle between a top leadership group that means well, but does not get it yet, and a workforce that means well, but does not yet trust these change efforts. Real change leaders are the linchpin, and we cannot afford to have them weaken. We also need all of them that we can possibly develop.

Our real dream is that the experiences of the more than 150 change leaders represented in this book will give others the inspiraton and insight they need to make their part of the change effort work, to stimulate those around them, and to influence their top leaders to build the necessary critical mass of RCLs. If they do so, we are sure they will advance their own careers and personal growth, as well as their company's performance and growth.

EPILOGUE

CHANGE IS ALL ABOUT *CRITICAL MASS*. IF YOU GET A CRITICAL MASS OF REAL change leaders in the middle, you have a much better chance of leading a successful major change effort. You cannot do it alone—and while there are isolated examples of the dynamic CEO driving change from the top, these are few and far between. CEOs get far too much credit, and far too much blame, for the results of transformational change efforts. Nor is it enough to have a committed team at the top. However you do it, you eventually need a critical mass of real change leaders throughout the organization.

This memo summarizes what we believe such change leaders would like top management to recognize about the RCL role, and how to develop a cadre of real change leaders. Most of those we interviewed were asked to comment either during the interview or in a special survey questionnaire afterwards. Drawing on those sources, this memo covers three basic topics:

■ **The RCL shortage;**

■ **The RCL mind-set; and**

■ **RCL needs and expectations.**

THE RCL SHORTAGE

The demand for change leaders already far exceeds the supply, and the continuing elimination of traditional middle management roles exacerbates this imbalance. You can find real change leaders in every major change situation from the decade-long struggles at Champion and NYCT to the "overnight" transformations at Compaq and Enron. In none of these situations, however, do either top management or the RCLs themselves believe there is an adequate number of change leaders in the middle to bring about the changes required.

The causes of the shortfall are obvious. Most organizations (corporations, government institutions, private enterprises) face what they consider major change—lots of people in lots of places needing to acquire new skills to improve organizational performance. The time frame to accomplish these changes is shortening, as are the intervals between such efforts. Such changes may not be continuous, but they are certainly recurring. Traditional managers have little experience with this kind of change, and their normal attitudes and skill sets make it difficult for them to adapt. Finally, top management cannot make it happen without change leaders in the middle.

The solution is equally obvious: obtain a critical mass of RCLs to fill the gap. Unfortunately, this is much easier said than done. You will have to answer these questions:

1. What is critical mass in your situation? It will vary. Do you need 250 real change leaders, or will 20 do the job?

2. Where do you need change leaders, and where can you get by with traditional managers? Do you need RCLs to fill normal management roles, or can you get by using them only on special assignment?

3. How do you get change leaders where you need them? Some argue that most traditional managers can readily convert if you make clear what that means. Others—particularly those in rapid-change situations—argue that you have to get at least a core by hiring from the outside. Most RCLs, however, believe that the answer lies in the middle, i.e., that a rigorous, high-priority development and support effort by top management can make the difference between being in short supply and having critical mass.

THE RCL MIND-SET

The real change leaders in your organization already recognize the bind you are in—and they want to help. They also recognize that your role is as critical to successful change as theirs—and they are seeking a realistic partnership with you. The difficulty of major change is something they have experienced firsthand, and their expectations reflect that experience. They do not expect every top management initiative to work, nor do they believe that every setback should be blamed on top management. On the other hand, they have little patience for denial, finger-pointing, or excuses—and they really become upset when they perceive top management being soft on the laggards. They hold themselves individually and jointly accountable for results, and they are strong supporters of consequence management at the top.

Moreover, they claim to be more interested in making a difference than they are in advancing up in the hierarchy. They obtain a surprisingly large proportion of their rewards from producing results beyond expectations, and from helping other people to perform beyond levels they thought possible. They expect to be recognized and rewarded for their change results by being given a chance to have higher impact the next time. We believe them.

Unfortunately, there are some pretenders to the throne. Most developing change leaders recognize their shortfalls and are honestly trying to build the skills and experience required. Some, however, continue to believe they have "always done it this way" and are fully able to handle change the same way they have always managed. Others cloak themselves in the jargon of change but miss the fundamentals. These are the people who refer to single-leader groups as teams, who think empowerment is the same as involvement, and who measure change progress in terms of activities rather than results. Both groups can do you in. You are better to deal with them as soon as you diagnose the fault.

RCL NEEDS AND EXPECTATIONS

What real change leaders ultimately need and expect from top management is probably unrealistic. They set high standards for both themselves and their leaders. The good news is they do recognize that it takes time, and that getting close enough is better than chasing the holy grail of perfection. Their needs and expectations fall into three groupings: performance discipline, unflagging support, and staying the course.

PERFORMANCE DISCIPLINE

Real change leaders seek performance results above all else. But they determine their success by more than financial numbers and they expect top management to do the same. A balanced performance ethic to them means that you are as rigorous about performance results that benefit customers and the workforce as you are about results that increase shareholder wealth. Striving for better and better results makes sense to them only within that context. *Using words we think they would use,* this is what they would urge their leaders to do:

1. Set goals and measures that make sense to customers and employees. We perform best when we have clear objectives that are central to your leadership agenda. We can set our own goals—and are not reluctant to do so—but the more that we can integrate them with what our top leaders want, the better we can motivate and focus the efforts of our people. We need to be able to measure results that reflect the marketplace situation—and that are in sync with your aspirations.

2. Be a demanding boss who walks the talk. We are not looking for a comfortable path of modest achievement. We want to excel, particularly relative to the competition, but also relative to absolute standards of excellence and quality. We need to be stretched and challenged to do more than we may think we can. We do not have your perspective on the opportunities or problems, nor do we always have the personal conviction to reach high enough. Moreover, it goes almost without saying that your admonitions are most compelling when we see you pushing yourself to the same extent—and when we sense that you expect no more of us than you expect of yourself.

3. Reward those who earn it, and punish those who deserve it. All too often the system protects people who are not with the change program. We find this to be discouraging, if not unfair. We think we know who the dedicated performers are—and when we see the less deserving being advantaged over them, we question how serious top leaders really are. Change is tough enough without being hampered by lack of consequence management. We expect to make a difference—and to be recognized accordingly. We expect others to be treated the same way.

4. Raise the bar in areas that are lagging. Every complex organization has some functions, departments or businesses that fall behind in performance results. If this is allowed to persist over time, those who are making a difference in other areas will become frustrated, if not antagonistic. Everybody should be expected to toe the same mark in the race for change. That does not mean that we expect no differences in results or rates of progress. It does mean, however, that we are unusually sensitive when some part of the organization seems to be protected from the change intensity that we must face.

5. Reward that which you are demanding. If you are seeking and urging team efforts, then you should find a way to reward team performance as well as individual performance. If you advocate superior customer service, then you should not be rewarding only volume. It is not good enough to talk a good game. You need to put your money where your mouth is—or at least provide comparable rewards for the different approaches and standards that you advocate.

Unflagging Support

The most troublesome top management trait for RCLs to live with is inconsistent support. It is far easier for them to work in a negative, or change-unfriendly situation, than it is to work in one where the support they receive is variable and unpredictable. They expect to be supported through the tough times as well as the easy times. When they take risks for the right reasons and fail, they need even more support than when they succeed. Most important of all, they need their leaders to be accessible, to solicit their views, and to listen to their concerns. And they need that accessibility well beyond the next level of supervision. *Again, in their words, we believe RCLs would urge you to:*

1. Encourage us to tell it like it is—and listen when we do. We need you to solicit our views and encourage us when they are unpopular—particularly if those views are consistent with what is happening in the marketplace. We also need you to back us up in public confrontations with those who resist change, or would divert and diffuse the effort. Our role is never popular among those who are comfortable with the status quo, and we need your visible support with these people.

2. Take the same kind of personal risks you expect of others. We need you to wade into the hard and unpopular issues. We recognize it is often necessary to delegate important aspects of the change effort to others, but if you remain above it all, our job is much tougher. Nothing is quite so effective in energizing people as seeing top leaders take personal risks to further the cause. Conversely, nothing is quite so debilitating as seeing top leaders protect themselves, while pushing others into high-risk situations.

3. Allow us to make mistakes and fail along the way. No two change efforts are ever the same. What works in one situation may not work in the next. To find the right set of tools and approaches for any particular change challenge often requires taking a chance on something we have not tried or proven before. This means we will sometimes make mistakes, and some of our efforts will fail. We need that experience, however, not only to find a particular solution, but also to build our skills and experience for the next set of change challenges.

4. Be consistent with your messages and actions. Explain anything that may be seen as inconsistent. Our people are always looking for signals that the change program is a passing fancy—or that "now we can get back to normal." They are susceptible to any indication that they personally don't need to change, or that those who stick their necks out in favor of change have been wrong. They do not need much of an opening to nourish their seeds of doubt, so be alert to opportunities which may cause you to inadvertently give them that excuse.

STAYING THE COURSE

Change demands time, hard work, and perseverance. RCLs need to believe that top management will stay the course, even when the going gets rough. You cannot make it an annual program, or declare victory early, and expect to cultivate and motivate a growing cadre of real change leaders. Moreover, it is easy for the organization (including change leaders) to misinterpret your intentions or misread your communications. Consistent reinforcement of the main themes of change is very important to change leaders. It is the one way they have of knowing, as well as indicating to their people, that top management is committed for the long haul. *We believe your change leaders would urge you to:*

1. Accelerate efforts to create change leadership opportunities. For us to develop the skills and experience required for change, we need a diversity of opportunities. This is not something that can be learned in books or classrooms; it demands on-the-job exposure and learning—in different settings with different approaches. Unless you take positive action to create such opportunities, the development of RCLs will continue to lag behind your growing need for them.

2. Get involved down the line—and stay involved over time. You need to have a firsthand knowledge of the change efforts down the line. You may not have the time to become as immersed in the effort as some of us, but try to spend some time working side by side with teams in problem-solving sessions or field pilots. This is more than symbolic participation; it is the best way you can begin to understand just how fundamentally challenging and exhilarating the experience of change can be at an individual level.

3. Help us build an increasingly diverse tool kit for change. Perhaps the most valuable support we can have in sustaining a change effort over time is a diversity of tools and approaches to draw upon. It is so easy for change efforts to stall, and for people to revert to more comfortable patterns. The more we can access different tools and approaches, the better we can deal with any loss of momentum and energy across the organization. While we can develop different tools and approaches on our own, anything that you can do to facilitate or add to those efforts will be extremely valuable and appreciated. We need all the help we can get.

4. Expand and diversify the skill mix. We are all learning on the job. It helps to get new blood and experiences into the mix that will enable us to build and strengthen the critical mass of RCLs. In rapid-change situations, bringing new experience in from the outside is often the only way to obtain it in time to do any good. In other change situations, however, new blood is also a plus. We are reluctant to have our good people overlooked for opportunities that they can fill—but we are not reluctant to have injections of skills that we cannot otherwise develop.

In sum, the RCLs that we interviewed do not believe you can leave the development of change leader attitudes, skills, tools and approaches to chance. It is true that in rapid-growth situations, the environment is more conducive to the new breed of change leaders. Even there, however, it seems foolish not to pursue a rigorous program for identifying, evaluating, developing, deploying, and accelerating the growth of a cadre of RCLs. They represent the single best source of new leadership capacity and talent for the future.

ORGANIZATIONS IN REAL CHANGE LEADER
RESEARCH BASE

	Industrial	Financial	Services/ Other
Abbot Laboratories			■
AT&T—Business Communications Services			■
Avon			■
BHP	■		
Browning-Ferris Industries			■
Burlington Northern Railroad			■
Champion International	■		
Compaq	■		
Citicorp		■	
Edmonton Public School District			■
Enron	■		■
GE Fanuc	■		
GE Motors	■		
Johnson & Johnson— Endosurgery	■		
Kaiser Permanente			■
Knight-Ridder			■
Kodak—Color Paper Manufacturing	■		
McKinsey & Company			■
Mobil—Exploration & Production U.S.	■		
New York City Transit			■
PeaceHealth Corporation— Sacred Heart Medical Center			■
Prudential—Insurance		■	
SBC (Southwestern Bell Telephone)			■
Sealed Air	■		
Shell—U.S.	■		
State Farm Insurance		■	
Texas Commerce Bank		■	
Unocal—Refining	■		

This book is the collective product of seven people. Because its origins differ from most books, Jon Katzenbach briefly describes herein the team process as a way of acknowledging the significant contributions of his fellow team members and the many extended team supporters.

THE PROCESS

There is no way I could have written this book on my own. The team was well under way when they recruited me to "do the writing." While they believed they already had the material for a book well in hand, none of them were prepared to do the actual writing. For over a year they had been working as a team to share change experiences and insights about change leadership and to develop material and approaches that would be of help to change leaders down the line. While they considered retaining an outside "professional writer," it became clear that this course would sacrifice a significant learning opportunity which only the discipline of book writing can provide.

When I joined the team, I submitted a detailed outline of my own point of view. The team had already developed a detailed chapter outline of their own. There were many similarities, but there were also significant differences that led us to embark on the fieldwork which eventually covered nearly thirty different change situations, and some 150 change leaders. We all learned much more than we expected from this effort and are obviously indebted to the many change leaders and executives who shared their experiences with us.

The teams' working approach focused on learning directly from the change leaders themselves. We selected the change situations based on the experience and advice of many of our colleagues and clients. The change leaders interviewed were selected based on the collective judgments of executives and consultants who had worked with them. Most interviews were conducted by more than one member of the team, and each major change situation was assessed and evaluated by the team as a whole. Most interviews were taped to ensure accuracy and detail, and each change situation was written up as a stand-alone case by the team members who did the interviews. The team then jointly assessed the relative impact of the change on the performance of the institution—at the level that the RCL was working.

I wrote the initial and the final drafts for each chapter to ensure continuity of voice, pace and style, but there were many redrafts in between that were done by other team members or by me as a result of intensive team discussion. No chapter was finalized until the team—both individually and collectively—was comfortable with it. What this effort lacked in writing efficiency, it more than made up for in substance and content quality.

MY TEAMMATES

It is impossible for me to do justice here to the contributions of each individual team member, particularly since so much was a collective effort. Nonetheless, I want to personally acknowledge each of them by highlighting the unique capability and insight that enriched both the process and the content of the book. I comment briefly in reverse order in which their names appear on the cover.

Tim Ling: A thoughtful pragmatist and realist, Tim likes getting things done more than talking about getting things done, and he spread this norm across the team. Moreover, those managers who do not meet the test of solid performance results do not make his RCL list. With an endless supply of quotes, and a determination to convince his mother that his expensive education was not in vain, he kept the team's values in focus.

Quentin Hope: The glue that held us all together, Quentin was responsible for more of the cases, interviews and chapter rewrites that the rest of the team combined. With strong midwestern roots and values, he combines the patience of Job with the determination of a bulldog. We were fortunate to have his full-time leadership of our fieldwork—and the "Real Change Leader Handbook for Action" is primarily the result of his diligence and insight.

Chris Gagnon: The informal leader of the team, Chris kept the rest of us focused on our mission and vision for the book. More than anyone else, he saw the potential and kept the team together. Whenever conflict or controversy threatened the effort, we turned to Chris. He found countless ways to inject fun, humor, and new energy into our discussions, particularly whenever the rest of us began to falter or lose heart. He also is responsible for the emphasis on practical tools for RCLs to use in several chapters.

Marc Feigen: The most creative and widely read member, Marc invariably caused us to think differently and to question the common wisdom. He is someone who understands that business is mostly about people and he helped us understand why such a diverse group of people decide to become RCLs. In addition to discovering George Devlin, he also somehow got us through the rough waters of process confusion in chapter 5.

Steve Dichter: The founder of the group, and its most experienced and thoughtful member, Steve did a "rigor review" of each chapter draft, and these were of inestimable value to the writer. On more than one occasion, his wisdom and sensitivity would lead us to a truly integrated resolution on critical differences of opinion. As the leader of the McKinsey Change Center, he tested our field conclusions against the broad base of the firm's change experience.

Rick Beckett: Open-minded and innovative, Rick also applies hard logic better than most. His insistence on "making it make sense" and seeking a logical fit led to a number of insights, not the least of which was enabling us to convert chapter 7 from a theme of integration to one of building momentum. He is also a big proponent of having fun along the way.

THE "EXTENDED" TEAM

The core team has benefited greatly from the assistance of a number of other people who worked with us along the way. Each in their own way made significant contributions without which the book would be less than it is. A few deserve some special comment as part of our extended team, in alphabetical order:

Rosa Cano-Calhoun, Janet Kiley, and Inez Roberts were all indispensable as keepers of our files, records and drafts, not to mention the correction of countless grammatical and substantive inconsistencies. Janet and Rosa deserve more thanks than we can provide, since they had to put up with all of us continually over the course of more than a year. Their professionalism, dedication, and sense of humor kept the team going on many, many occasions.

Alan Kantrow provided unique skills as a "development editor" for the early drafts, and helped us realize that the best RCLs are truly proto-types of future top corporate leaders.

Linda Katzenbach fulfilled the invaluable role of critical reader for each and every chapter draft and redraft, enhancing both the substance and readability of the book. She was also our in-house line editor and grammarian throughout the entire process.

Mary Lou Kelley served a critical research role for two months when we were badly in need of professional assistance in finishing our casework. Her insights as well as her case research made it possible for us to com-plete the book on schedule.

John Mahaney of Random House epitomizes the "gentleman pub-lisher." John was truly a pleasure to work with. More important, his skills as an editor are manifold and always gently employed. He asks smart and probing questions, forces clarity and conciseness, yet provides authors with the freedom they need. John helped us write a much clearer and more interesting book.

Chris Meyer signed on for several months to help us with our inter-views at GE Motors, Compaq, and Enron. As a newcomer to both the team and this subject, he quickly picked up on the RCL perspective and pro-vided very helpful contributions and insights.

Rafe Sagalyn saw the potential of our work earlier than any of us, and through a mix of very insightful coaching, wise counsel, and front work helped provide a platform of publishing support. We are very grateful to Rafe. He believed in us first.

Doug Smith was an early and ongoing thought partner and a contin-uing source of intellectual stimulation, even as he worked on his own book, *Taking Charge of Change*.

Several McKinsey colleagues helped directly by drawing on their close and well-earned relationships to arrange interviews, help with inter-views, and review case material. We owe special thanks to Bill Barnett, Damon Beyer, Jim Crownover, Russ Fradin, Christine Hardcastle, Jeff Hawn, Ken Kurtzman, Keith Meyer, Suzanne Nimocks, Dave Noble, Andy

Steinhubl, and Warren Strickland. We also drew on the support and experience of Dick Cavanaugh, Watters Davis, Vince DePalma, Bernie Ferrari, Jon Harris, Tom Hedrick, Gil Marmol, Mike Pritula, Bruce Roberson, Charlie Schetter, Robert Taylor, and Tom Tinsley. The experience of all of these colleagues and supporters provided a deep base of understanding from which we could develop the RCL story.

Finally, we thank our administrative assistants for their able assistance and forebearance through the research and writing process: Ann Boettcher, Jodi Elkins, Kathy Featherman, Michelle Marigliano, Leslie Marvin, Vicki Nicholas, Jedi Ochuonyo, Thia Rentas, and Jeanne Westrup.

THE RCLS THEMSELVES

Most important, the team wants to acknowledge the contributions of the 150 change leaders that we learned from in this effort. In every way they could, they helped us to understand what the world of change looks like from their window, and were open and generous in sharing with us—and therefore with you—what has worked for them. We are truly grateful for their invaluable help and cooperation—and wish we could pay tribute to each individually.

We believe learning from real world stories is critical, which explains why this book is based on the experiences of RCLs. However, many of our clients and colleagues have also asked for specific ideas, guides, and tools to help accelerate their change efforts and their personal development. Unfortunately, there is no magic seven-step program for developing as an RCL and leading successful change programs (despite the fact that many have been promoted). Nor are there any "cookbook" formulas for handling specific situations. We have, however, put together a "Real Change Leader's Handbook for Action" which you may find helpful in either starting or accelerating your change efforts.

This handbook provides:

1. A simple, informal self-assessment guide for each of the change leader topics covered by the first seven chapters of this book. The diagnostic questions for each chapter are designed to quickly and simply give you a general reading on whether you are in good shape or have a lot of work to do.

2. Ideas, checklists, and frameworks for getting started in areas where change leadership help is needed.

3. Pictures (charts) you may find useful in remembering and communicating to others some of the key ideas in this book.

You can obtain a copy of the handbook by completing the reply card attached to this book or, if the card has already been removed, by writing Times Business/Random House, 201 East 50th St., N.Y., N.Y. 10022 and asking for the "Real Change Leader's Handbook for Action."